Donated to

**Visual Art Degree
Sherkin Island**

HOUSEY HOUSEY

A Pattern Book
of Ideal Homes

Designs by Pierre d'Avoine Architects
Words by Clare Melhuish & Pierre d'Avoine

Written by Clare Melhuish and Pierre d'Avoine
Designed by bc, mh (www.bcmh.co.uk)

© 2005 Black Dog Publishing and the authors

Black Dog Publishing Limited
Unit 4.04 Tea Building
56 Shoreditch High Street
London E1 6JJ

Tel: +44(0)20 7613 1922
Fax: +44(0)20 7613 1944
Email: info@bdpworld.com

British Library Cataloguing-in-Publication Data

A catalogue record for this book is available from the
British Library

ISBN 1-904772-10-2

HOUSEY
HOUSEY

Contents

Introduction

The aim of this book is to present a collection of house designs, which have been developed by Pierre d'Avoine Architects over some years, as a source of ideas and models for application today and in the future. In making this compilation, we see ourselves following in the tradition of the historic 'pattern books' of architecture and construction, which were used by architects, builders and clients over the centuries to present and acquire new ideas about design and technical realisation.

Perhaps the most famous of these is Andrea Palladio's Four Books of Architecture, of 1570, which became immensely important in Britain in the seventeenth and eighteenth centuries as a source for the dissemination of classical ideas about architecture in the hands of Inigo Jones and his successors. During this period, two British architects, Colen Campbell and James Gibbs, drew on the model to produce their own treatises, Vitruvius Brittanicus, 1717, and A Book of Architecture, 1728, which were also widely circulated and used, and effectively transformed the face of public and private architecture in Britain. Later, Batty Langley, a carpenter, pirated many of the Gibbs designs to produce a more technical volume of his own, aimed primarily at builders and craftsmen, called The City and Country Builder's and Workman's Treasury of Design, 1740, which helped to ensure the hegemony of classical models as the dominant influence in the explosion of speculative housing. In the following century, J C Loudon's Encyclopaedia of Cottage, Farm and Villa Architecture, 1833, was perhaps the most influential of the pattern books, presenting a vast treasury of different styles of domestic design for public consumption.

Our pattern book doesn't aspire to be anything as wide-ranging and exhaustive as those historic publications, containing a mere 23 designs, developed in response to different types of site condition, that are more-or-less typical of the opportunities for house construction today. Although some of them were designed as individual projects and others were always intended to be built as developments of multiple dwellings, they are all intended for potential mass production, with scope for customisation by individual clients.

In our opening essay we discuss the conditions which govern house-building today, and which the designs presented here are intended to challenge by offering opportunities for new approaches appropriate to modern living patterns and aspirations. The following diagram presents the characteristics of the different projects defined by location, type, site condition, materials, and construction agenda. This leads straight into the pattern book of houses, organised chronologically — the earliest designs first, the most recent at the end.

The final section of the book is made up of words — a series of 12 essays written by Pierre d'Avoine and Clare Melhuish over a period of years. The essays elaborate on the various issues which have shaped the projects, some focusing specifically on individual schemes, others describing more broadly aspects of the context in which the work has developed. The book concludes with a bibliography of sources for further reading.

Note: The main elevations, plans and sections are shown at 1:200 scale.

The Pattern Book Approach in the Twenty-first Century

Shortage and monopoly

For the past 30 years there has been a significant decline in house building in the UK. As a result, the opening decade of the twenty-first century has been marked by an acutely felt shortage of homes. The local authorities responsible for the surge of house construction in the period of rebuilding following the Second World War were forced, for political reasons, to relinquish their role as providers of new housing in the 1980s. They have since been pushed to the limit to maintain their existing stock – or what remains of it in the wake of the 'right to buy' initiative instituted by the Thatcher government, giving council tenants the right to buy their homes at an advantageous rate. Meanwhile, new house building has been more or less monopolised by private house-building companies, offering, for the most part, a standard model of large scale, suburban density development, and a basic catalogue of conventional, detached and semi-detached house types styled in a range of 'traditional' looks.

This approach has been founded in an aggressive rejection of the forms of modern architecture which were embraced in the post war years as an expression of social idealism and progress, and are now largely condemned as elitist, oppressive, and impossible to maintain. But it offers no acknowledgement that the patterns and values of contemporary life have changed from those of the past, or that the public has any interest in inhabiting new homes designed in response to the conditions of today. For those people who yearn for the opportunity to inhabit an appropriate twenty-first century home there is virtually no choice. They are offered either housing stock which is on average 60 years old, or simplistic reconstructions of those same models which pepper the land and make a mockery both of the originals they emulate, and of the house buying public. Only a very small minority of people will ever be in a position to employ an architect to design a new house entirely in accordance with their particular requirements, taste, and values. There is a great opportunity, therefore, to introduce into the housing supply a greater range of choice, by instituting new procedures of developing land in smaller parcels, on a more individual basis, using standardised construction systems which can nevertheless deliver 'desirability' and accommodation suitable for today's lifestyles, within a plausible budget.

Pattern book

Throughout the history of building, architects and builders have used pattern books to present and disseminate new ideas about architecture and practical information about construction and decoration. Pattern books characteristically presented a large selection of exemplary models of design and construction, accompanied by more or less textual elaboration on the ideas and procedures involved. The very earliest of these was the Ten Books of Architecture by the ancient Roman writer Vitruvius, which set out the principles of classical architecture for the first time. Rediscovered in the fifteenth century, it was the inspiration for the great surge of interest in classical architecture, and the many architectural treatises on it which were published up until the eighteenth century. These were essentially intended to inform and direct the taste of architectural patrons. But at the end of the seventeenth century, builders' manuals, orientated towards craftsmen rather than patrons, also began to circulate, presenting classical designs in a more practical and technical way, intended for reproduction by builders. During the nineteenth century these became stylistically more varied, as the Gothic Revival and Picturesque movements took off. The books became more explicit, showing designs, plans and descriptive texts for each project. They were aimed increasingly at influencing the ideas of the middle classes, identified as a burgeoning mass market for domestic design, during the first period of extensive suburban development around major cities. These books, in turn, were to develop into the mail order catalogues and house plan books that became popular in the USA during the twentieth century. However, in the UK they were to fall into something of a decline.

The fundamental idea behind the pattern book approach is that of a reproducible formula, which, nevertheless, has an inherent quality and originality and can respond to different situations and contexts, both physical and cultural. Unlike the one-off, individually commissioned, architect-designed house, the pattern-book home is essentially a standard product, that minimises the cost and increases the accessibility of design, while allowing for customisation by the individual client. For today's architects, like those of the past, the pattern book offers the possibility of producing high quality, 'original' designs for a potential mass market, using standardised construction methods.

Interstitiality

During the heady eras of suburban construction, from the nineteenth century until the 1930s and 40s, vast tracts of land were made available for fairly low-density house building around cities. Today, cities are tightly bounded by green belts, and the reigning consensus is that urban sprawl must be contained within existing conurbations, with a corresponding increase of density to accommodate demand. In rural areas, there has been an equally strong resistance to encroachment on the countryside, and new development has been strictly limited to replacement of existing building stock, or to the peripheral areas of existing settlements – although an exception has been made for the construction of one-off, substantial new houses of exceptional architectural quality. This has raised the pressing question of where and how to build new homes in sufficient quantities, and at affordable prices. Since the election of the Blairite government in Britain in 1998, two main strategies have been mooted, reflecting developments throughout the post-industrial world. On the one hand, there is brownfield development, or recycling of wasteland in towns and cities, which has been greeted with dismay by those resistant to the idea of increased density and the potential for a return to high-rise residential construction. On the other hand, large scale urban extensions have appeared in a number of areas earmarked for strategic development, notably the Thames Gateway area to the east of London, and the Milton Keynes area in the Midlands, which are also resisted by those who fear the spread of fast-track, uncoordinated, unsustainable housing construction lacking adequate infrastructure.

Despite government protestations of commitment to high quality design and planning, the continuing reliance on established procurement channels means that large scale developments, entrusted to the corporate housing developers, continue to be given preference over smaller sites and operators. The corporate developers rely heavily on in-house design services, or on those of the biggest architectural firms. Thus, independent practitioners are left to wrestle with the red tape and fierce local interests involved in working with the small scale, left-over, interstitial spaces, which become available for recycling. Such spaces are too problematic, and offer insufficient financial incentive, to attract big developers. In both urban and especially rural areas, however, where the shortage of affordable housing has reached crisis levels, they are eminently suitable for the application of pattern book concepts tailored to particular kinds of physical context. Furthermore, they have the potential to yield a surprising supply with scarcely visible consumption of land, quickly settling into and merging with the existing landscape.

This book proposes a number of identifiable categories of valuable interstitial site characteristic of urban, suburban, 'exurban', and rural environments in the twenty-first century. These sites, for example, exist along the edges of motorways, canals, rivers, railways and planning zones, on redundant industrial and agricultural sites, on rooftops, in back gardens, and so on. Working on this basis, design proposals start to be shaped and defined primarily by site characteristics, spatial parameters, and cultural conditions, as opposed to stylistic and aesthetic dogma. Rather than imposing a preconceived 'look' or 'lifestyle concept' on a particular site, they absorb the existing conditions of the city and its fabric, relying on an incremental approach that allows them to adapt and invent new spaces and volumes from old. The problem, to date, is how to free up this kind of land for small scale individual development. A heavy bias towards the large scale commercial developer is apparent in planning policy at every level. A corresponding discrimination undermines the efforts of small scale groups and individuals interested in working with fragments of the built environment at a more detailed level,

with greater attention to the reality of local environments and the long term impact of construction.

Society
The major house builders always maintain that what they offer in terms of housing 'products' meets public demand, as assessed by market research exercises, but in fact they represent a deeply patronising view of public taste as uninformed, unsophisticated and, ultimately, unquestioning and gullible. Every society is built on historic traditions of domestic building and design that are rich, varied, eclectic and unique. The Disneyfication of design and the built environment, or the reduction of the built heritage to a few identifiable 'brands', speaks volumes about the low opinion held by big construction companies of their customers.

The 'brand leaders' in off-the-peg mass housing are not exactly designed, but rather formulated in response to surveys which set the parameters of possible debate very narrowly. They are also shaped to satisfy, at the lowest level of sophistication, the requirements of planning authorities throughout the country for 'contextual' development — that is, developments which 'fit in' with their surroundings. Imaginative interpretation and speculation are viewed as unacceptably risky, in terms of both the market and the restrictive planning system, and factored out. As a result, the vast majority of new houses in Britain are fairly crudely fabricated reproductions of particular historical models identified as having public popularity. They evoke a quintessentially 'British' past which no longer properly exists. Twenty-first century society in the UK is a great deal more varied than it has ever been before — both ethnically, having been host to great incoming flows of migrants from almost every part of the world for nearly 100 years, and also culturally, in terms of the values and mores which constitute a wide spectrum of frames and reference points for public and private life. This situation, though familiar throughout Europe and the USA, is particularly entrenched in the UK, which has developed a peculiar preoccupation with heritage and its conservation.

It might be argued that the construction of inauthentic reproductions of historic models allows people to orientate themselves and take root in the 'instant' new communities which the house builders specialise in, by referencing a memory bank which links them to a reassuring, collective cultural past. But ultimately, the inauthenticity itself generates further cultural disorientation, shaping narratives of identity that may have little or no relation to reality. Perhaps, then, housing models should reflect the eclectic constitution of today's society, particularly in the post-colonial cities of the West, and the multifarious points of reference of its citizens; certainly, the housing surveys give no hint of the complexity and ambiguity that challenge the validity of current easy assumptions about the ideals and expectations of home owners and occupiers.

Architects, on the other hand, learn a great deal, in immense detail, about the reality of the needs and desires of individuals and families when they work with clients on the design of projects. This process demands the most intense commitment and engagement from both parties, however, which for the majority of people is completely unrealistic in terms of the time-scale and financial undertaking involved. This fact again points to the value and relevance of the pattern book approach, which offers a viable alternative: a range of imaginative, desirable, architect-designed products appropriate to different situations, and capable of replication on various scales, which can be tailored by individual customers, or clients, to match their particular site, circumstances, background and outlook on life within a reasonable budget.

Status quo and future practice

Mounting evidence in recent years has shown that the public is not particularly happy with the standard output of the volume house builders, and 'official questions' have been asked in the UK through the Office of the Deputy Prime Minister about the rash of so-called "Noddy houses" spreading across the land. Nevertheless, governments, under intense pressure to solve the housing shortages of the new millennium, continue to rely on the same channels of procurement which promise little in the way of innovative thinking about housing design, and also threaten to desecrate large tracts of hitherto undeveloped rural land. The pattern book approach offers, instead, a viable method of incremental, small scale development, harnessing the extensive training, skills and experience of architects. This method is suitable for urban and rural areas alike, and empowers future users to have a far greater say in the way they want to live.

This book presents 23 house designs conceived to meet the constraints and opportunities of different kinds of sites, some more unconventional than others. Some have been implemented, some not, but all have been developed in response to real briefs and programmes, and the desires of real people from various walks of life. As such, they provide a small but valuable insight into the make-up and aspirations of post-industrial, post-colonial twenty-first century society, as expressed in the home. They demonstrate that there is scope for a more confident, experimental approach to housing design, which is, perhaps paradoxically, based on the principle of timelessness. None of the models presented in this book is intended to be overtly 'futuristic' in appearance or agenda. Rather, the experimental approach they represent is about drawing on and reinvigorating a much wider, hence unconventional, range of historical and cultural sources, combined with the latest strategies for reducing environmental impact. They all subscribe to an essentially traditional low-rise concept of living, but incorporate the potential for high-density occupation, emulating older models of housing in eras pre-dating the tightly-defined, self-contained

nuclear family. In so doing, they simply reflect the great changes which have taken place in family structure, household configuration, and working practices in the latter half of the twentieth century, and embrace the opportunities presented for new approaches to housing design.

Design principles

From the end of the nineteenth century onwards, domestic planning became progressively tighter and more cellular. This was a response to an increasing segregation of private, domestic and public life, a reduction in the size of families, and, eventually, the demise of household staff and servants at all levels of society. The social and economic conditions of the nineteenth century, particularly the rise of office-based work and commuting, led to a conflation of women's identities with a feminised domestic sphere, and a proliferation of clubs and other venues where men would socialise outside the home. This so-called 'privatisation' or 'domestication' of the home had a far-reaching effect on domestic design, resulting in a compartmentalisation of the house interior which was quite a substantial shift away from earlier models of design. In the past, bigger, multi-purpose spaces were the norm, and circulation passed directly through habitable rooms, instead of around them. Even bedrooms would be subject to a flow of people passing through, and double-up as conference and entertainment spaces when necessary. Privacy had been provided only by the curtained four-poster or cupboard bed. Today, surprisingly, the occupation of the home in the Western world has, in some ways, started to shift back to pre-nineteenth century norms. The increasing incidence of step-families, extended families, home-working, a de-formalisation of hospitality, and the near-universal use of central heating throughout the house, has generated a certain loosening up of the home. Larger living rooms, or 'family rooms', which incorporate kitchen and dining areas, are growing in popularity along with bedrooms that absorb the characteristics of multi-purpose living and working spaces. The central difference between the European and North American homes of today and those of the past is the enormous emphasis now placed on bodily hygiene and well-being. This difference is reflected in the widespread expectation of not merely one, but multiple bathrooms provided per household. What a contrast to former times, when bathing was an occasional activity accommodated in a portable or roll-top tub in the bedroom or kitchen.

In the pattern book models shown here, 'loose-fit', flexible space becomes the norm, with the potential for adaptation over the life-span of a house to accommodate changes in household configuration and occupancy patterns. This allows for a major shift towards more spacious, more accommodating houses for modern times – qualities lost in the drive towards more compartmentalised homes. Combining a rigorous implementation of low energy solutions with the use of flexible, recyclable, construction systems, this principle provides the foundation for the longevity and durability of a house: it does not become outdated or dysfunctional, nor does it simply wear out. The design has an inbuilt capacity for adaptation and renewal.

While most of the houses are presented here as individual units, the majority also have the capacity to be combined, with modifications where necessary, in smaller or larger groups, to create tight-knit, cohesive environments with outdoor spaces of various kinds — private and communal gardens at ground or roof level, terraces, verandas, streets and paths — integrated into the mix. It is the traditional street which remains the fundamental connective tissue, accommodating wheeled transport on the one hand, and parties on the other. During decades of spatial experimentation, the street has proved unchallengeable as a conduit of social and spatial integration and order. But the principle of complementary internal and external space in varying shapes and forms provides the basis of a strategic approach to a whole range of household issues, including internal light levels, views out, ventilation and temperature control, privacy, and pollution limitation.

The pattern book houses were designed for specific urban, suburban, and rural sites ranging from London, to Wales, Iran, India, Ghana, and the Caribbean, but the aim of each project is to present a generic approach which can be applied and adapted to comparable conditions anywhere else. They demonstrate the possibility of a way forward for people who would prefer not to live in a 'Noddy' house, if there were more choice, and who would enjoy the opportunity for greater involvement in the design of their own home, challenging the monopoly of the big house builders on housing provision.

CATEGORIES		109 Sheendale Studios	151 White House	175 Invisible House	175 Invisible House 2	195 Mehr House	254 Highstone Rooftop	255 Slim House	255 Slim House 2	261 Big House	264 Monad House
LOCATION	Backland	...	...	*	*	...	...	...	...	...	*
	Countryside	...	...	...	...	*	...	...	...	...	*
	Suburban	*	*	*	*	*	...	*	*	*	*
	Urban	...	...	*	*	...	*	*	*	...	*
TYPE	Bungalow	...	...	...	...	...	...	...	...	...	...
	Courtyard	...	*	*	*	...	...	*	*	...	*
	Detached	...	...	*	*	*	...	...	...	...	*
	Flat/Apartment	...	...	...	...	...	*	...	...	...	...
	Live/Work	*	...	*	*	...	...	*	*	*	*
	Maisonette	...	...	...	...	...	...	...	...	...	...
	Semi-detached	...	*	...	...	...	...	*	...	*	*
	Show House	...	...	...	...	...	...	*	...	...	...
	Terrace	*	...	...	...	...	...	*	*	...	*
	Tower	...	...	...	...	...	...	...	...	...	...
	Town House	*	...	...	...	...	...	*	*	*	...
	Villa	...	...	...	...	*	...	...	...	...	...
CONDITION	Adapted	...	*	...	...	...	*	...	...	...	...
	Buried	...	...	*	*	...	...	...	...	...	...
	Converted	...	...	...	...	...	...	...	...	...	...
	Elevated	...	...	...	...	...	*	...	...	...	...
	Embedded	...	...	...	...	...	...	...	...	...	*
	Extended	...	*	...	...	...	...	...	...	...	...
	Horizontal	...	...	...	...	...	...	*	*	...	...
	Hybrid	...	...	...	...	...	...	...	...	...	...
	Inserted	...	...	*	*	...	...	...	...	*	...
	Infill	*	...	...	...	...	...	*	*	*	*
	Invisible	...	...	*	*	...	*	...	...	...	...
	Plinth	...	...	...	...	*	...	...	...	...	...
	Repeatable	*	...	*	*	*	...	*	*	...	*
	Verandah	...	...	...	...	*	...	...	...	...	...
	Vertical	*	...	...	...	...	...	*	*	*	...
	Viral	...	*	*	...	...	...	...	...	...	...
MATERIALS	Block	*	*	...	...	...	...	...	...	...	...
	Brick	*	*	...	...	...	...	...	...	*	...
	Concrete	...	...	*	...	*	...	...	...	*	...
	Hybrid	...	...	*	...	...	*	...	...	*	...
	Inflatable	...	...	...	...	...	...	*	...	...	...
	Pre-fab	*	...	...	...	...	*	*	*	...	...
	Stone	...	...	...	...	...	...	...	...	...	...
	Steel Frame	...	...	...	*	...	*	*	*	*	...
	Timber Frame	...	...	...	*	...	...	*	...	...	*

265 Maisonette	269 Pudding Mill House	278 Rooftop Houses The Piper Building	307 Baffoe House	319 Collins House	335 Rough Grounds Octagon House	335 Rough Grounds Belvedere House	335 Rough Grounds Lodge	336 Climate House	342 Swaythling Housing	344 New Battery House	350 Sam House	358 Drum House
	*			*								*
					*	*	*		*	*	*	*
								*	*		*	*
*		*	*	*				*				*
									*		*	
	*			*	*	*			*			
	*		*		*	*	*	*	*			*
									*			
	*			*								*
*		*							*			
								*				
*				*								
						*						*
				*								
			*		*		*	*		*	*	*
*		*										
				*				*				
*												
*		*			*							*
				*	*	*	*	*				
	*		*	*						*	*	
*		*										
*	*			*				*				
				*								
				*								
			*					*		*	*	
*	*	*	*					*	*			
			*					*			*	
*						*						*
			*					*			*	
*												
				*				*			*	
*		*									*	*
	*			*					*			
					*	*	*	*				
*	*	*	*						*	*		*
												*

HOUSES

109
Sheendale Studios

The kitchen is screened from the main, triple-height living space by folding double doors.

These apartments were designed on the site of an old factory in south-west London. There are six units, arranged as two rows of three, placed back-to-back. The aim was to create the feeling of a house, in the space of a flat. Each unit has a triple-height living-room, with kitchen facilities screened behind a folding door, and very large studio windows lighting up the whole interior volume from one side. A spiral staircase is tucked into the back of the space, leading up to the bedroom and bathroom on the overhanging upper floor, past a built-in desk on the landing in between.

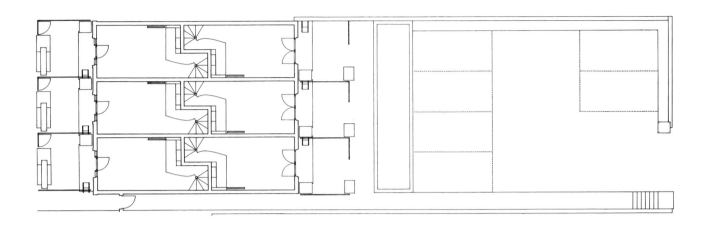

EAST ELEVATION TO SHEENDALE ROAD

The east elevation to Sheendale Road (middle and bottom) shows how the scale and proportions of the studios match those of the existing houses along the street, while maintaining a distinct contemporary character. The site plan (top) reveals a long narrow site with the studios grouped back-to-back in line with the adjacent villas. Three studios address the street, and three, accessed via a side passage, address a garden and a car-parking area at the back. The six dwellings are interlocked at the centre of the block around their staircase units.

(top) Sheendale Studios is in a conservation area and it was a requirement that the street elevation was designed to match the facades of the adjacent villas. Each studio house has its own front garden with copper clad meter boxes, and rendered bin and boiler enclosures.

(bottom) The garden facade features full height windows bringing maximum daylight into the three storey space within.

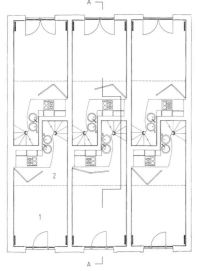

GROUND FLOOR PLAN

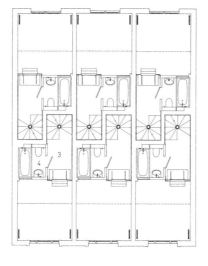

FIRST FLOOR PLAN

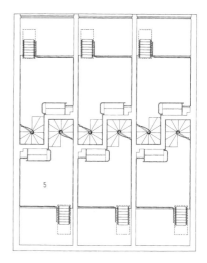

SECOND FLOOR PLAN

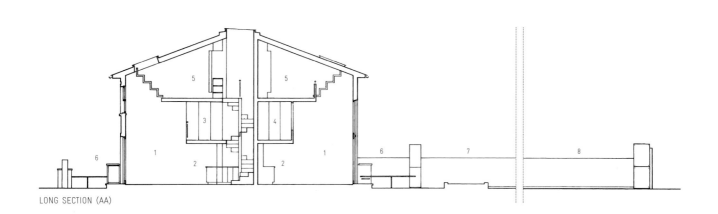

LONG SECTION (AA)

The long section from back to front
shows how the triple-height living
spaces work in tandem with the
bedrooms suspended in the roof spaces.

1	Living/Dining
2	Kitchen
3	Landing/Study
4	Bathroom
5	Bedroom
6	Private Garden
7	Communal Garden
8	Parking

1:50

0   2m

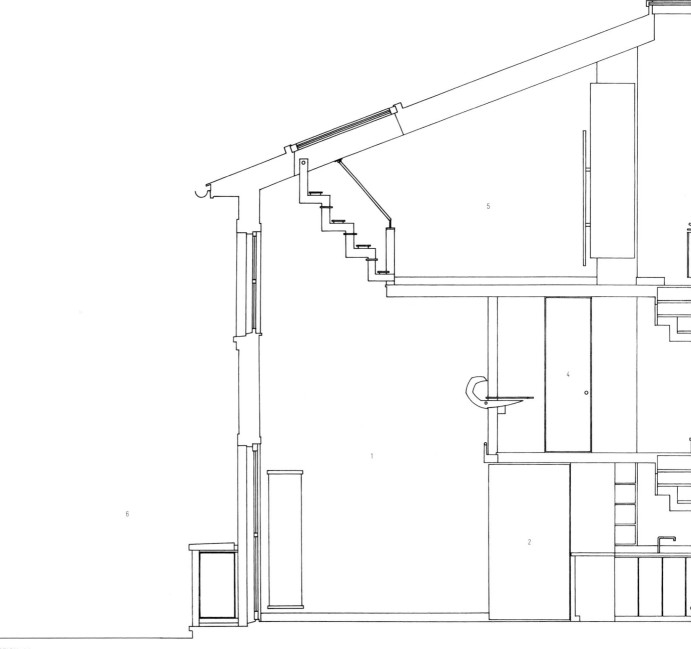

SECTION AA

The building has cavity walls to the exterior, made of blockwork insulated with styrofoam, and faced in brick. The party walls between each studio are built in blockwork. The roof is constructed using timber joists and finished in slates. These are fixed to battens laid on sarking felt, which covers the insulation between cross battens fixed to plywood decking.

The internal faces of the exterior walls to each studio are finished in plaster, and the sloping undersides to the roofs are finished in plasterboard and skim. Interior ceilings and walls are built in timber stud clad in painted plywood panels. The floors, joinery and staircases are in oak. The staircases have mahogany centreposts and aluminium handrails. The small staircase at second floor provides access to a rooflight as an alternative means of escape in case of fire.

1   Living Room
2   Kitchen
3   Bathroom
4   Landing/Study
5   Bedroom
6   Private Garden

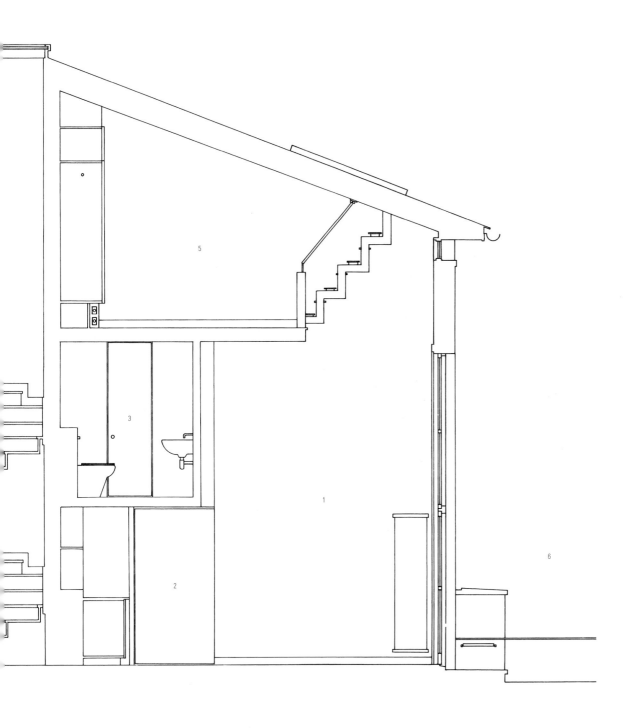

(top) Steel and perspex desk on landing overlooking triple-height living room with aluminium light cowl.

(bottom) The view up to the skylight in the roof reveals the extent of the vertical space. The desk on the landing can pivot to form a balustrade.

(top) Facade of studio house to rear
with two storey window/entrance door.

(bottom) View to rear garden and
parking court from landing.

151
White House

The extension of the White House was determined by the desire to make strong connections with the garden.

The clients for this project have always maintained that it transformed their lives. They made the decision to extend their existing 1920s house in suburban London, rather than buying a second home in the country. The approach was to open up the back of the house onto the garden, which featured a beautiful wisteria, now framed by sliding French windows. The new part of the house incorporates an open-plan kitchen, dining room and garden room, which double up as gallery space for the family's art collection. The garden can be glimpsed from the front of the house through glazed screens, and connections are also forged between the garden and the upstairs bedrooms by means of a pivoting steel staircase which can be lowered into position, or drawn up out of the way, as required.

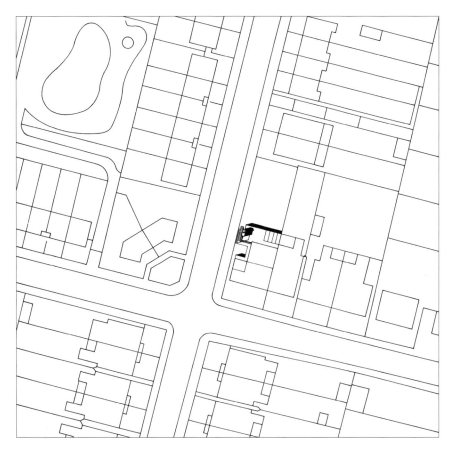

The location plan (top) shows how
the significance of the corner site is
enhanced. The side elevation (bottom)
takes on a new formality, and gives the
house an increased sense of enclosure.

1:200

0   10m

BEFORE

AFTER

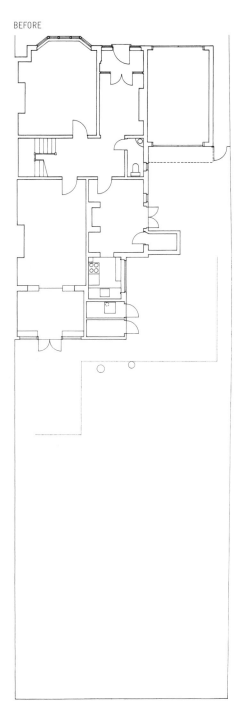

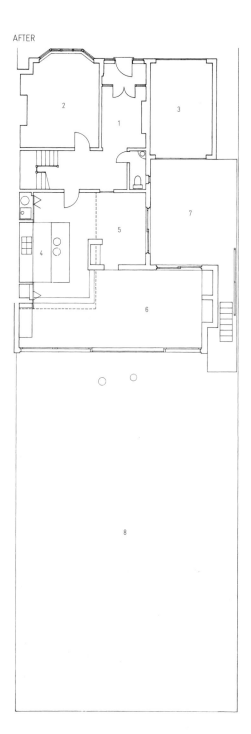

GROUND FLOOR PLAN

The new ground floor plan (right) shows
a vista through the house from the front
door out to the garden, focussing on
two wisteria trees, compared to the
layout of small rooms which existed
before (left).

1	Entrance Hall
2	Study
3	Garage
4	Kitchen
5	Dining Room
6	Garden Room
7	Courtyard
8	Garden

BEFORE

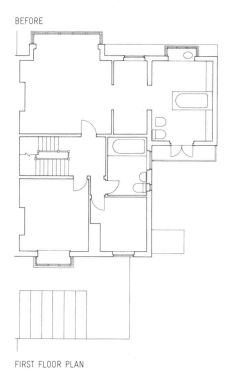

FIRST FLOOR PLAN

AFTER

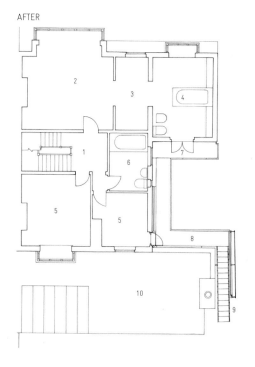

(right) The first floor plan shows how the new external staircase provides direct access from the en-suite master bedroom down to the garden (compare with original layout, left).

1 Landing
2 Master Bedroom
3 Dressing Room
4 Master Bathroom
5 Bedroom
6 Bathroom
7 Balcony
8 New Walkway
9 Pivoting Staircase
10 Roof to Extension

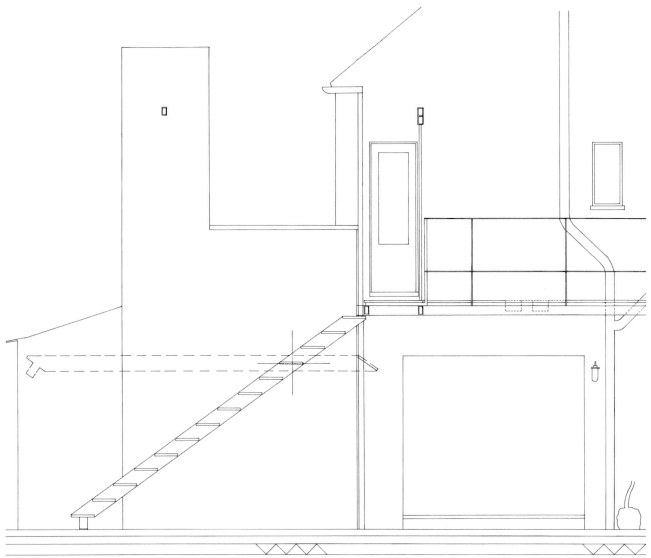

SECTION THROUGH THE PIVOTING STAIRCASE

The staircase connects the walkway at
first floor to the rear garden. When it
is winched into the horizontal position
(shown dotted) an alternative connection
is made between rear garden and
courtyard.

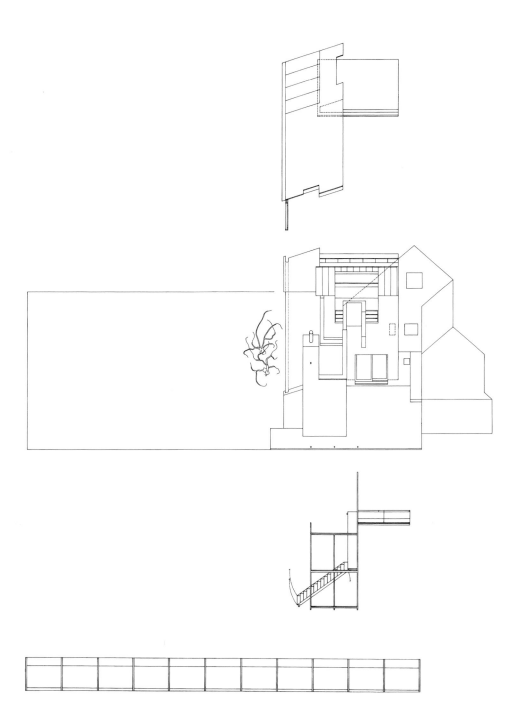

The exploded planimetric drawing
shows the various elements of the
project, including the glazed roof to
the extension (top), the wisteria and
internal fit-out (second from top), the
pivoting staircase behind the steel
frame structure (third from top), and
the existing fence (bottom).

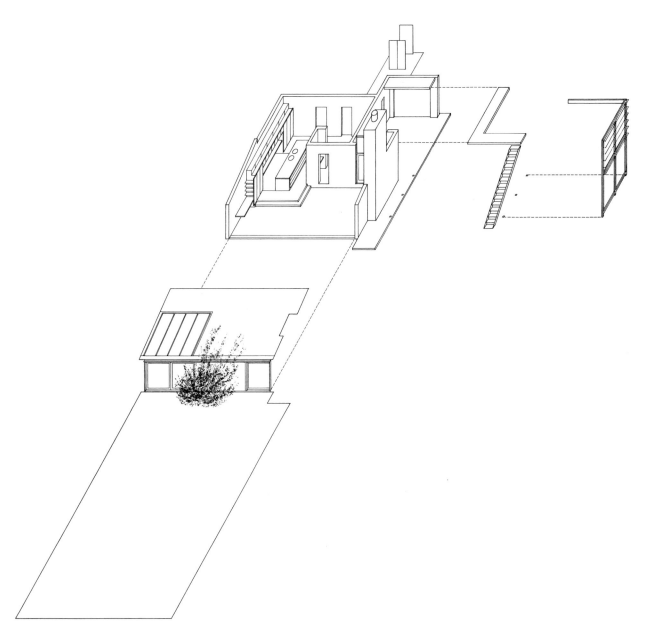

Drawing showing the various elements
of the ground floor layout, including
the glazed garden facade and roof
(foreground), the garden room and
opening (centre) and the pivoting
external staircase and steel frame
to the street (right).

(bottom) The new garden elevation gives
a grandeur and presence to the back
of the house, compared to its previous
appearance (top), and blurs the
boundary between indoors and outdoors.

(left) First phase of the project showing the new garden room extension with its tall chimney, which anchors the composition.

(right) Second phase of the project showing the suspended metal grille walkway and staircase to the rear garden. The courtyard is paved with concrete slabs inset with stone strips and oak spacers.

(top) The wisteria and garden are visible from the entrance hall of the house.

(bottom) The new physical route through the house to the main garden room and garden passes through the kitchen zone, turning it into the lynchpin of household activities and social events.

The garden room is bathed in light from
north, south, and above. The seating
arrangement can be focussed around
the fireplace, or towards the view of
the garden.

(top) The view from the garden room towards the kitchen and dining spaces shows the change in floor levels which mark the differentiation of these spaces.

(bottom) An oblique view from the dining area to the rear garden across the corner of the garden room.

(top) View from west with heather
screen now overgrown with ivy to
the left.

(bottom) Oblique view of the house
showing the ivy covered garden fence
merging with the heather screen.

A series of family Christmas cards, photographed and produced by Guy Montagu-Pollock, show how the new living spaces are colonised and inhabited by family members.

(middle) View through the wisteria into the garden room by night; (top) left angled perspective into the illuminated garden room and kitchen. (bottom) View from the first floor level external walkway into the courtyard and garden room below.

175
Invisible House
Invisible House 2

The 'invisible' approach to this design made it possible to obtain planning permission for construction of a new home on a back garden site in a residential suburban area of houses dating from the 1920s and 30s. By digging one storey of the house into the ground, around a central open courtyard, a substantial family house, in a contemporary style, could be fitted onto the site without causing problems of overlooking or infringing rights of light. The internal layout is designed as flexible open space which can be customised to fit specific requirements, and enjoys plentiful daylight by virtue of a fully glazed facade to the courtyard on three sides. The scheme includes an integrated parking space.

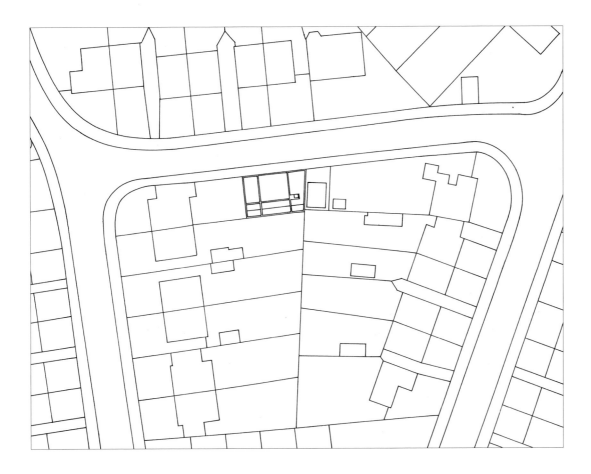

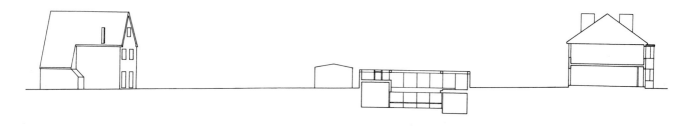

The location plan (top) shows the relationship between the new house, a three-sided volume round a courtyard, and its neighbours. The plot is excavated up to the boundaries, using the space to its maximum potential.

The section through the site (bottom) shows how, by digging the house into the ground, the existing line of vision between the houses is maintained with minimum disruption. The roof height of the two storey 'invisible house' is slightly lower than the adjacent garage structure.

175
Invisible House

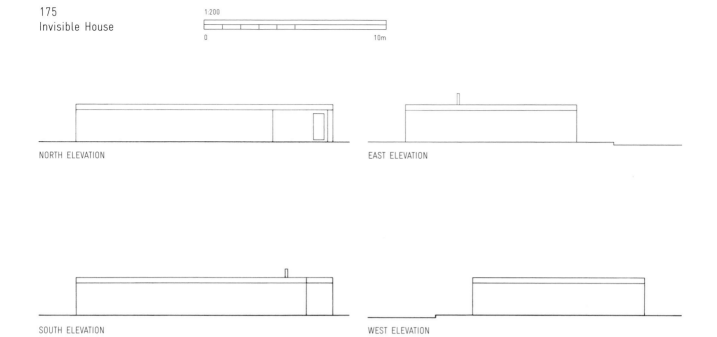

1:200

0   10m

NORTH ELEVATION

EAST ELEVATION

SOUTH ELEVATION

WEST ELEVATION

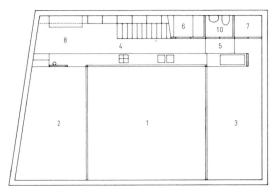

LOWER GROUND FLOOR PLAN

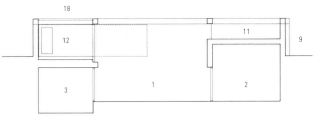

SECTION AA

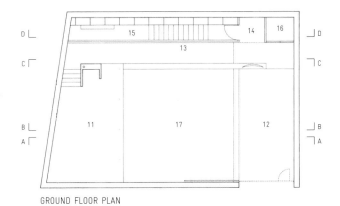

GROUND FLOOR PLAN

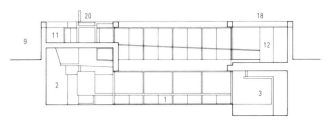

SECTION BB

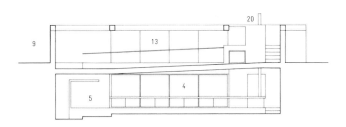

SECTION CC

ROOF FLOOR PLAN

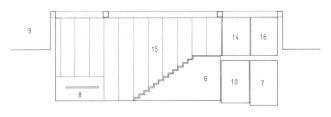

SECTION DD

1	Courtyard	8	Study	15	Stairwell
2	Living Room	9	2 Metre Garden Wall	16	Store
3	Bedroom	10	WC	17	Courtyard Below
4	Kitchen	11	Garden	18	Pergola
5	Bath	12	Driveway	19	Conservatory
6	Utility	13	Walkway	20	Barbeque
7	Wardrobe	14	Entrance		

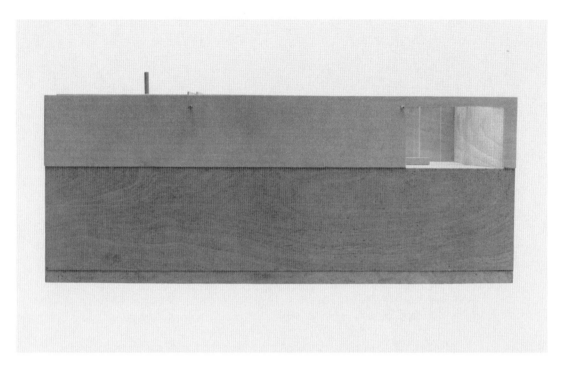

(top) Model shown closed. The
horizontal line indicates ground level
with the lighter fence and entrance
opening above and the retaining wall
to the excavated site below.

(bottom) Side of model removed to
reveal the Invisible House arranged
around a courtyard with raised roof
garden above the living room and
entrance ramp and parking space above
the bedroom. To the rear is the glazed
lean-to conservatory which encloses the
entrance staircase to the house at lower
ground level. Storage is provided in
cupboards adjacent to the staircase.

(top) View of living room with fireplace and small study beyond.

(bottom) View of bedroom with bath. The horizontal beams above the roof form a planting box. Both views reveal the spacious, airy quality of the interior.

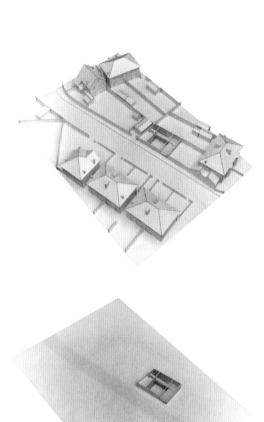

The Invisible House is inserted into a hole in the ground and is set behind the garden fence in the back garden of an existing semi-detached house in suburban west London. The roof of the Invisible House is mainly at ground level and is laid out as a garden with lawn, pergola and planting boxes. As the planting matures the Invisible House disappears into the existing landscape of suburban back gardens.

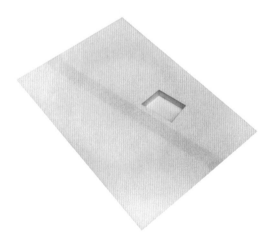

The map of interwar suburban Acton,
west London, shows how the Invisible
House infiltrates its suburban context,
by stealth, to increase density without
loss of garden space. The Invisible
House may be used as a 'granny' flat
or office connected to the existing
house, or as a separate house, studio
or even communal building serving
the neighbourhood.

The potential of constructing the Invisible House using an all dry construction system has been explored using sheet steel piling to provide a retaining wall to the site boundary. The piling system uses a method of vibrating each pile into the ground (this system is less noisy and disruptive than the more traditional method of piling — an important consideration especially in residential areas). The piles act as a vertical cantilever enabling the soil within the site to be excavated to the required depth. A steel frame is constructed to form the structure of the house with mini piles providing intermediate support. Within the frame an insulated timber plywood interior is formed. The driveway and roof are waterproofed with asphalt and the roof is laid with a soiless lawn. Feather edged vertical timber boarding is used for the elevations to the street and neighbouring properties to match materials used locally.

Typical use of sheet steel piling to excavate a tight site opposite Hawksmoor's Church of St Alphege in Greenwich.

NORTH ELEVATION

SOUTH ELEVATION

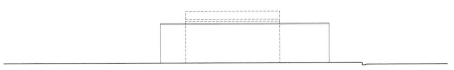

EAST ELEVATION

WEST ELEVATION

The external elevations to each side
show that the house is completely
concealed behind its perimeter fence.
The only clue to its presence is the
gate to the street (top).

1:200

0   10m

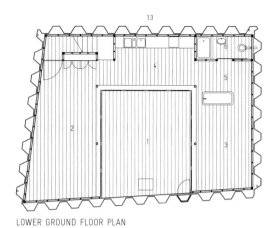

LOWER GROUND FLOOR PLAN

Invisible House 2 was designed around the idea of using sheet steel piling for the retaining structure. The lower ground (top), ground (middle) and upper level (bottom) floor plans show the relocation of the main entrance to the south-east corner, and a double height volume to the living room.

1   Courtyard
2   Living Room
3   Bedroom
4   Kitchen
5   Bath
6   Shower Room
7   Entrance
8   Void
9   Courtyard Below
10   Walkway
11   Driveway
12   Grass Roof
13   Sheet Steel Piling

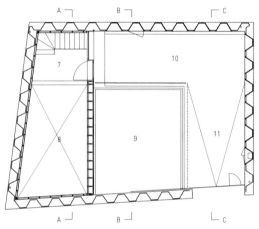

GROUND FLOOR PLAN

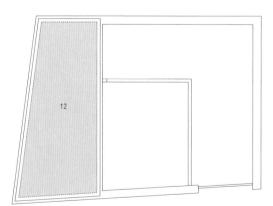

ROOF PLAN

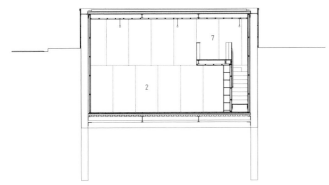

SECTION AA

The introduction of the double-height volume to the living room enables the alteration of Invisible House 2 in the future, to accommodate up to four bedrooms without increasing the size of the house. This is achieved by simply inserting a mezzanine floor into the double height space of the living room.

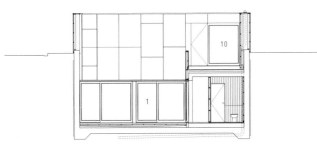

SECTION BB

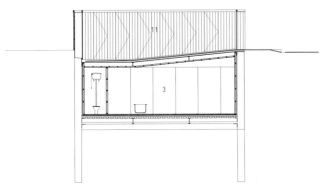

SECTION CC

1:50

0   2m

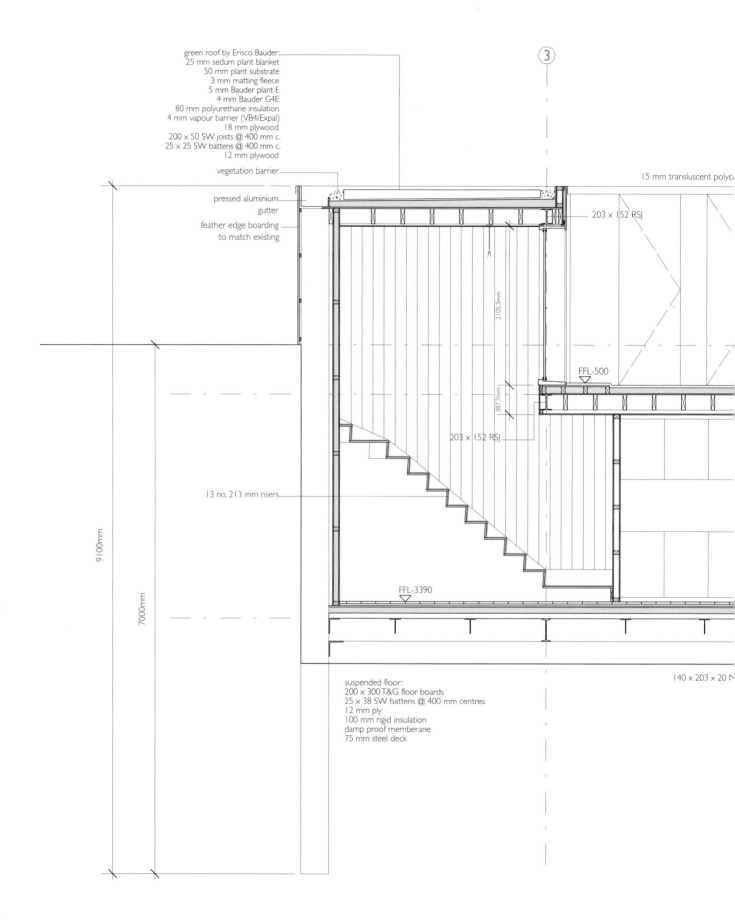

green roof by Erisco Bauder:
25 mm sedum plant blanket
50 mm plant substrate
3 mm matting fleece
5 mm Bauder plant E
4 mm Bauder G4E
80 mm polyurethane insulation
4 mm vapour barrier (VB4/Expal)
18 mm plywood
200 × 50 SW joists @ 400 mm c.
25 × 25 SW battens @ 400 mm c.
12 mm plywood

vegetation barrier

pressed aluminium
gutter

feather edge boarding
to match existing

15 mm transluscent polyca

203 × 152 RSJ

2105.3mm

FFL-500

387.7mm

203 × 152 RSJ

13 no. 213 mm risers

9100mm

7000mm

FFL-3390

140 × 203 × 20 N

suspended floor:
200 × 300 T&G floor boards
25 × 38 SW battens @ 400 mm centres
12 mm ply
100 mm rigid insulation
damp proof memberane
75 mm steel deck

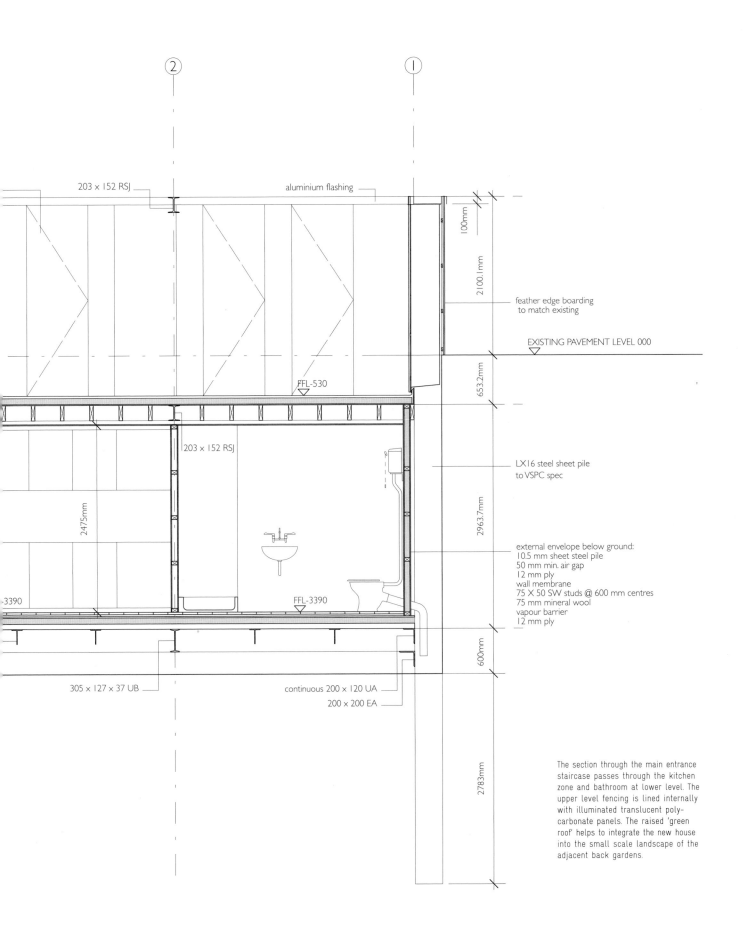

203 × 152 RSJ

aluminium flashing

100mm

2100.1mm

feather edge boarding
to match existing

EXISTING PAVEMENT LEVEL 000

FFL-530

653.2mm

203 × 152 RSJ

LX16 steel sheet pile
to VSPC spec

2475mm

2963.7mm

-3390

FFL-3390

external envelope below ground:
10.5 mm sheet steel pile
50 mm min. air gap
12 mm ply
wall membrane
75 X 50 SW studs @ 600 mm centres
75 mm mineral wool
vapour barrier
12 mm ply

600mm

305 × 127 × 37 UB

continuous 200 × 120 UA
200 × 200 EA

2783mm

The section through the main entrance
staircase passes through the kitchen
zone and bathroom at lower level. The
upper level fencing is lined internally
with illuminated translucent polycarbonate panels. The raised 'green
roof' helps to integrate the new house
into the small scale landscape of the
adjacent back gardens.

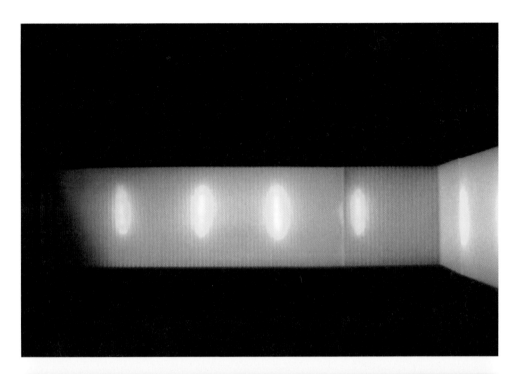

In Invisible House 2, the ceiling height
is raised, and polycarbonate sheeting
is used to generate a bright glow of
light through the upper level wall, in
the manner of a clerestorey (opposite
bottom and bottom this page). The same
material is used for cladding the inside
face of the enclosure to the side and
back of the site, back-lit at night to
illuminate the exterior spaces at ground
level (opposite top, and top and bottom).

195
Mehr House

This house was designed as part of a speculative development of retirement and holiday homes on a site in the foothills of the Western Ghats, three hours' drive north of Bombay. It is built out of reinforced concrete, following the local tradition, and designed to maximise air flow through the house. There are large open verandas to front and back, and the flat roof to the north can be used as a terrace commanding views of the hills, and as an outdoor sleeping space. Screens, blinds, canopies and shutters are used to provide additional shade when the house is in occupation.

PHASE II 'C'

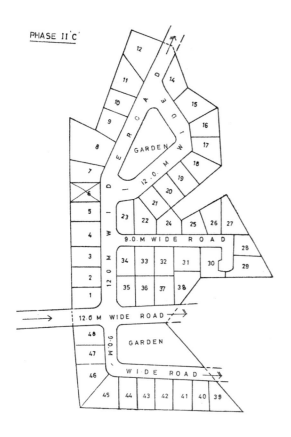

The layout of the site (top) is typical of speculative suburban developments all over the world, characterised by a linear arrangement of plots around cul de sacs.

The red earth landscape which forms the backdrop to the Mehr House site (bottom) is at the foot of the Western Ghats, in the hinterland of Bombay.

1:200

0   10m

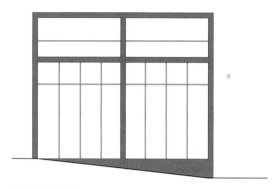

NORTH ELEVATION

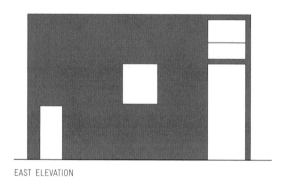

WEST ELEVATION

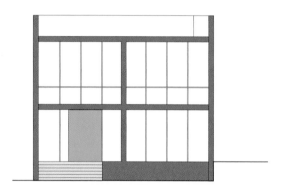

SOUTH ELEVATION

EAST ELEVATION

The three storey house is designed as a simple perforated cube, which can be opened up or closed by means of a layered arrangement of screens, blinds, canopies and shutters. The interior is set back from the frame to form verandas to north and south. The flat roof terrace with its pergola provides an area for shaded open-air living and may be used for sleeping in the hot season, in line with local tradition. The west and east elevations (top and bottom right) are less permeable, but articulated by smaller openings in the surface of the wall.

The ground floor plan (opposite top left) shows the main entrance, located on the south side, opening into a flexible, multi-dimensional space for living, eating and cooking, which flows through to the verandas on both sides.

The first floor plan (opposite top right) comprises two bedrooms and a bathroom, entered off a gallery looking into the double-height living space below.

The second floor provides outdoor living space on the north side set beneath a pergola with views of the hills (opposite bottom left and right). The raised south terrace may be used to put the washing out to dry.

1   Entrance
2   Living
3   Dining/Kitchen
4   Verandah
5   Landing Gallery
6   Bedroom
7   Bathroom
8   Void
9   Terrace
10 Pergola
11 Parking
12 Courtyard

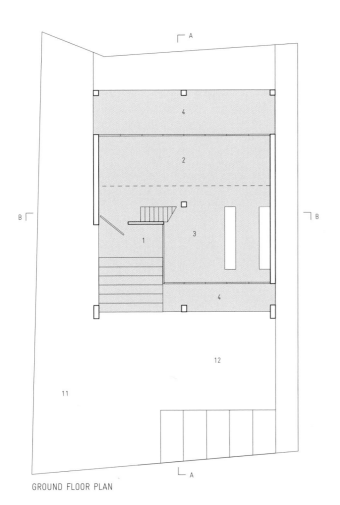

A

B

B

A

4

2

1   3

4

12

11

GROUND FLOOR PLAN

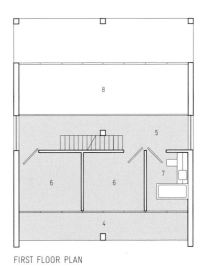

8

5

6   6

7

4

FIRST FLOOR PLAN

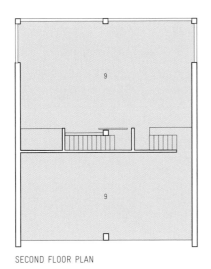

9

9

SECOND FLOOR PLAN

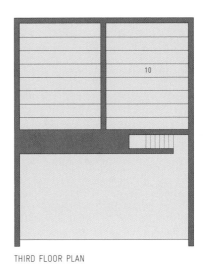

10

THIRD FLOOR PLAN

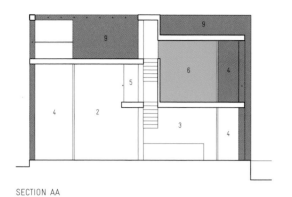

SECTION AA

SECTION BB

The east-west cross section AA (top) reveals a pattern of painted solid walls and voids. The north-south cross section BB (bottom) shows the interleaved floor plates hinging around the centrally located staircase. The concrete walls are painted externally in red to match the local earth and internally in shades of green. The floors are terrazzo throughout. The house provides a framework for living that may be customised with blinds and canopies when in occupation.

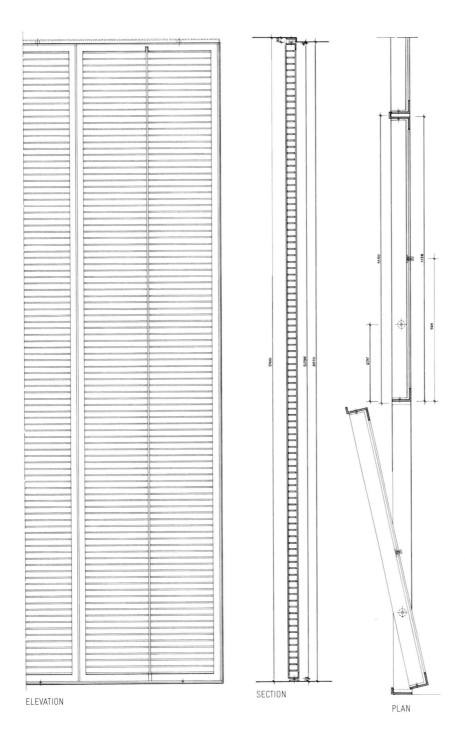

ELEVATION

SECTION

PLAN

All openings to the house, with the
exception of the solid pivoting front
door, are fitted with floor to ceiling
pivoting louvred doors, constructed
in locally available hardwood set in
galvanised steel frames and painted.
The louvres are adjustable. The doors
are also fitted with stainless steel fly
screens. This arrangement omits the
use of any glass which is not really
necessary in a tropical climate.

Views of the east (top) and west
elevation (bottom) showing the
sloping site excavated to provide a
private courtyard and the ground
floor of the house set at the highest
level of the site.

(top) View from the north-west. The driveway runs alongside the west elevation.

(bottom) View from the south-west. The rear courtyard may be fitted with an awning to provide shade and extend the public spaces of the interior when the occasion demands.

The existing building (top) is one storey higher on the road elevation than on the canal elevation. The proposed addition to the building (bottom) would create a more even profile on the skyline. The two bedroom flat on the front rooftop, addressing the main road, is very discreet, barely visible from street level.

254
Highstone Rooftop

This is a pair of flats designed to sit on top of an existing 1930s mansion block in north London. The flats are relatively lightweight, prefabricated structures that can be craned into position on top of the steel frame building in a matter of days. Access to the new dwellings is provided by the existing lift and staircases. The design accommodates the various housings already projecting above the roof-line (the lift motor room, water tanks, and staircase tower), and creates a smooth, uniform profile, 'completing' the building. Both units have two bedrooms and spacious living areas with glazed facades framing magnificent views out over the surrounding city landscape.

The site plan shows the location of
the L-shaped block on the corner of
a busy main road and an elevated
terrace along the Regent's Canal. The
building is a highly visible landmark.

1 Highstone Mansions
2 Elevated Terrace
3 Regent's Canal
4 Main Road
5 Railway Viaduct

254

Highstone Rooftop

1:500

0 25m

BEFORE AFTER

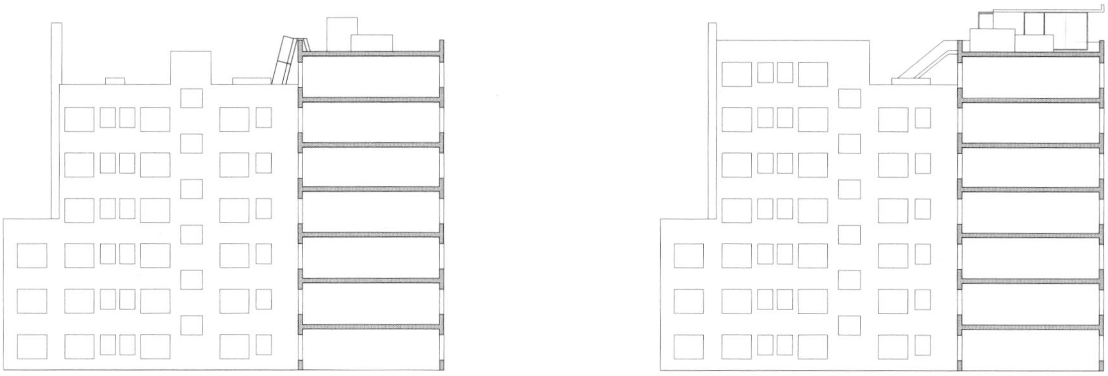

SOUTH-EAST ELEVATION

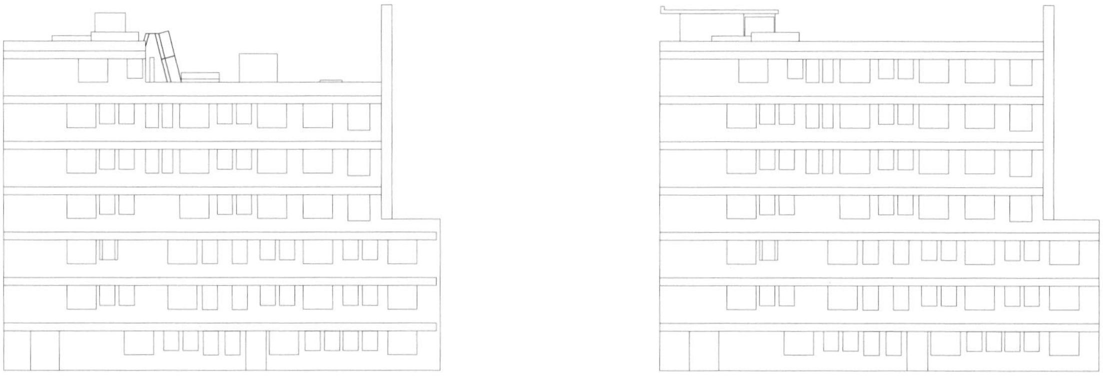

NORTH-WEST ELEVATION

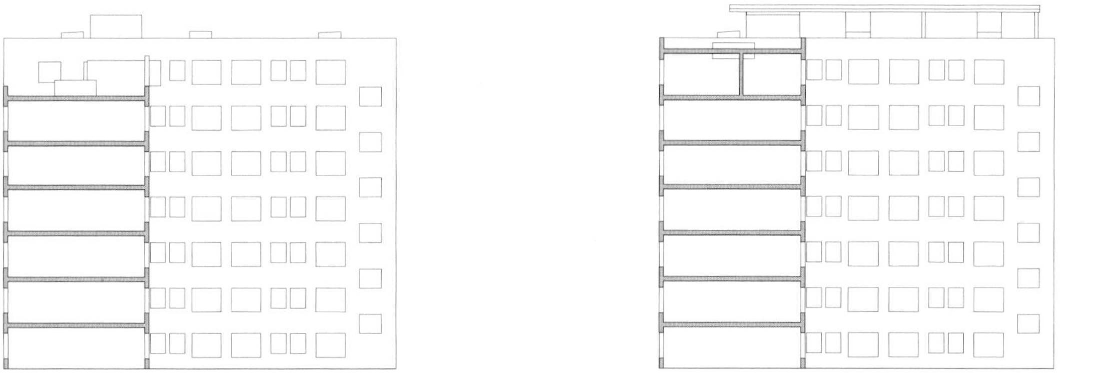

SOUTH-WEST ELEVATION

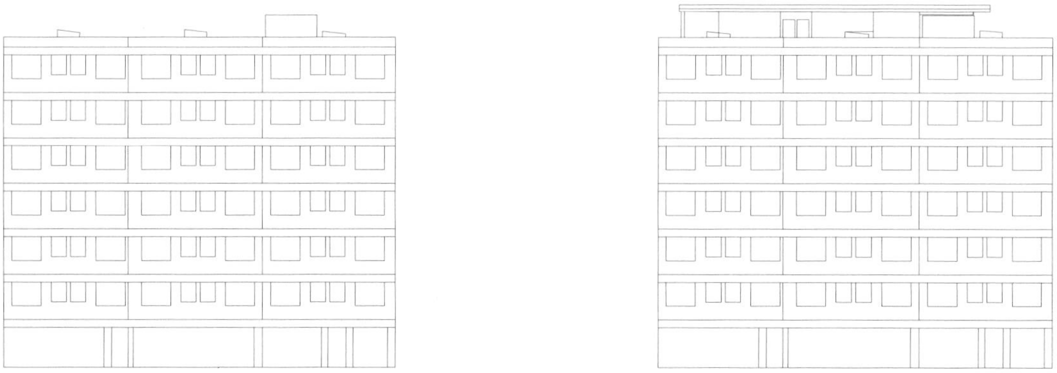

NORTH-EAST ELEVATION

BEFORE AFTER

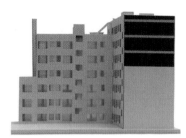 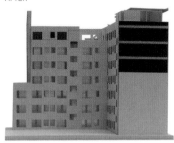

SOUTH-EAST ELEVATION

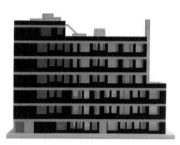 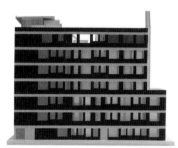

NORTH-WEST ELEVATION

SOUTH-WEST ELEVATION

NORTH-EAST ELEVATION

Photographs of the model show how
Flat A is integrated with the existing
facades and Flat B is designed as a
glazed pavilion set on top of the roof.

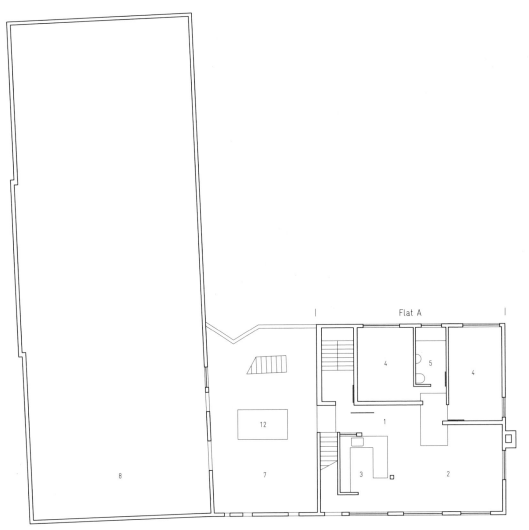

SIXTH FLOOR PLAN

Two flats are proposed for the existing
rooftop, with access via the existing
internal staircase and lift (not shown).

Flat A is constructed on the existing
lower flat roof by extending the
elevations upwards to form the external
walls to the south, east and west, and
enclose the existing stair tower.

Flat B (opposite) is constructed on the
existing upper flat roof in the form of
a pavilion with a balcony on four sides.

1   Entrance Hall
2   Living/Dining
3   Kitchen
4   Bedroom
5   Bathroom
6   Roof Garden
7   Courtyard
8   Existing Flats
9   Gallery/Library
10 Study
11 Lift Motor Room
12 Existing Tank Housings

The section (opposite bottom) shows
the staircase access to the roof garden
of Flat A, at the same height as the
existing upper roof. The courtyard space
between the existing and new structures
presents an opportunity to create a
small roof garden for residents of the
existing building

Flat B

10

12

3

4

5 4

9

12 1

2

11

12

12

12

6

A A

SEVENTH FLOOR PLAN

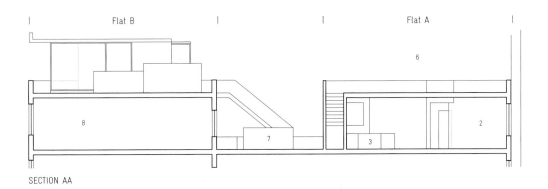

Flat B   Flat A

6

8

7 3 2

SECTION AA

The 'urbane' front elevation of Slim
House could be realised in a number of
different materials, according to context.

255
Slim House
Slim House 2

The Slim House was the winning design in a competition, Concept House 99, organised by the Daily Mail Group, and built as a show house at the Ideal Home Show. It is a scheme for a contemporary re-interpretation of the traditional British urban terrace house, to provide greater flexibility and comfort for twenty-first century living. The scheme offers a design prototype which could be built widely using prefabricated building methods and components, while maintaining a high standard of internal and external finish, and is intended to form part of a terrace of houses. The house is mainly single storey (90 square metres in volume), with a double-height room addressing the street at the front, which could also be subdivided horizontally to provide an upstairs space, possibly an office. Alternatively, the ground floor could be used as a shop, with a separate entrance and living accommodation above it. The remaining rooms are arranged in a linear sequence from the front to the back of the plot, each having full-height glazed sliding doors opening onto private courtyards, while the garden is situated on the roof, forming part of a sheltered, communal open space for relaxation and leisure above street level. The front of the house is designed with a three storey high facade which could be adapted to suit any particular street context, or designed as an artwork, advertising hoarding or fitted with photovoltaic panels on south facing elevations.

(top) Slim House was constructed as a show house at the Ideal Home Show, 1999, with a shimmering inflatable facade.

(bottom) The Model Terrace can be inserted into the traditional fabric of the city, maintaining the existing pattern of streets and terraces.

Five principles for the Slim House:

#1 Loose Fit/Flexible Accommodation
#2 Raised Threshold
#3 Roof Garden
#4 Active Facade with 'urbane' Front
      and DIY Back
#5 Vertical Extension

255
Slim House

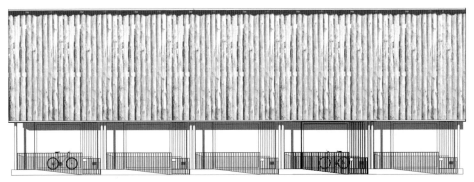

FRONT STREET ELEVATION

| 2 bedroom house and shop | 2 bedroom house | 3 bedroom house and office | 3 bedroom house | 3 bedroom house |

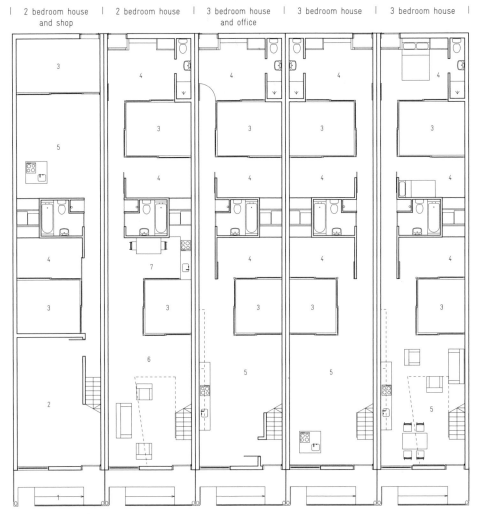

GROUND FLOOR PLAN

(Top) The front elevation and plans show a terrace of five Slim Houses grouped together, each arranged internally into different configurations (see key for details) to accommodate different living arrangements.

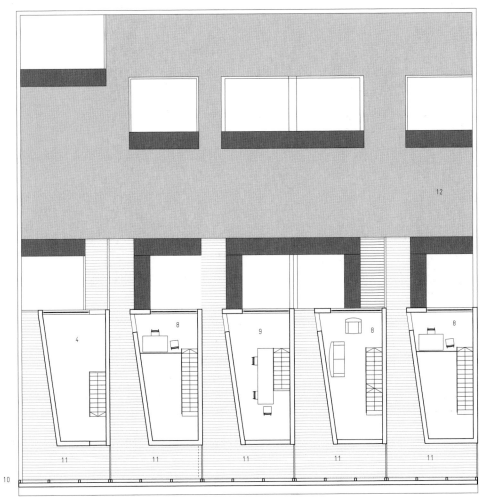

FIRST FLOOR PLAN

1   Porch
2   Shop
3   Courtyard
4   Bedroom
5   Living/Dining/Kitchen
6   Living/Dining
7   Kitchen
8   Study
9   Office
10 Active Facade
11 Private Yard
12 Communal Garden

1:200

0   10m

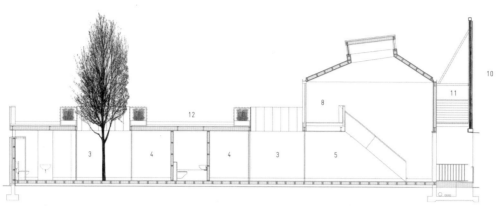

SECTION THROUGH THREE BEDROOM HOUSE

The long section (top) and model
photograph (bottom) show the
relationship between the facade,
the two storey pavilion, and the
rest of the house stretching out
behind.

1	Porch	7	Kitchen
2	Shop	8	Study
3	Courtyard	9	Office
4	Bedroom	10	Active Facade
5	Living/Dining/Kitchen	11	Private Yard
6	Living/Dining	12	Communal Garden

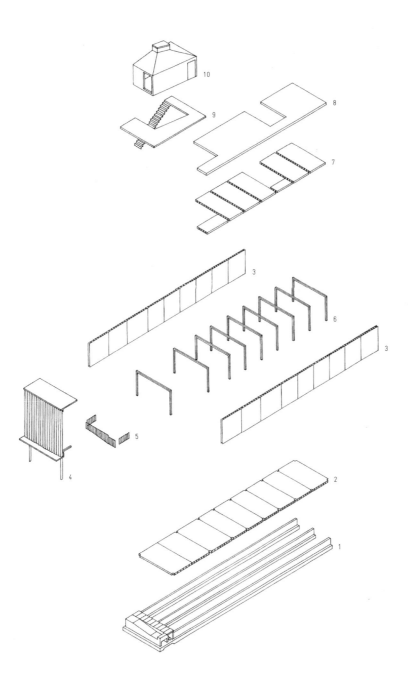

The house is designed as a series of prefabricated components which can be transported to the site and quickly assembled.

1 Concrete Foundations
2 Timber Floor Panels
3 Timber Wall Panels
4 Active Facade
5 Railings
6 Steel Portal Frames
7 Timber Roof Panels
8 Roof Covering
9 Timber Stair and Mezzanine
10 Timber Framed Pavilion

(top) Show house front with two storey inflatable entrance porch.

(bottom) Oblique view of the show house entrance.

(top) View of the show house from the side and close up of the DIY back (bottom).

(top) Perspective view showing the
living room interior with a sequence
of courtyards and rooms opening off
the wide corridor.

(bottom) Interior perspective view into
the courtyard.

(top) Double-height living room of the show houses at the Ideal Home Show.

(bottom) View of the show house interior looking toward the front door.

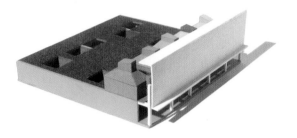

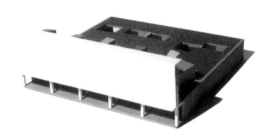

The model photographs (left) illustrate
the relationships between the closed
and open elements of the houses. The
internal courtyards bring daylight and
sunshine into the deep plan.

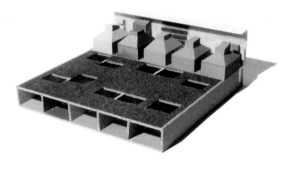

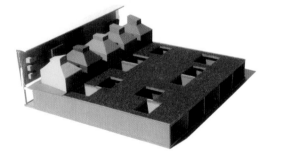

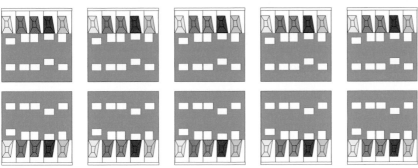

It is envisaged that Slim House could work well organised into short terraces grouped back-to-back into blocks on a regular grid layout. A narrow service route is provided through the centre of each block, allowing ease of access for the collection of rubbish, maintenance and deliveries (bottom).

(top) Suburban Mortlake.

The Model Terrace can be inserted into the traditional fabric of the city, maintaining the existing pattern of streets and terraces.

Further intensive design development on Slim House was
undertaken in conjunction with Yorkon Limited, the modular
building specialists, with the intention of constructing an
economically marketable prototype using Yorkon's steel frame
modular building system. In line with the recommendations
of the Egan Report, Rethinking Construction, 1998, the aim
has been to develop a new approach to residential buildings
using a method of lean construction that reduces waste and
improves efficiency. The intention is to deliver Slim House to
its customers in the same way as the best consumer-led
manufacturing and service industries to provide consistency,
continuity, innovation and value for money.

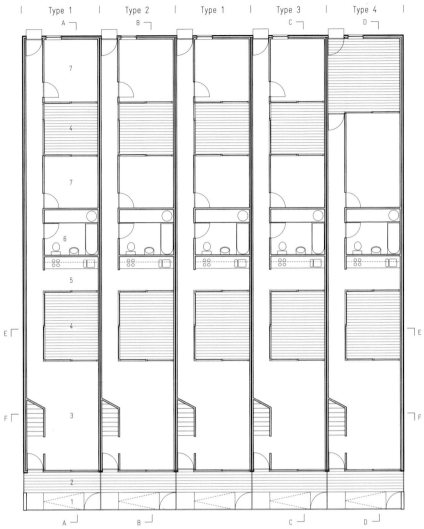

GROUND FLOOR PLAN

The further development of the Slim
House scheme, as a volumetric modular
construction, entailed a reduction in
the width of the house from 5 metres
to 4.2 metres, and an increase in the
height of the front pavilion from two
to three storeys. The kitchen is relocated
to the far side of the first courtyard,
back-to-back with bathroom services,
and the number of bedrooms on the
ground floor is reduced to two or one.

1   Ramp
2   Porch
3   Living/Dining
4   Courtyard
5   Kitchen
6   Bathroom
7   Bedroom
8   Bedroom/Office
9   Mezzanine
10 Void
11 Roof Garden
12 Covered Deck

255
Slim House 2

1:200

0   10m

| Type 1 | Type 2 | Type 1 | Type 3 | Type 4 |

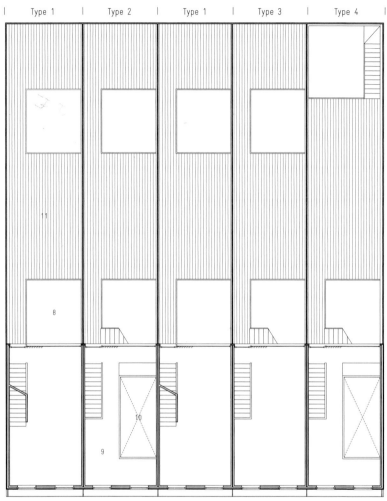

FIRST FLOOR PLAN

The first floor plan demonstrates the
scope to create a second or third
bedroom or office.

8   Bedroom/Office
9   Mezzanine
10   Void
11   Roof Garden
12   Covered Deck

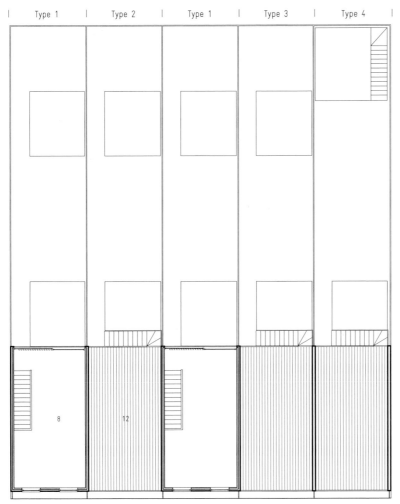

| Type 1 | Type 2 | Type 1 | Type 3 | Type 4 |

SECOND FLOOR PLAN

The second floor plan comprises a
further internal or external habitable
space, accessed either from within or
via an external staircase.

1:200

0   10m

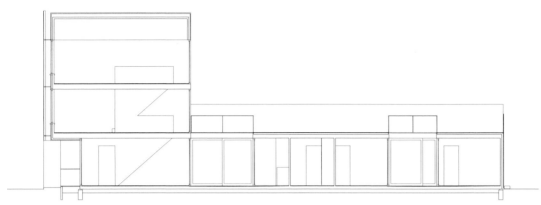

SECTION AA THROUGH HOUSE TYPE 1

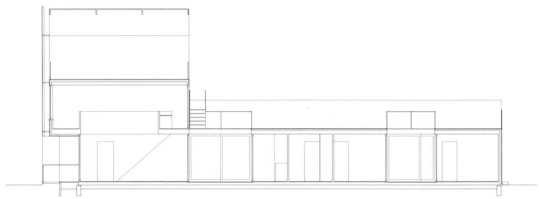

SECTION BB THROUGH HOUSE TYPE 2

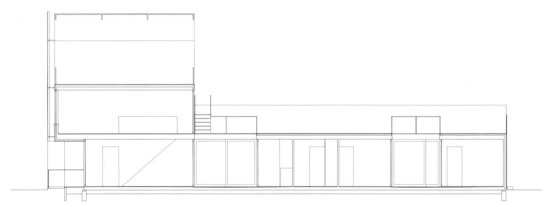

SECTION CC THROUGH HOUSE TYPE 3

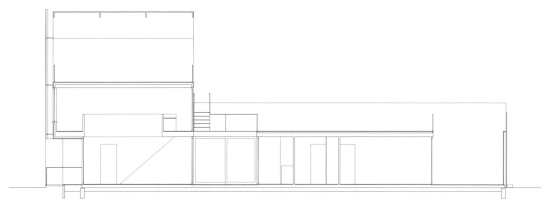

SECTION DD THROUGH HOUSE TYPE 4

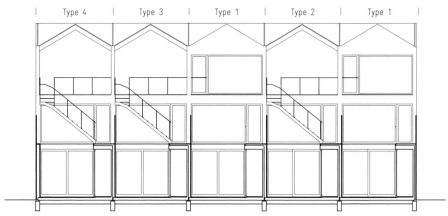

| Type 4 | Type 3 | Type 1 | Type 2 | Type 1 |

SECTION EE

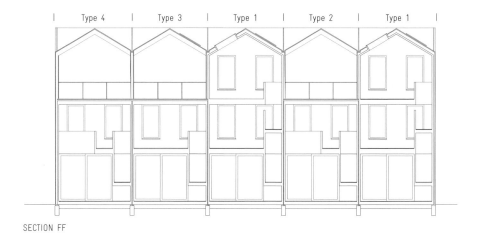

| Type 4 | Type 3 | Type 1 | Type 2 | Type 1 |

SECTION FF

The sections show the various ways in which the three storey volume at the front of the house may be designed to provide a variety of spaces including three separate enclosed floors – Section AA, a double-height living room, and covered open space at third floor – Section BB and Section DD.

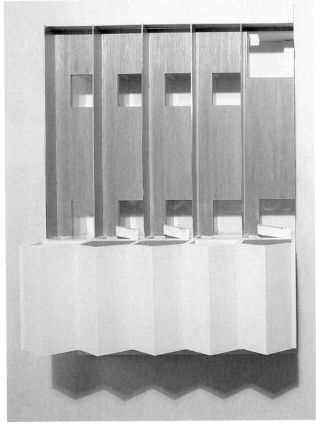

(top) View of the model showing the
house type with rear courtyard and
covered roof deck.

(bottom) Model, view of the roof and
roof garden.

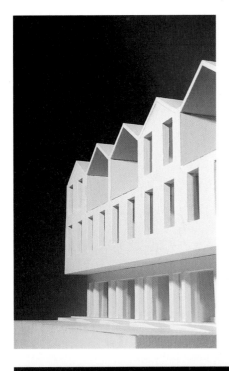
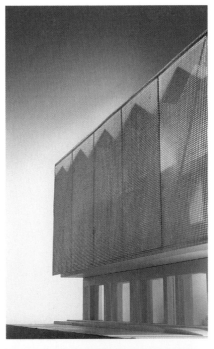
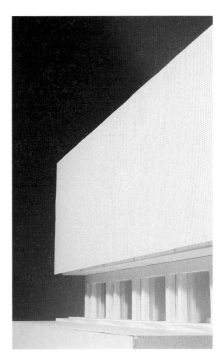

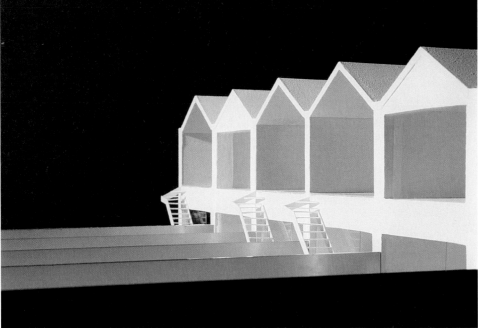

(top left) Oblique view of model
without screen.

(top centre) Shown with translucent
screen, back-lit.

(top right) Shown with translucent
screen, providing views out, but not in.

(bottom) Rear view with external
staircases to the covered roof decks.

Big House sits end-on to the river, forming a new landmark in a suburb of London characterised by mixed residential and industrial development. The blank street elevation protects the interior from the disturbance of busy passing traffic, while the Douglas fir boarding and brick plinth generate a warm, natural texture.

261
Big House

Building in conservation areas is always difficult from a planning point of view, but this house was nominated for several awards on completion, even though no attempt had been made to produce a traditional-looking building. On the other hand, the design and choice of materials were intended to give a sense of continuity with the existing built and natural environment, on a historic urban riverside site. The house is a four storey high, rectangular-shaped box clad in vertical timber boarding made from Douglas fir, with large windows framing oblique river views. It stands at right angles to a busy road, achieving a sense of privacy and detachment without disappearing behind a high wall. Inside the house, the main living space is elevated on the second floor, extending its full length, with a garden room and roof terrace on the top, bedrooms on the first, car-parking at ground level, and a cinema room in the basement.

STREET ELEVATION

1   Big House
2   Street
3   Brewery
4   Church
5   River

261
Big House

1:200

0   10m

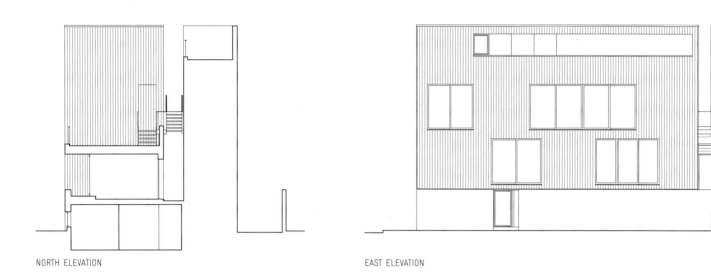

NORTH ELEVATION

EAST ELEVATION

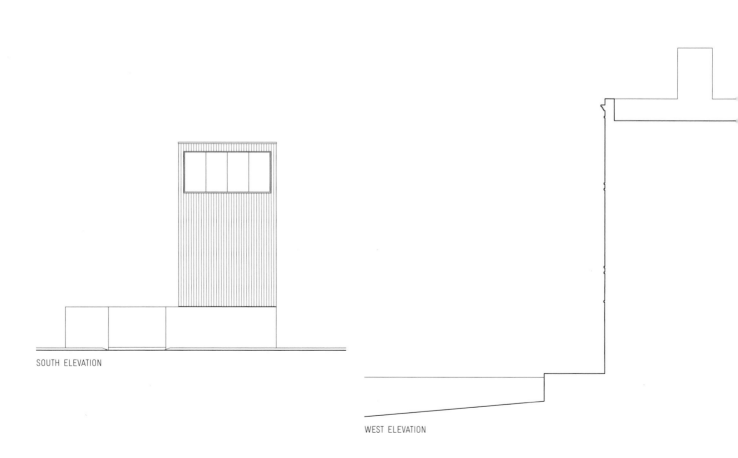

SOUTH ELEVATION

WEST ELEVATION

Little | Existing |

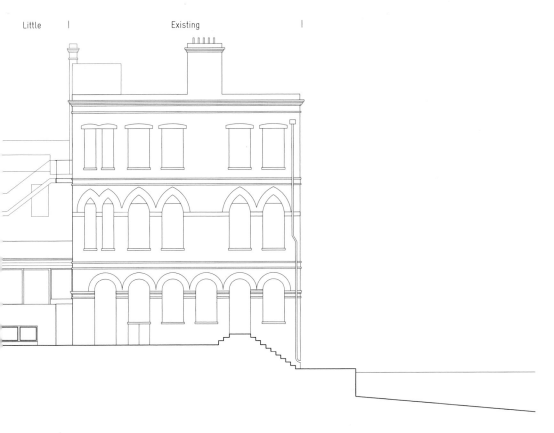

The enclosed north facade (top left) of Big House is viewed from the existing building on the site across the terrace over the Little House. The east facade (top right) reveals the similarity in scale and proportion between the old and new buildings, and the contrast in architectural detail. The south elevation (bottom left) is glazed at the top. The west facade (bottom right) is the most open, with its glazed garden room and visible roof terrace.

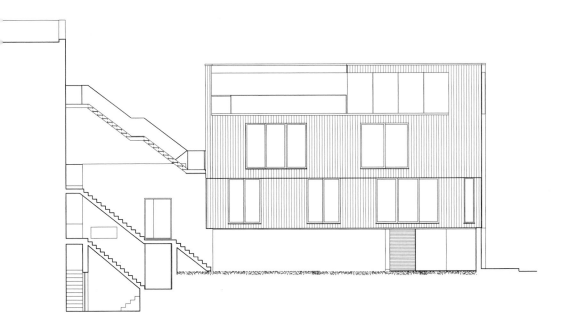

1:200

0   10m

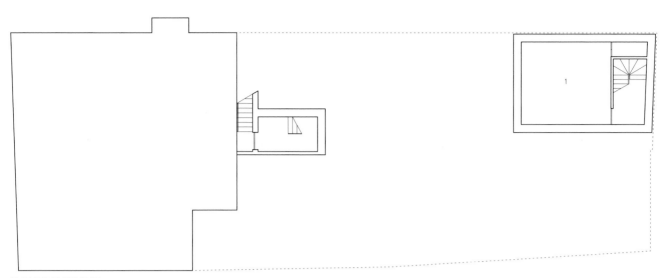

BASEMENT FLOOR PLAN

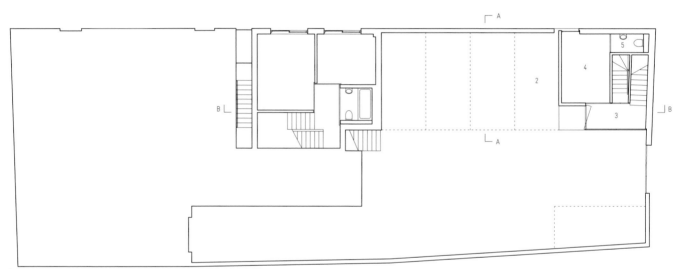

GROUND FLOOR PLAN

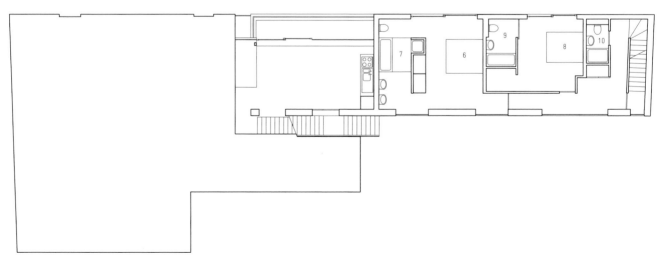

FIRST FLOOR PLAN

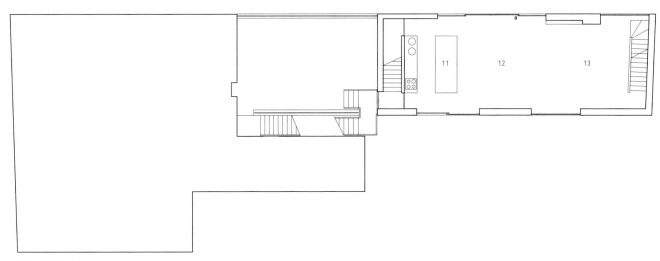

SECOND FLOOR PLAN

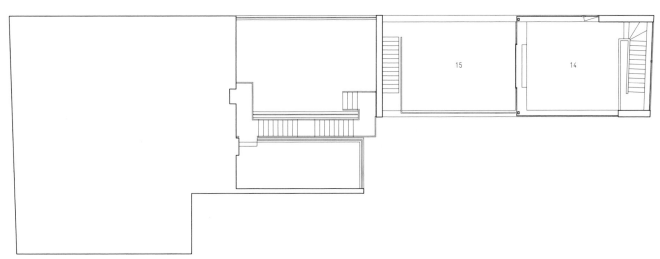

THIRD FLOOR PLAN

(opposite top to bottom) Basement, ground, and first floor plans of Big and Little Houses.

The second floor plan (top) of Big House contains the main living space, incorporating kitchen and dining area. The third floor (bottom) contains the roof terrace and garden room.

1	Cinema Room
2	Carport
3	Entrance Hall
4	Bedroom/Study
5	WC
6	Master Bedroom
7	Master Bathroom
8	Bedroom
9	Bathroom
10	Shower Room
11	Kitchen
12	Dining
13	Living
14	Garden Room
15	Roof Garden

1:200

0   10m

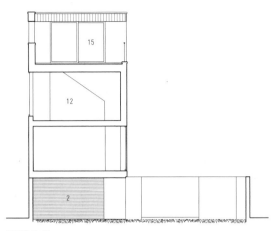

SECTION AA

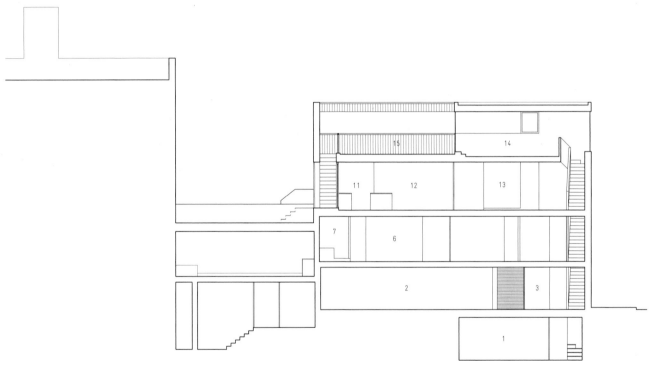

SECTION BB

The section through Big House (top) shows the relationship between the more closed and open sides of the roof terrace. The long section (bottom) shows the location of the staircase hugging the inside of the street edge of the house, with a separate staircase leading to the roof terrace from behind the kitchen area.

1   Cinema Room
2   Carport
3   Entrance Hall
4   Bedroom/Study
5   WC
6   Master Bedroom
7   Master Bathroom
8   Bedroom
9   Bathroom
10 Shower Room
11 Kitchen
12 Dining
13 Living
14 Garden Room
15 Roof Garden

Big House is a steel frame construction, pictured here in progress. The mass of the building is clearly outlined against the sky.

The undercroft (top) provides sheltered space to the front door and for car parking.

The east elevation (bottom), viewed obliquely from the river, shows the balcony and roof terrace to the Little House, and the juxtaposition between the old and new buildings.

Big House viewed from the street (top) appears as a glazed timber boarded box sitting on a brick plinth. The east elevation (bottom) with large asymmetrical openings is simultaneously transparent, reflecting and marked with the shadows of the trees in the foreground.

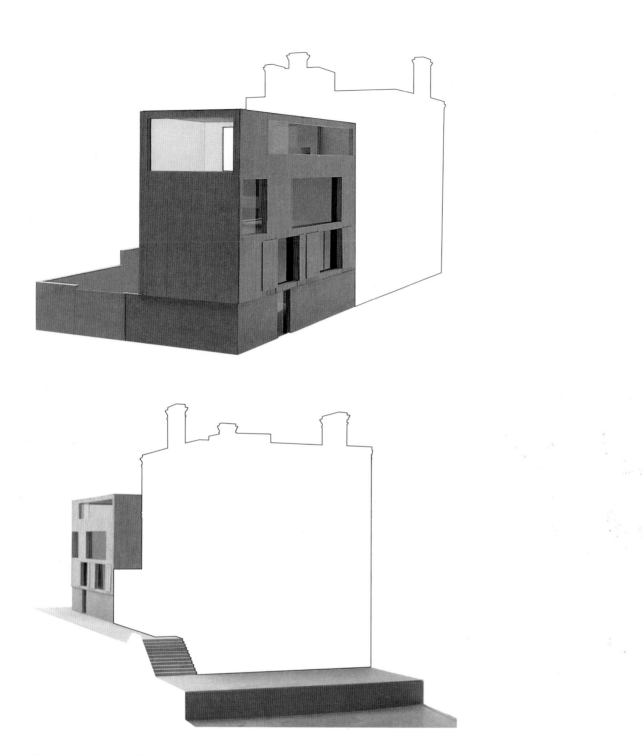

The model (top) is pictured from the
south-east addressing the street face
on and (bottom) from the north, with
oblique views of the river.

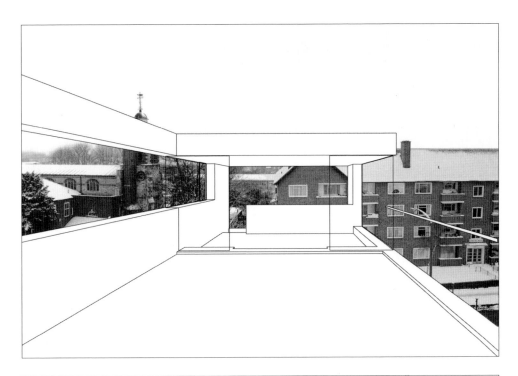

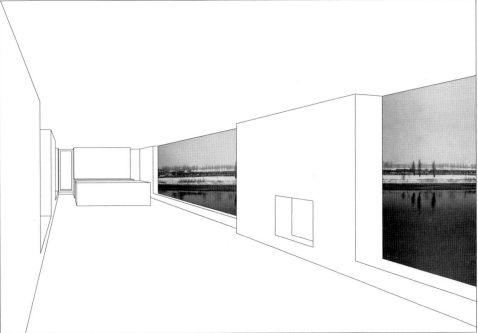

(top) The garden room is a highly
transparent pavilion at roof level,
looking out over the high street, and
opening onto the roof terrace. This
drawing reveals the eyrie-like quality
of the whole roof space.

(bottom) The open plan living/dining
room/kitchen occupies the whole of
the second floor.

(top) View of river from living room.

(bottom) Main bedroom and bathroom.

(top) Garden room looking towards
staircase.

(bottom) Garden room and roof garden.

(top) Staircase to garden room
from living room.

(bottom) View from ground floor
study window.

(top) Big House from the towpath.

(bottom) The river viewed from the
roof garden.

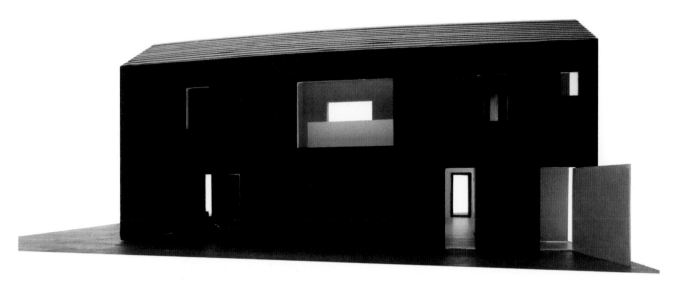

264
Monad House

This is a model for a house which can be built as a single unit, but can also be combined as courtyard or terrace developments, depending on the site — whether rural, suburban, urban fringe, or inner city brownfield. The basic model is a linear, timber frame construction, which can be wrapped around a central space, and extended or shortened as desired. The width is approximately 4.2 metres, the distance easily spanned by a joist in traditional domestic construction. The internal layout is essentially 'loose-fit' in character, with open-plan living and kitchen areas on the ground floor, providing the focal point for gathering, relaxing and entertaining, like a traditional farmhouse kitchen. Two further enclosed rooms at ground level could be used as bedrooms (suitable for the elderly, infirm or disabled), or as workspace, plus a bathroom and further storage. On the upper level is a large open landing suitable for family activities and two further rooms with attached bath/shower rooms, one of which has independent access via an external staircase to the courtyard below.

The central courtyard, which can be covered over if desired, allows the house to 'breathe', as well as providing storage space for awkward objects, such as bikes and pushchairs. It can also be used as a carport.

A variety of cladding materials can be used. The pitched roof over the two storey wing is suitable for photovoltaic panels, while the flat roof over the one storey section could be used as a garden in a development of several units, or turned into a pond to improve thermal performance of the building envelope.

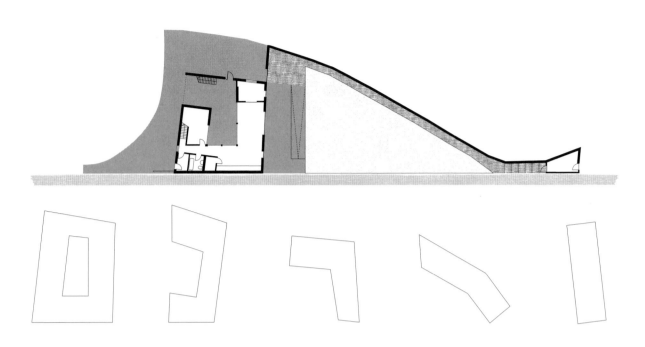

The diagrams (middle) present the
different ways in which the linear layout
of the house could be configured. The
scheme was specifically designed to be
adaptable for awkwardly shaped sites.

(bottom) View of the competition site at
the Museum of Welsh Life at St Fagans,
Cardiff.

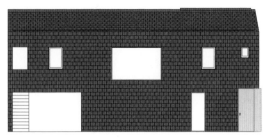

NORTH ELEVATION

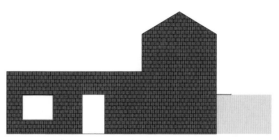

EAST ELEVATION

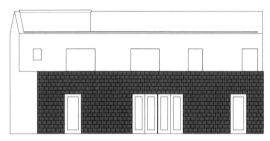

SOUTH ELEVATION

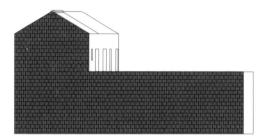

WEST ELEVATION

The north facade (top left) contains the
main entrance and vehicular access to
the courtyard, while a secondary
pedestrian entrance is located in the
east facade (top right). The west facade
(bottom right), along the boundary edge
is blank, and the south facade (bottom
left) contains French windows opening
onto a garden.

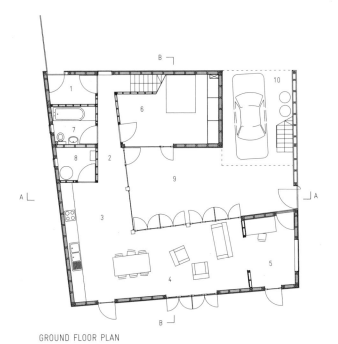

GROUND FLOOR PLAN

FIRST FLOOR PLAN

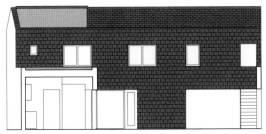

SECTION AA

The ground and first floor plans (top left and right) show the house wrapped around a courtyard, with a two storey wing on the north side. The upper floor has its own external staircase allowing potential use as separate office accommodation or 'granny flat'. The courtyard elevation of the north wing (bottom) shows the pitched roof with photovoltaic panels.

1	Entrance Lobby
2	Hall
3	Kitchen
4	Living/Dining
5	Study
6	Bedroom
7	Bathroom
8	Utility
9	Courtyard
10	Carport
11	Landing

1:50

0   2m

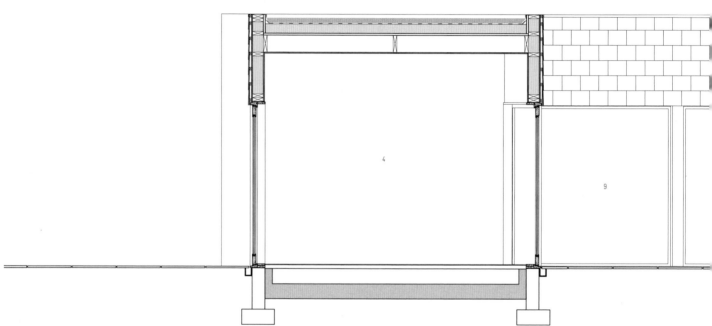

SECTION BB

The section through the house shows
the flat roof of the south wing, which
is designed to take a pool of water,
enhancing thermal insulation and
providing a pond for water storage.
The roof structure of the north wing
is engineered to be truss-free, creating
greater volume to the rooms at first
floor. The courtyard may be roofed
over with a horizontal insulating blind
(not shown) to provide the potential
for using the courtyard in cold or
inclement weather.

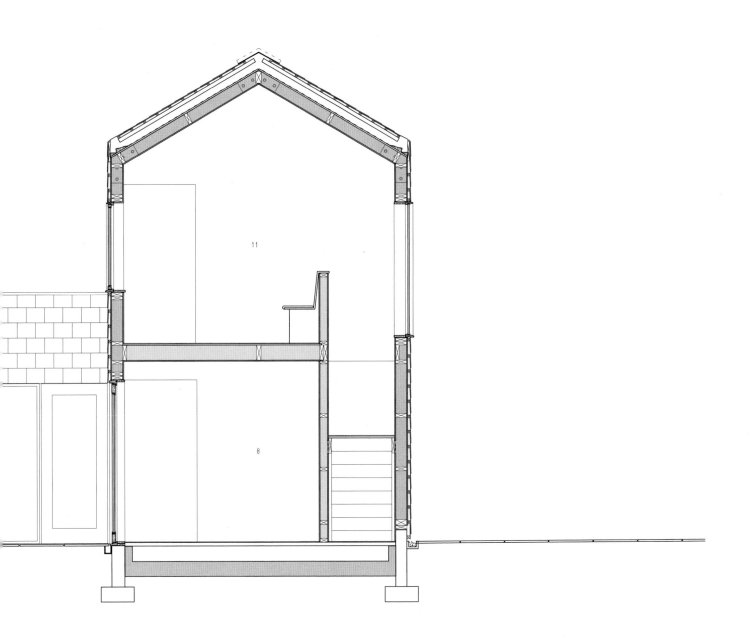

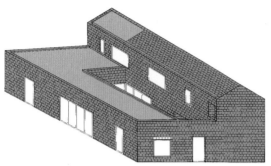

4

Four diagrams show the layering
of the structure:

1   Concrete Strip Foundations
2   Timber Frame with Sheep Wool
     Insulation
3   Plywood Sheeting
4   Artificial Slate Cladding

3

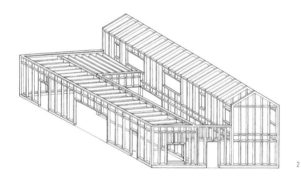

2

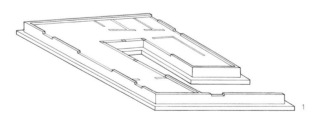

1

INVENTORY

walls and ceilings plasterboard 9.5mm and plaster skim finish ground floor sheet rubber flooring (dalsouple or similar) first floor wool carpet on underlay partitions soft wood studwork 100 x 50 100 mm insulation (warmcel) doors standard flush solid core timber doors joinery standard softwood shelving kitchen fittings welsh slate worktop 50 mm thick freestanding base units on castors kitchen appliances calor gas hob electric oven fridge/freezer dishwasher stainless steel sink with chromium plated mixer tap bathroom fittings proprietary white porcelain basins (three no) wc (three no) shower (one no) white enamelled steel baths (two no) with chromium plated spray mixer taps to basins, baths and shower utility fittings washing machine spin drier central heating calor gas fired balanced flue condensing boiler (potterton) panel radiators (runtal) with thermostatic radiator valves electrical fittings white plastic flush mounted sockets and switches (mk) decorations emulsion paint to plasterwork eggshell paint to all internal joinery (crown) ironmongery lever handled door furniture in nickel plated steel (allgoods) stairlift to interior staircase exterior – finishes and fittings paving to entrance, courtyard and terrace welsh blue black slate offcuts front entrance screen pale gold painted galvanised steel panel on steel frame front entrance door pale gold painted galvanised steel plated flush timber door walls artificial blue black slates pitched roof artificial blue black slates proprietary photovoltaic modules flat roofs pond and rainwater storage on asphalt soffit and awning galvanised sheet steel soffit and awning to carport ceiling decorations oak external doors and windows dark stained to match slate (sadolins or similar) garage roller shutter door in galvanised steel garden wall artificial blue black slates on battens on timber frame garden gates oak ledged and braced gates dark stained to match slate (sadolins or similar) stairlift to exterior staircase exterior quality ironmongery interior – furniture and furnishings ground floor entrance lobby coat rack shoe rack umbrella stand light fitting hall carpet runner light fittings blind curtain kitchen cutlery crockery cooking utensils spice rack food mixer chopping boards tea towels sundry bits and pieces living/ dining room dining table six no chairs sofa armchairs rug coffee table side tables television video hi-fi speakers light fittings blinds curtains study table two no chairs shelving computer monitor keyboard printer modem telephone fax shelving filing cabinet cupboard rug light fittings blinds curtains utility room calor gas storage shelving general purpose cupboard linen cupboard ironing board iron household tools ladder light fittings blind bedroom double bed bedside cabinet desk chair armchair dressing table cupboard chest television rug blinds curtains table lamp light fittings bathroom bathmat towel rail bathroom cabinet toothbrush holder soap dish shower curtain blind light fittings staircase handrail fitted carpet first floor landing table two no chairs armchair bookcase shelving unit mobile cabinet anglepoise computer monitor keyboard modem telephone/fax television video hi-fi posters paintings photographs fitted carpet blinds cupboards main bedroom double bed two no bedside cabinets two no armchairs dressing table bookcase chest television hi-fi speakers telephone fitted carpet blinds curtains two no table lamps light fittings bathroom bathmat towel rail bathroom cabinet toothbrush holder soap dish shower curtain blind fitted carpet light fittings dressing room wardrobes fitted carpet light fittings bedroom/study single bed bedside cabinet armchair table chair bookcase chest of drawers cupboard television hi-fi speakers telephone fitted carpet blinds curtains bedside lamp table lamp light fitting shower room showermat towel rail cabinet toothbrush holder soap dish shower curtain blind fitted carpet light fittings exterior – furniture and loose items carport storage cabinets bicycle rack four no dustbins for recycling waste materials terrace barbeque

The inventory is a resumé of the materials, fixtures and fittings to be used in the construction of Monad House.

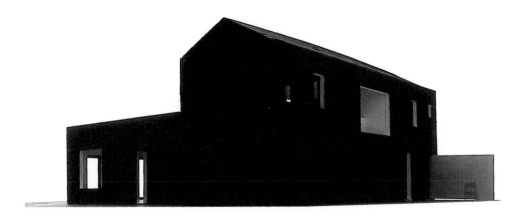

(top) Model photographed showing the
view from the north-east.

(bottom) Model photographed showing
the aerial view from the south-east,
with pond on the flat roof.

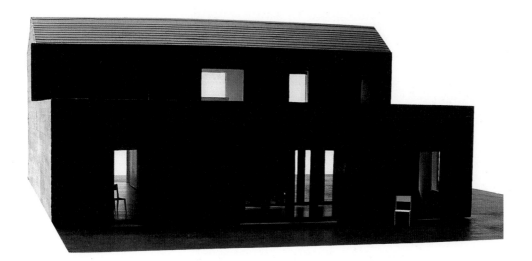

(top) Model photographed showing the view from the east, with glimpse into the courtyard.

(bottom) Model photographed showing the view from the south, illustrating the permeable quality of the house.

Views into the courtyard (top) and
courtyard with canopy to carport just
visible (bottom).

South-east corner (top), and view
through the living room looking east
(bottom).

One house

Two houses

Four houses

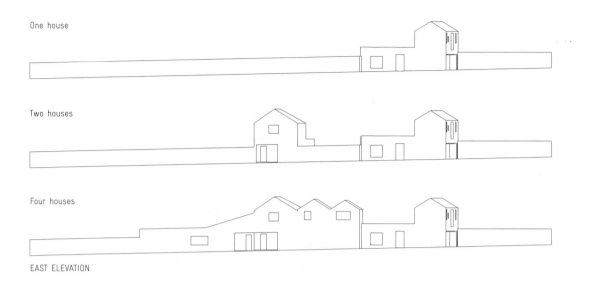

EAST ELEVATION

One house   Two houses   Four houses

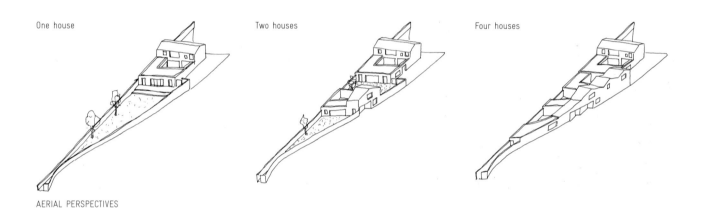

AERIAL PERSPECTIVES

The east elevations (top), aerial
perspectives (bottom) and site plans
(opposite) show how the basic house
model can be modified and multiplied
on a site to generate tight-knit
developments at various scales.

One house	Two houses	Four houses

GROUND FLOOR PLAN

FIRST FLOOR PLAN

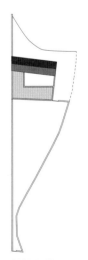  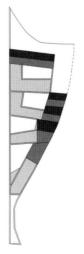

ROOF PLAN

265
Maisonette

The rear elevation (viewed from a passing train) shows large sliding windows to the new upper space, looking out over the back garden to the railway viaduct.

This project extended a first floor studio flat vertically into the roof space to create a spacious maisonette, with a bedroom on the upper floor, and living space below. The first floor living space is daylit from front and rear as well as from a skylight over the stairs, and provides a hanging space for the client's own artwork. The bedroom above opens onto narrow roof terraces on both sides, one, to the front, screened from the public gaze by a high parapet wall, the other, to the rear, opening onto views of the ivy-covered railway viaduct running behind the gardens. The provision of adequate storage was central to maintaining the spacious, open feel of the living spaces, with a storage wall containing the fireplace and kitchen, running the full length of the living space. In the bedroom, built-in cupboards are screened by large sliding panels.

Maisonette

STREET ELEVATION

The site plan (top) and street
elevation (bottom) show a typical
Victorian street layout of terraced
two storey houses, many of which
have been vertically extended into
their roof space.

1:200

0   10m

FIRST FLOOR PLAN

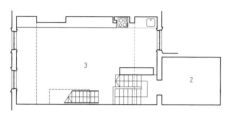

SECOND FLOOR PLAN

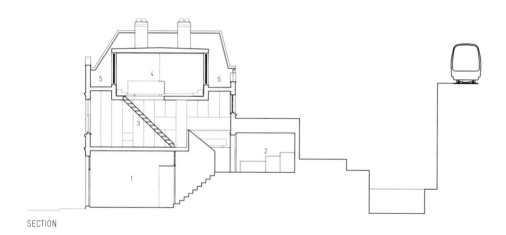

SECTION

The first and second floor plans (top
and middle), and the section from front
to back (bottom) demonstrate the
principle of extending a house vertically
without recourse to a 'mansard' roof
solution. The new room at second floor
level is constructed in place of the old
'butterfly' roof to form a simple box
volume that is inserted into the first
floor below. Because it is set back from
the parapet to the front facade its
impact from the street is less obtrusive
than a mansard roof structure.

1 Entrance Hall
2 Bathroom
3 Living/Dining/Kitchen
4 Bedroom
5 Terrace

(top) View of preliminary model. The staircase has been repositioned in the scheme as built (see section on opposite page).

(bottom) View into living room from bathroom half landing showing the storage wall to the right and top-lit staircase to the left.

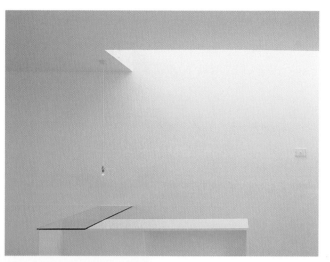

(top left) Second floor bedroom with view of roof terrace to rear with railway viaduct.

(top right) Second floor bedroom with view of rooflight over staircase.

(bottom) First floor living room with view of staircase from kitchen.

(top) Second floor bedroom with view
of roof terrace to front.

(bottom) First floor living room with
view of storage wall.

Bedroom at second floor with rooflight
over the staircase.

Detailed view of the wardrobe interior
to the bedroom on the second floor.

269
Pudding Mill House

The house occupies a narrow linear site bordered by a river on one side, and a busy road on the other.

Pudding Mill House is a linear building on a busy road in east London. The house is designed for a couple — a graphic designer and a photographer — each of whom has their own studio separated from their domestic accommodation by a covered courtyard. The elevation to the road forms a protective barrier between the outside world and the internal spaces, while the other side of the house, overlooking the Pudding Mill River, is mainly glazed to enjoy the open views across the landscape. This house offers space for living and working in one structure assembled out of prefabricated industrial building components.

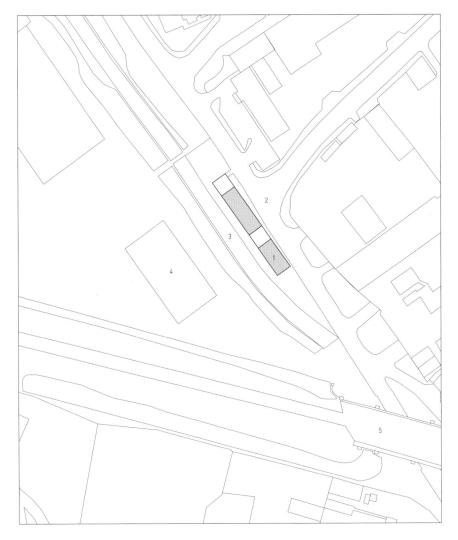

Pudding Mill House uses the simple
construction system of a modular steel
framed building by Parklines (Buildings)
Limited, illustrated here with corrugated
galvanised steel cladding.

1   Pudding Mill House
2   Road
3   Pudding Mill River
4   Tennis Courts
5   Disused Viaduct

1:200

0   10m

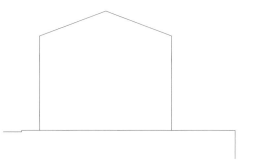

NORTH-WEST ELEVATION

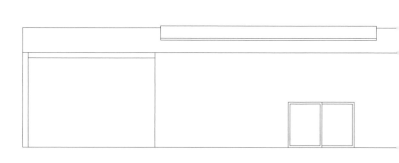

NORTH-EAST ELEVATION

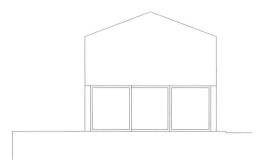

SOUTH-EAST ELEVATION

SOUTH-WEST ELEVATION

The north-east elevation (top right) is designed with few openings to provide protection against the busy road. The south-west elevation (bottom right) is more open to the river. The north-west elevation (top left) encloses the carport, while the south-east elevation (bottom left) is glazed to the double-height living room. The steel frame roof and walls are clad in profiled steel panels with standard aluminium 'patio doors' and windows and patent glazed rooflights.

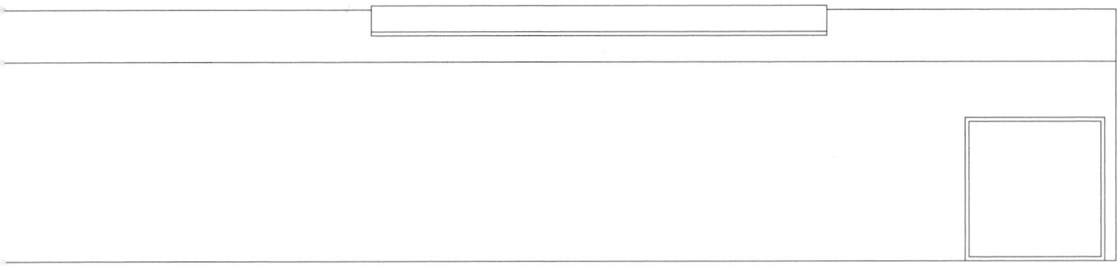

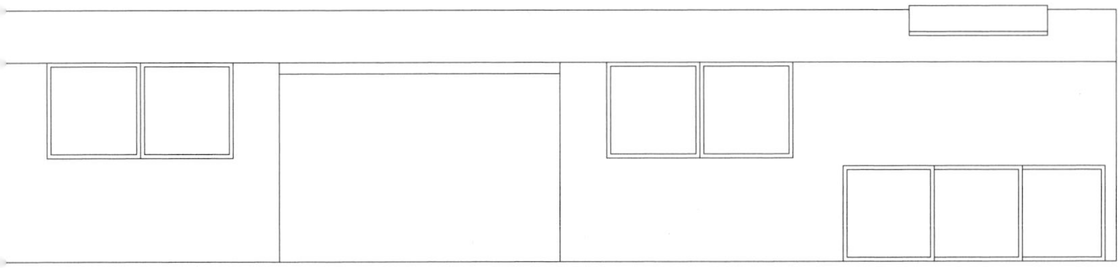

269
Pudding Mill House

1:200
0 ——————————————— 10m

| Unit 1 | Unit 2 | Unit 3 | Unit 4 | Unit 5 |

11

10

9   8   7

6

5

A

GROUND FLOOR PLAN

12   10   14   13

FIRST FLOOR PLAN

ROOF PLAN

11   10   13

10   6

SECTION AA

Unit 6 | Unit 7

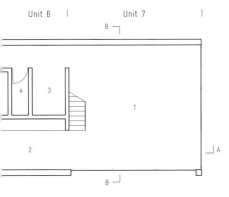

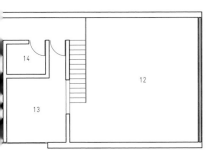

The ground (top) and first floor (second from top) plans show the division of the building into two zones, for living and working.

The roof plan (second from bottom) shows a large skylight over the double-height studio space, and a small one over the living space. The long section (bottom) shows the workspace at the west end, separated from the domestic quarters at the other end by a covered courtyard.

(bottom) Section through the double-height living room with staircase to the bedrooms on the first floor.

The plan consists of seven units, each 7 x 7 metres on plan, built using a proprietary steel frame.

The construction of the house may be phased and extended to suit the client's budget and requirements.

The frame is insulated to a high standard. Upper floors, wall and ceiling are lined with plywood and the ground floor finished in power floated concrete.

1	Living/Dining
2	Kitchen
3	Coats
4	WC
5	Utility
6	Courtyard
7	WC
8	Dark Room
9	Store
10	Studio
11	Carport
12	Void
13	Bedroom
14	Bathroom

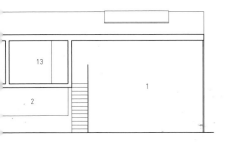

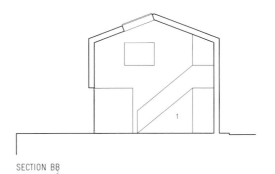

SECTION BB

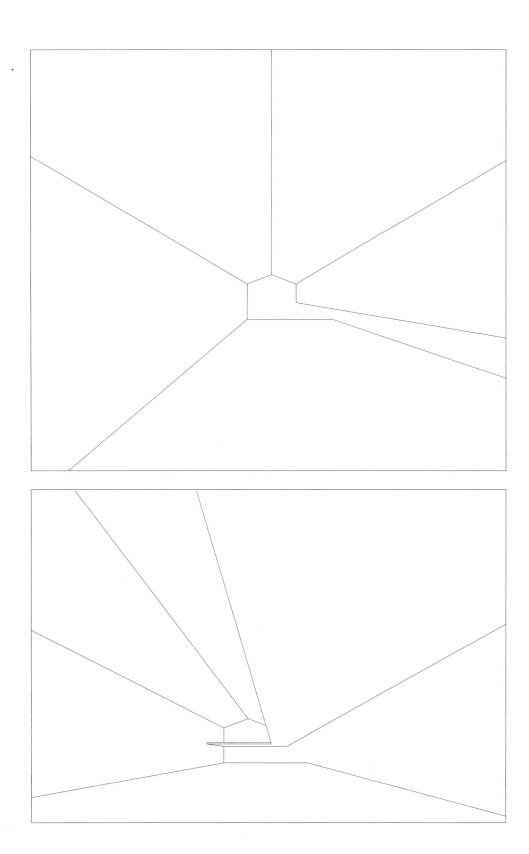

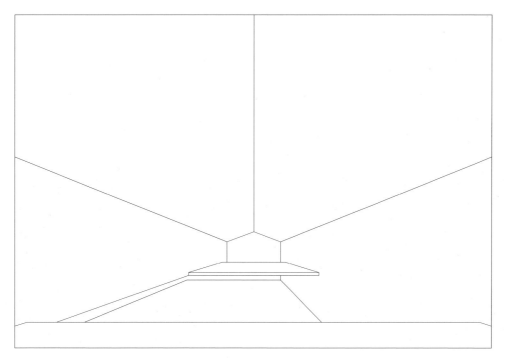

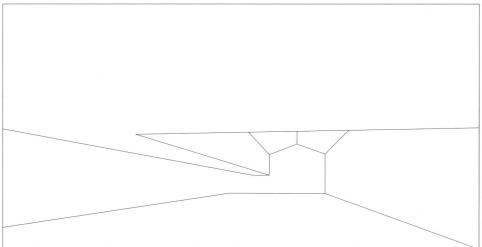

The house is intended to be built out
of prefabricated industrial components
which may be customised and
'domesticated' to suit budget, taste and
context. The diagrams here illustrate the
smooth-skinned linearity of the concept.

278
Rooftop Houses, The Piper Building

These rooftop houses were converted out of two tank rooms on the roof of a former British Gas laboratory, altered in the mid-1990s into luxury flats. A modular, steel-framed construction system was used, allowing the units to be assembled and fully fitted out internally in the factory, transported by truck to London and installed by crane in a few days. The two ends of each unit are fully glazed, framing panoramic views over the Thames River, while the remaining facades are solid with smaller windows and clad in metal mesh, which catches and shimmers in the light. Each house has two bedrooms with en-suite bathrooms, and a spacious living area with integrated kitchen and dining areas.

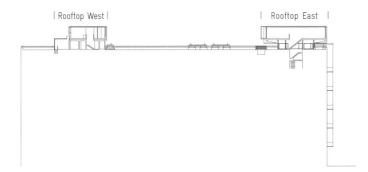

| Rooftop West | | Rooftop East |

The Piper Building roof forms the datum
for the two new roof top houses. (top)
Section, (middle) roof plan and (bottom)
view from across the River Thames.

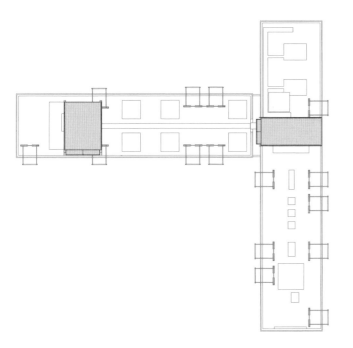

1:200

0   10m

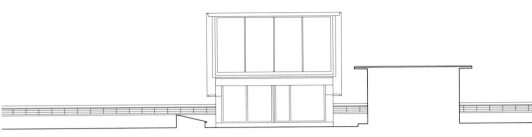

EAST ELEVATION

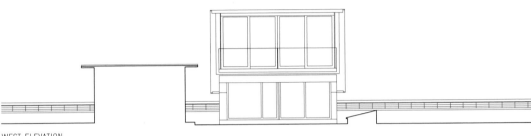

WEST ELEVATION

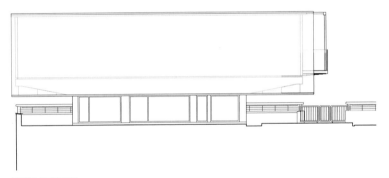

NORTH ELEVATION

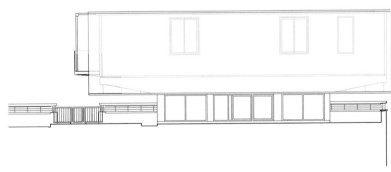

SOUTH ELEVATION

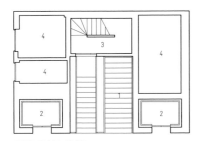

FIFTH FLOOR PLAN

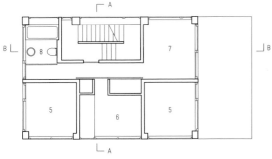

LOWER LEVEL PLAN

Rooftop East

The lower level plan is a conversion of the existing rooftop plant room. The upper level consists of five volumetric modular units craned into place and bolted together to form a single building.

1   Main Staircase
2   Lift
3   Entrance
4   Plant
5   Lift Motor Room
6   Study
7   Bedroom
8   Bathroom
9   Living/Dining
10   Kitchen
11   Balcony

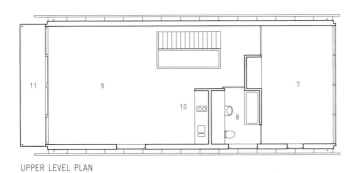

UPPER LEVEL PLAN

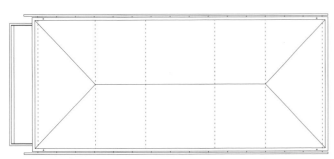

ROOF PLAN

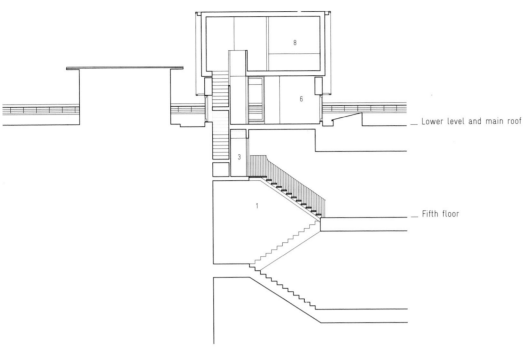

— Lower level and main roof

— Fifth floor

SECTION AA

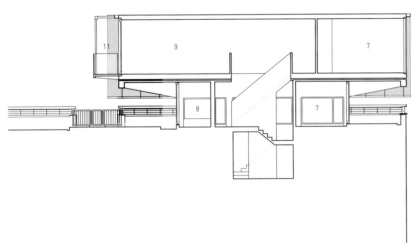

SECTION BB

1   Main Staircase
2   Lift
3   Entrance
4   Plant
5   Lift Motor Room
6   Study
7   Bedroom
8   Bathroom
9   Living/Dining
10   Kitchen
11   Balcony

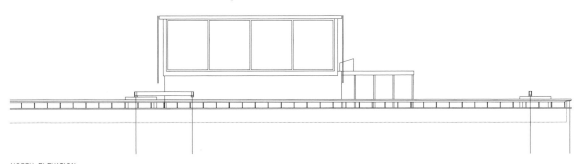

NORTH ELEVATION

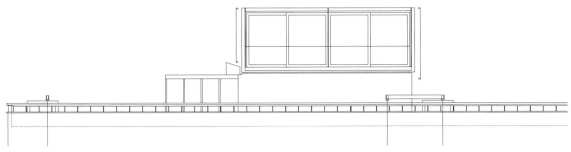

SOUTH ELEVATION

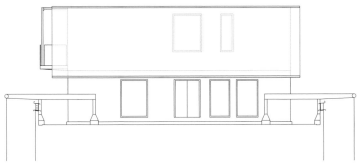

EAST ELEVATION

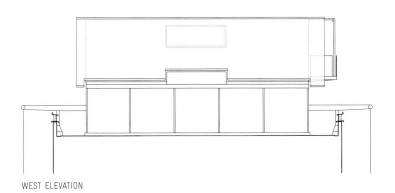

WEST ELEVATION

Rooftop West

The glazed north and south elevations
(top and second from top), contrast with
the more enclosed elevations to east
and west (third from top and bottom).

1:200

0   10m

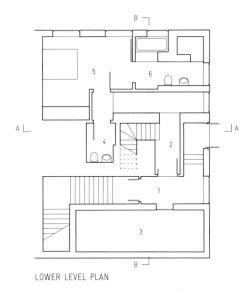

LOWER LEVEL PLAN

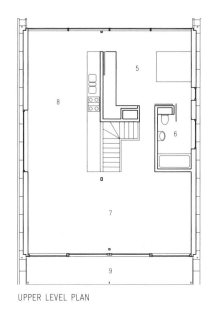

UPPER LEVEL PLAN

ROOF PLAN

Rooftop West

Lower (top left), upper (top right) and roof (bottom) plans, showing loose-fit flexible living space on the upper floor, opening onto the balcony. The lower floor contains a bedroom with en-suite bathroom. Rooftop West's lower level is a conversion of the existing plant rooms and circulation block. The upper level consists of three pre-fabricated volumetric modular units.

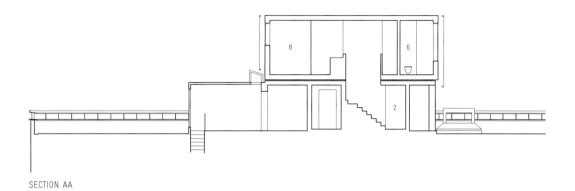

SECTION AA

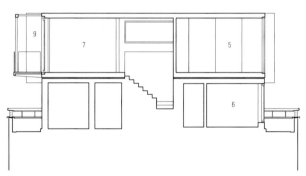

SECTION BB

1 Landing
2 Entrance Hall
3 Plant
4 WC
5 Bedroom
6 Bathroom
7 Living/Dining
8 Kitchen
9 Balcony

The houses were assembled in the
factory, transported to the site by truck,
and craned into position on the roof.

(top) Upper level Rooftop East in the
foreground with Rooftop West in the
background.

(bottom) Craning of first module onto
Rooftop West.

INVENTORY

to construct, on the roof, three prefabricated modules (rooftop west) and five prefabricated modules (rooftop east): kalzip aluminium standing seam roof and aluminium
guttering; stainless steel flashings; locker wire weavers stainless steel mesh screens
with folded edge seams and stainless steel framing; levolux silver coloured fabric
blinds to balcony with stainless steel framing; clear structural glass balustrades
with stainless steel fixing plates; painted structural mild steel balcony frame; 50 mm
wide square edge iroko balcony decking; reynaers international silver anodised
aluminium external doors, windows and curtain wall with clear and opaque acid
etched double glazed units; 50 x 5 mm silver anodised aluminium projecting frames
around windows; light grey sto external render system; light grey powder coated
aluminium wall end flashings; external walls – 10 mm viroc render board bonded
to hanson tis 100 mm composite wall panel comprising of 100 mm high density
insulation framed with fibre glass pultrusions and sandwiched between 1 mm
bonded sheet metal, bolted to structural steel frame; rolled hollow section mild
steel structural frame, steel sections not exceeding 160 x 80 x 10 mm, with welded
joints; floating floor – 19 x 190 mm solid oak floor boards, 12 mm and 9 mm
bonded plywood, 55 x 45 mm profloor dynamic floor battens, under-floor heating
pipes and insulation between dynamic battens; structural floor – 126 mm deep
floor deck comprising ward multideck 80 metal decking fixed between two sheets
of 18 mm structral plywood; internal walls – two layers of 12.5 mm plasterboard,
fixed to 70 mm galvanised metal studs, 50 mm mineral wool insulation, with skim
coat plaster finish painted with white matt emulsion; varnished; painted white mdf
skirtings; white 'velour' formica colorcore on mdf kitchen units with 'cameo-white'
corian counter top and moulded inset sinks; gaggenau stainless steel electric hob,
fan extract, oven, refrigerator, freezer, dishwasher, bosch condenser washer-dryer;
a-lite pendant and surface mounted light fittings with stainless steel reflectors and
white braided cord; low-voltage downlighters above kitchen units and in bathrooms;
bette 'classic' white enamelled steel baths, armitate shanks 'braemar' white wall
hung wc's, armitage shanks 'portman' white wall hung basins, chrome wall mounted
bath and basin taps, flush mounted silver mirror bathroom cupboard doors; chrome
habitat wall mounted shaving mirror; domus 'porcelanico' green grey and turquoise
25 x 25 mm wall tiles to bath and basin walls; full height painted white emulsion
cupboard doors with coburn sliding door gear; allgood 'modric' range of silver
anodised aluminium ironmongery; mk white plastic surface mounted switches and
sockets; fire and smoke alarm; under-floor heating throughout; 'white aluminium'
colour painted mild steel staircase with pre-cast off-white terrazzo treads; tretford
'blackberry-584' cord carpet to existing stair lobby

The inventory is a resumé of the
materials, fixtures and fittings to
be used in the construction of the
Rooftop Houses, The Piper Building.

145

(top) View from east of Rooftop East overlooking The Piper Building's main entrance.

(bottom) Rooftop West viewed from the north-east.

The former gas headquarters building is
surrounded by small scale mixed use
development and open spaces typical
of the inner city.

(top) View from the north-west across
the bowling green.

(bottom) View from the south-west.

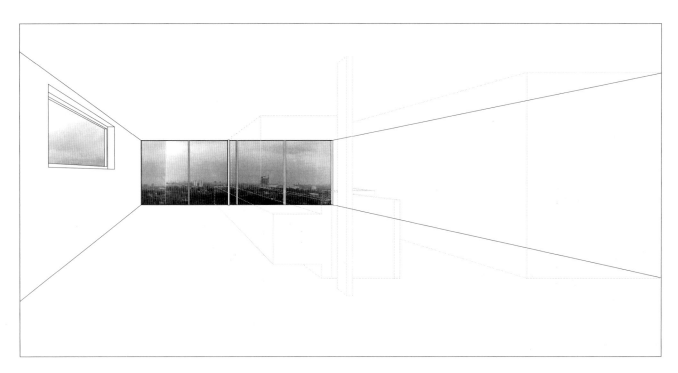

(top) Rooftop West interior, the view of
the west London skyline to the north.

(bottom) Rooftop West interior, the view
of the river to the south.

(top) Rooftop East living room interior,
framing the view of Rooftop West.

(bottom) View of the river from the
bedroom of Rooftop East.

The rooftop of The Piper Building was seen by the client as an opportunity for 'brownfield' development. The pavilions help to pull together a roofscape that is constantly changing as a result of small scale garden interventions made by residents. The metal mesh screens change quality dramatically given different light conditions.

(top) East elevation of Rooftop West.

(bottom) Rooftop East in close-up with Rooftop West in background.

(top) Rooftop East overlooking the London skyline at night.

(bottom) Night view of the west elevation of Rooftop East.

307
Baffoe House

The long section through the model, viewed from the west, reveals a double-height entrance hall and living space, enhancing air flow and environmental ambience.

The client for this house lived and worked in London but owned land on the outskirts of Accra in Ghana, part of a larger site blocked out for suburban density residential development at the edge of a rapidly expanding city. Drawings for a house in a grand neoclassical style had been produced by a previous architect. This scheme represented a significant reworking of that project, in response to local architectural traditions, climatic conditions and available materials. The plan is one room deep, with a linear sequence of spaces all opening onto a verandah running the length of the house. The organisation of the house, including a double-height living room, and two first floor bedrooms opening onto their own first floor verandah ensures that it is well ventilated and comfortable even when very hot. The drawings and photographs of the model were taken by the client to Ghana and interpreted by his builders at the site without supervision by the architect.

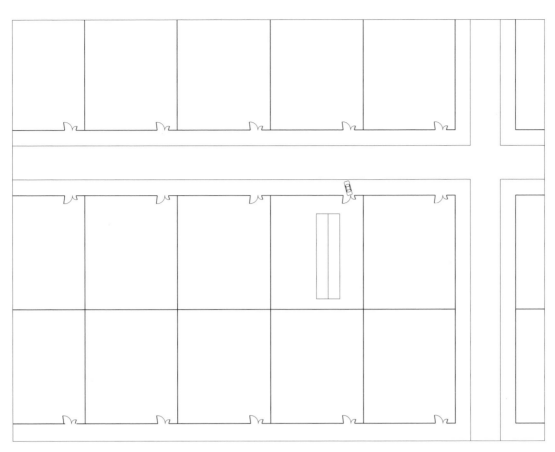

Site works. Digging out the
foundation trenches.

1:200

0   10m

NORTH ELEVATION

SOUTH ELEVATION

(from top left clockwise) North, east,
west and south elevations of the
house, designed to be built in rendered
block-work with concrete floors and
verandah structure, and double-skin
corrugated sheet steel finish to roof.
The main entrance and entrance to the
carport are located on the east facade.

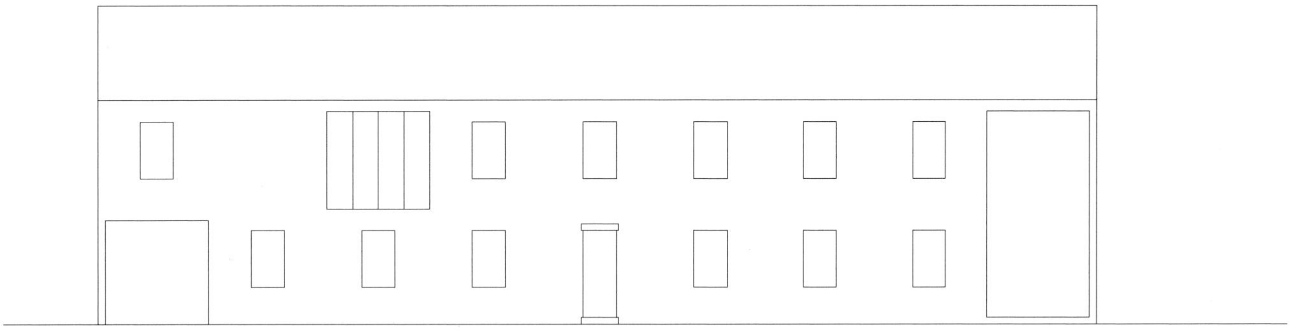

EAST ELEVATION

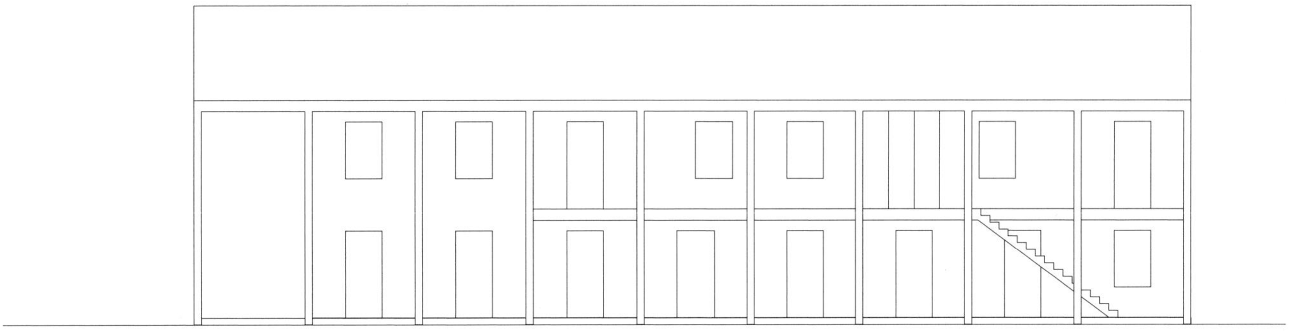

WEST ELEVATION

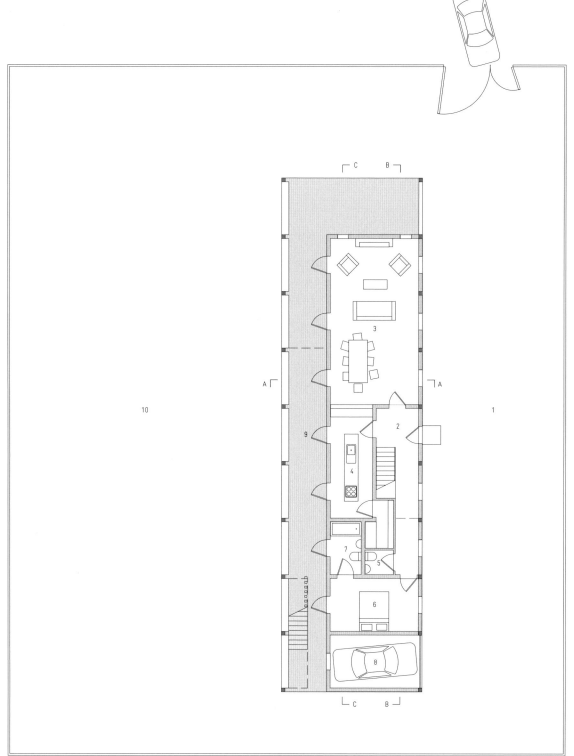

SITE AND GROUND FLOOR PLAN

The ground floor plan shows the kitchen
and staircase located at the core of
the house and en-suite guest bedroom
and bathroom to the south.

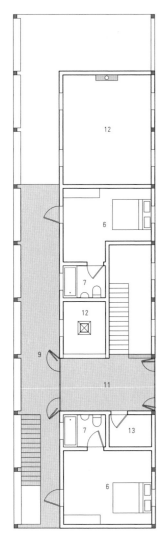

FIRST FLOOR PLAN

ROOF PLAN

The first floor plan comprises two further bedrooms and a large open landing. The pitched roof (right) is in corrugated sheet metal, following local practices.

1   Drive
2   Entrance Hall
3   Living/Dining
4   Kitchen
5   WC
6   Bedroom
7   Bathroom
8   Garage
9   Verandah
10 Garden
11 Landing
12 Void
13 Linen Cupboard

1:200

0   10m

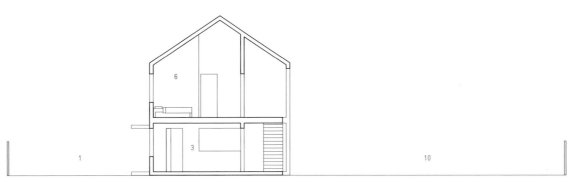

SECTION AA

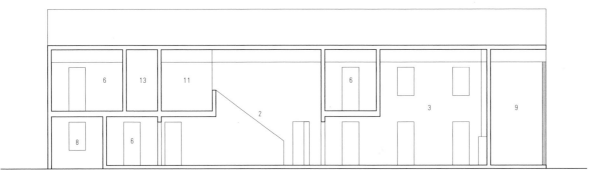

SECTION BB

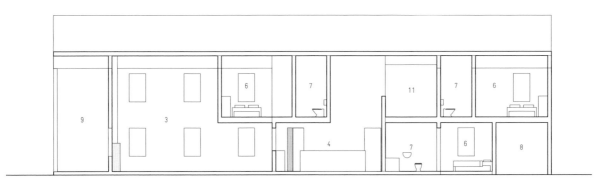

SECTION CC

(top) The model, viewed from the south, reveals a glimpse of the double-height verandah facing west onto the garden.

(middle and bottom) Views of the house under construction.

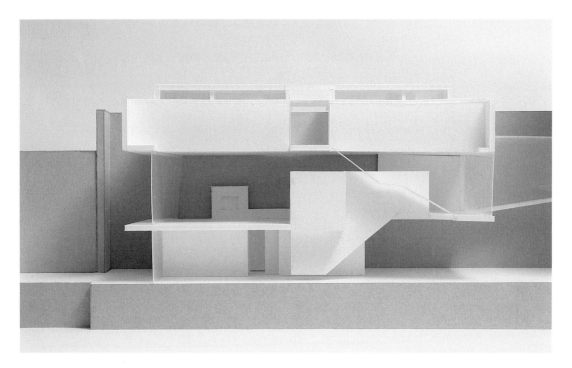

319
Collins House

This house is designed for a concealed site in Chelsea, part of a densely developed urban neighbourhood. It consists of three separate buildings, linked by small courtyards. There is a two storey studio/library, the main house on three floors and a two storey service wing beneath an existing building. The whole site is excavated and a reinforced concrete basement formed. Walls and openings are arranged to maximise sun and daylight into the courtyards and interiors throughout the day, but also privacy to the house from its neighbours. Each floor is glazed at both ends creating long vistas within the interior to increase the sense of scale and openness. Within the site the roofs, walls and floors of the courtyards and interior spaces will be lined with slabs of pale stone and the end walls triple glazed with full height sliding screens framed in dull finished stainless steel. Detailing will be restrained and lean and lighting discreet and glowing. Externally the wall to the north side pedestrian passage is rendered and painted to blend into the existing context so that the house all but disappears from public view.

The site is long and narrow, sandwiched
between houses and gardens.

319
Collins House

1:200

0   10m

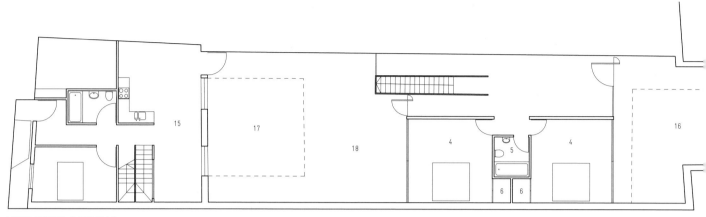

LOWER GROUND FLOOR PLAN

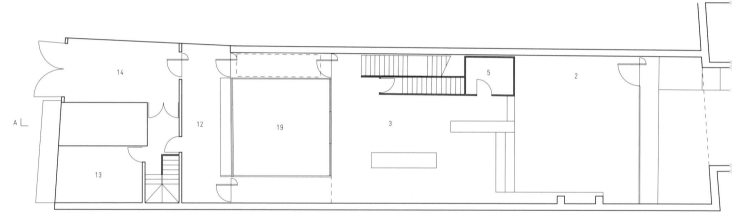

A L

GROUND FLOOR PLAN

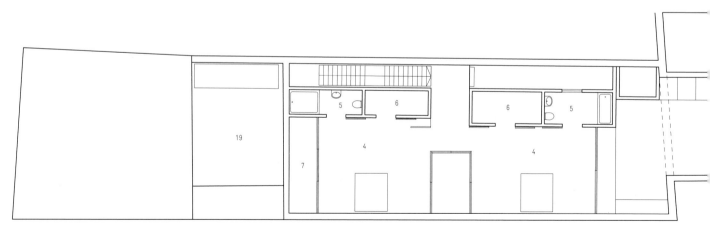

FIRST FLOOR PLAN

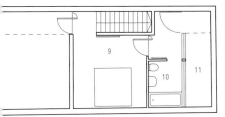

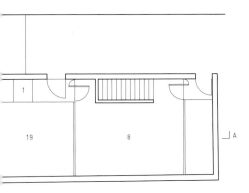

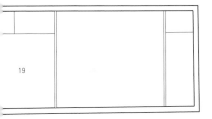

The lower ground, ground and upper
floor plans (top to bottom) reveal three
principal components of the house
linked by small courtyards. From east
to west the accommodation includes
a two storey studio/library, the main
house on three floors and a two storey
service wing below the existing building
on the street.

Main House
1   Entrance Ramp
2   Living Room
3   Dining Room
4   Bedroom
5   Bathroom
6   Wardrobe
7   Terrace

Studio/Guest Wing
8   Studio
9   Bedroom
10   Bathroom
11   Lightwell

Service Wing
12   Kitchen
13   Office
14   Garage
15   Staff Flat

Outdoor Spaces
16   Entrance Courtyard
17   West Courtyard
18   Grotto
19   Void

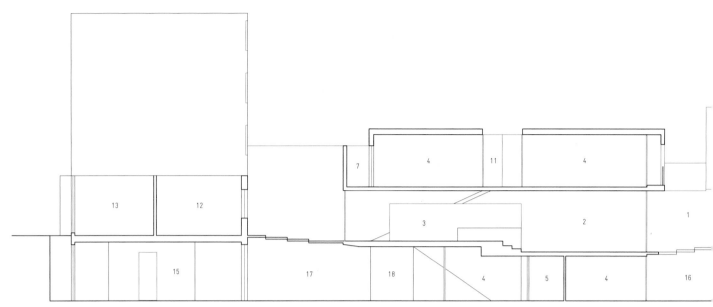

SECTION AA

The long section shows the interplay of
solids and voids, organised to generate
light and vistas through the heart of
the enclosed site. The house has been
designed to be built in reinforced
concrete construction, with walls and
floors lined in pale stone slabs.

Main House
1   Entrance Ramp
2   Living Room
3   Dining Room
4   Bedroom
5   Bathroom
6   Wardrobe
7   Terrace

Studio/Guest Wing
8   Studio
9   Bedroom
10   Bathroom
11   Lightwell

Service Wing
12   Kitchen
13   Office
14   Garage
15   Staff Flat

Outdoor Spaces
16   Entrance Courtyard
17   West Courtyard
18   Grotto
19   Void

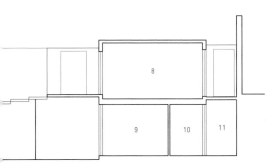

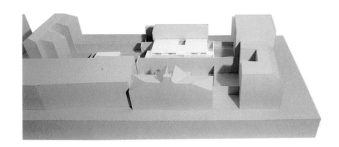

The model shows the new house dug
into the ground to form part of the
garden landscape behind the street
frontages. It is conceived as a secret
hidden volume embedded in the site.

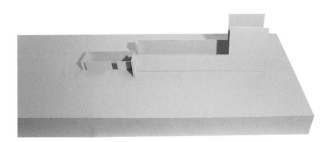

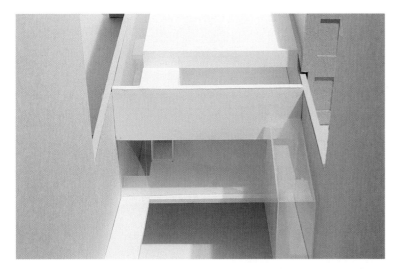

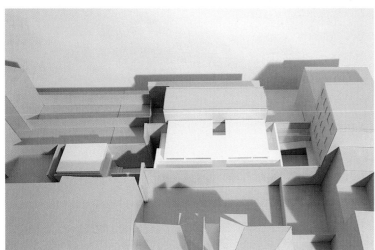

(top) Aerial view of main house across west courtyard.

(middle) Aerial view of house from the north.

(bottom) View of main house from the entrance courtyard (entrance ramp not shown).

335
Rough Grounds Houses: Octagon House, Belvedere House and Lodge

The site is in Rough Grounds, a heart shaped woodland plantation on the Westonbirt estate in Gloucestershire.

These houses are an integral part of a larger rural development for an equestrian centre, which has been conceived as an initiative in agricultural diversification. The site is part of a Grade I listed landscape on the Westonbirt Estate in Gloucestershire. Octagon House, Belvedere House and Lodge have been designed together with indoor and outdoor schools and stables, embedded in clearings formed within the woodland plantation known as Rough Grounds.

The Octagon House is designed for a family of five – two parents and three children. It is freestanding on two storeys, with a central atrium garden covered by a retractable horizontal sliding rooflight and a covered deck to the south, providing a natural extension to the open-plan living, dining and kitchen accommodation on the ground floor. The bedrooms, with en-suite bathrooms, are on the first floor. The house has a steel frame, with fully glazed, clear or gold tinted elevations, and a flat roof. It is highly insulated, with a system of layered blinds and insulating curtains which not only provide privacy, but also a flexible and efficient means of controlling the temperature inside the building.

The Belvedere House is five storeys high and uses the same construction as the house. It is situated on the edge of a 'ride' with a dining room at the top with wonderful views of the landscape and Westonbirt House in the distance. The Belvedere House is primarily intended for entertainment but may also be conceived of as a one bedroom house, as drawn here. It is constructed in a similar manner to Octagon House. However the Grooms' Lodge, a two bedroom house designed as a seven metre cube on two storeys, is built using load-bearing blockwork walls and clad in vertical panels of external quality plywood finished with scumbled gold paintwork to match the finish of the equestrian buildings on the site.

(above) A view from within the Rough
Grounds woodland plantation.

The site plan shows how the buildings
are placed in the woodland which is
sliced through by two rides, that focus
on the garden terrace of Westonbirt
House, part of the original Picturesque
landscape laid out in the mid-nineteenth
century and now Grade I listed.

1   Octagon House
2   Belvedere House
3   Lodge
4   Stables
5   Indoor School
6   Outdoor School

1:200

0   10m

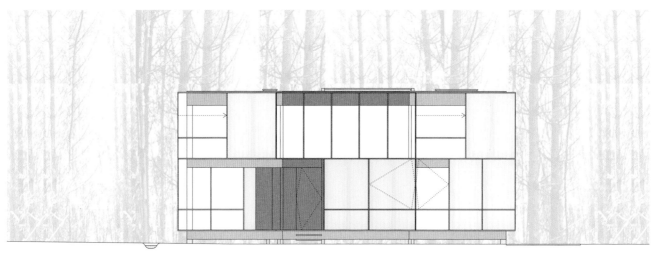

NORTH ELEVATION

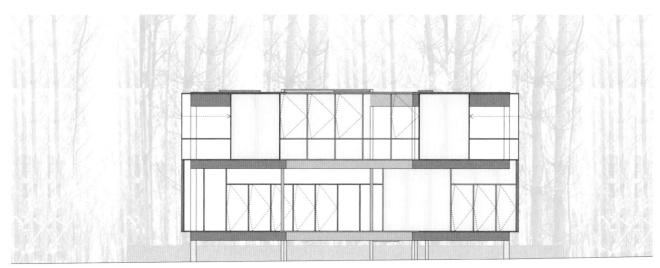

SOUTH ELEVATION

The Octagon House is one of a group
of buildings that make up a new
equestrian centre. The steel-framed
house is raised on stilts and clad in
clear and gold-tinted glazing in gold
anodised aluminium frames.

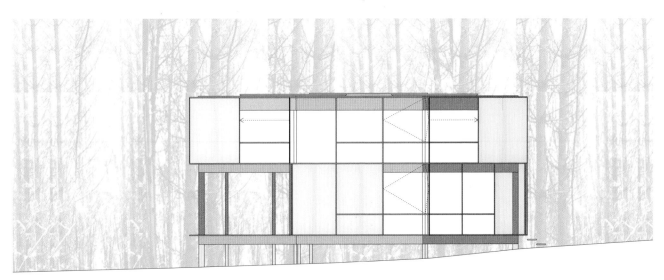

EAST ELEVATION

WEST ELEVATION

1:200

0   10m

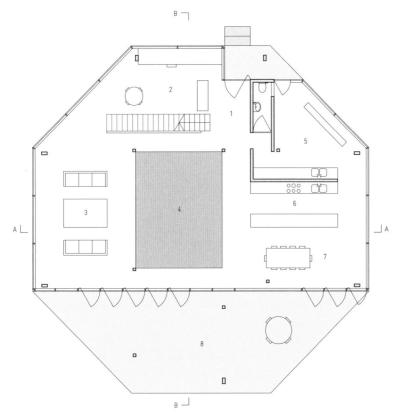

GROUND FLOOR PLAN

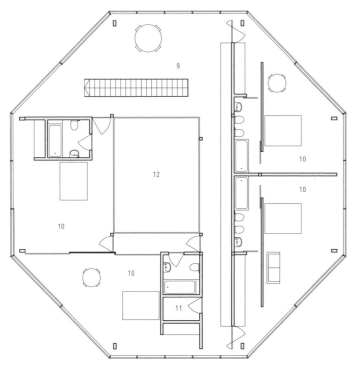

FIRST FLOOR PLAN

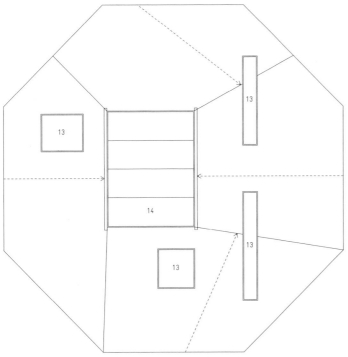

ROOF PLAN

The ground floor plan shows a generous
deck facing south, a courtyard garden,
and loose-fit, flexible living space
around it. The first floor plan shows
four bedrooms with en-suite bathrooms
arranged around the central void. The
organisation of the plan allows all the
internal spaces to enjoy generous
daylight views out through the glazed
facades.

1   Entrance Hall
2   Study
3   Living Room
4   Garden
5   Utility Room
6   Kitchen
7   Dining Room
8   Deck
9   Landing
10 Bedroom
11 Laundry
12 Void
13 Rooflight
14 Sliding Rooflight

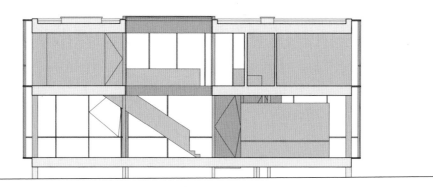

SECTION AA

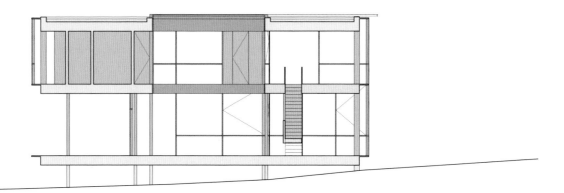

SECTION BB

The roof plan and section AA show the
sliding rooflight over the central garden.

The house viewed through the trees
is designed to appear as a shining
jewel-like object in the woodland.

1:200

0   10m

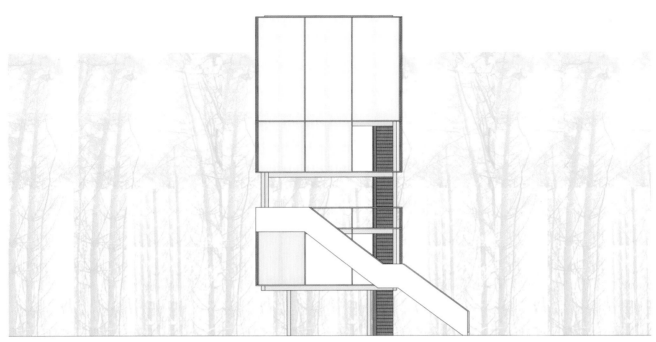

NORTH-WEST ELEVATION

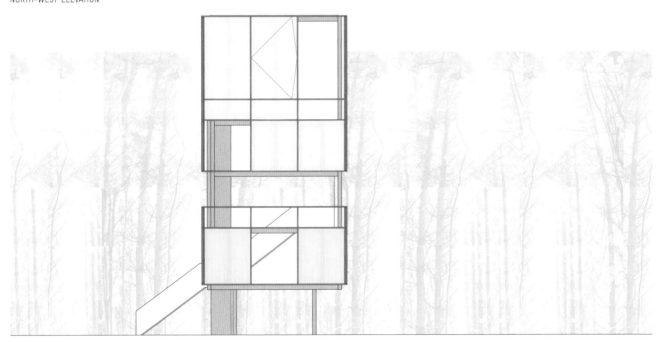

SOUTH-EAST ELEVATION

Belvedere House is conceived as a
vertical marker in the wood, projecting
into the principal ride just visible from
the garden terrace of Westonbirt House.
The elevations indicate the same palette
of materials used for the Octagon House.

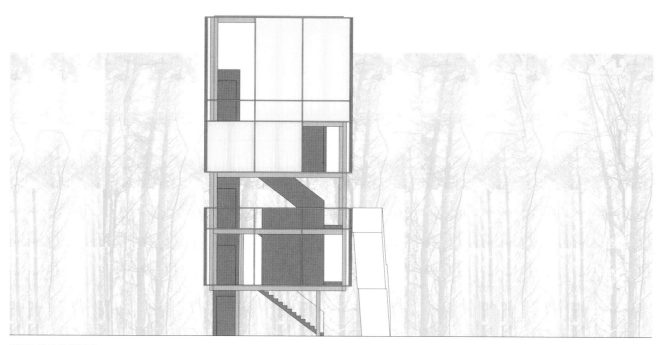

NORTH-EAST ELEVATION

SOUTH-WEST ELEVATION

1:200

0   10m

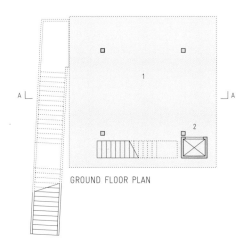

GROUND FLOOR PLAN

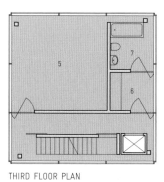

THIRD FLOOR PLAN

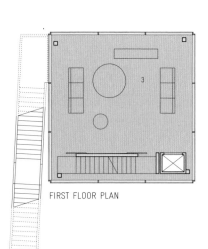

FIRST FLOOR PLAN

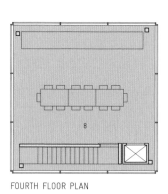

FOURTH FLOOR PLAN

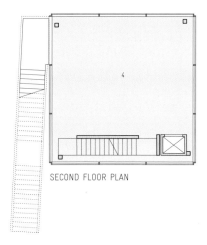

SECOND FLOOR PLAN

ROOF PLAN

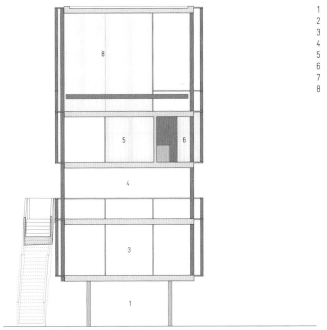

1 Undercroft
2 Lift
3 Living
4 Deck
5 Bedroom
6 Dressing Room
7 Bathroom
8 Dining/Kitchen

SECTION AA

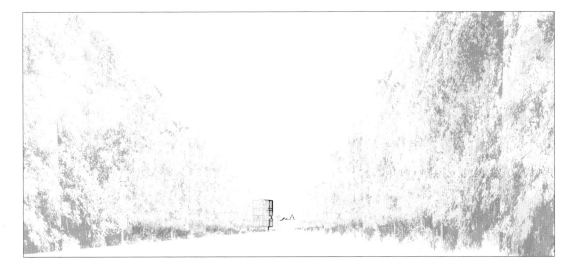

(bottom) The Belvedere House is glimpsed at the edge of the main vista through the woods with Westonbirt House viewed on axis with the ride.

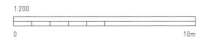

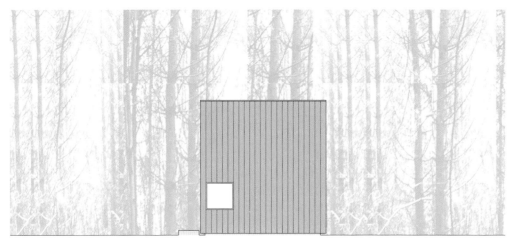

NORTH ELEVATION

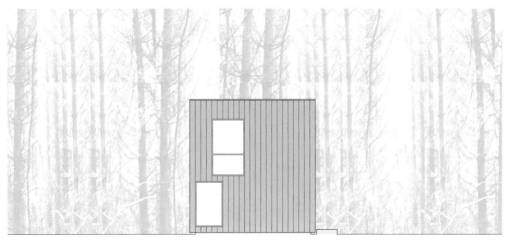

SOUTH ELEVATION

The Groom's Lodge is a two storey cube
clad in painted plywood boarding.

EAST ELEVATION

WEST ELEVATION

335
Rough Grounds
Lodge

1:200

0   10m

GROUND FLOOR PLAN

FIRST FLOOR PLAN

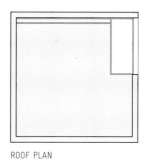

ROOF PLAN

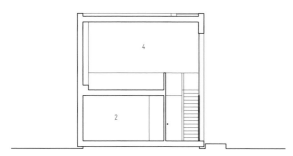

SECTION AA

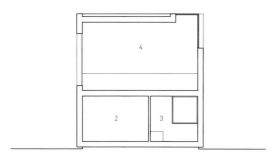

SECTION BB

(top) The plans show two bedrooms on
the ground floor and an open-plan living
space on the first floor, with a skylight
in the roof.

1   Entrance Hall
2   Bedroom
3   Bathroom
4   Living/Dining/Kitchen

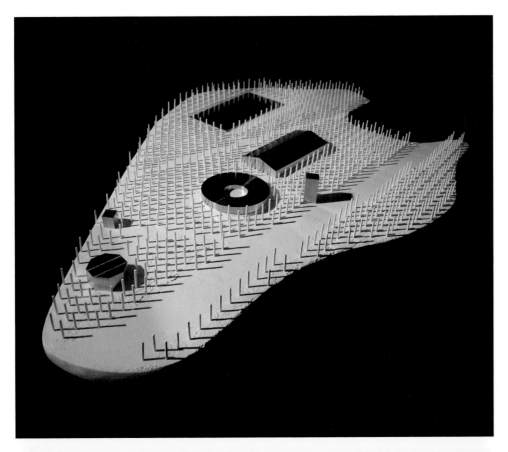

The equestrian centre is part of an ambitious ten year plan to restore the historically important Picturesque landscape laid out in the mid-nineteenth century. The project involves constructing a new road and bringing services to the site 200 metres across a field to the south. A major aim of the project is to evolve principles for creating new initiatives for sustainable rural development.

The site model without tree canopy (top) shows the buildings in relation to each other. The site model with tree canopy (bottom) shows the two rides and clearings in Rough Grounds woodland marking the location of the buildings.

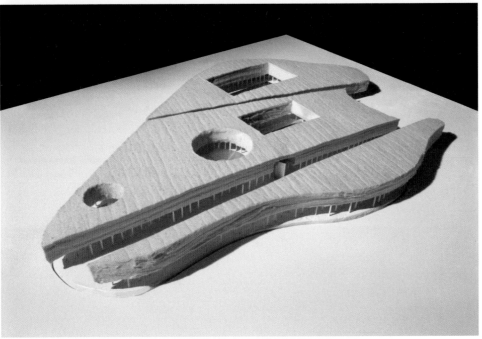

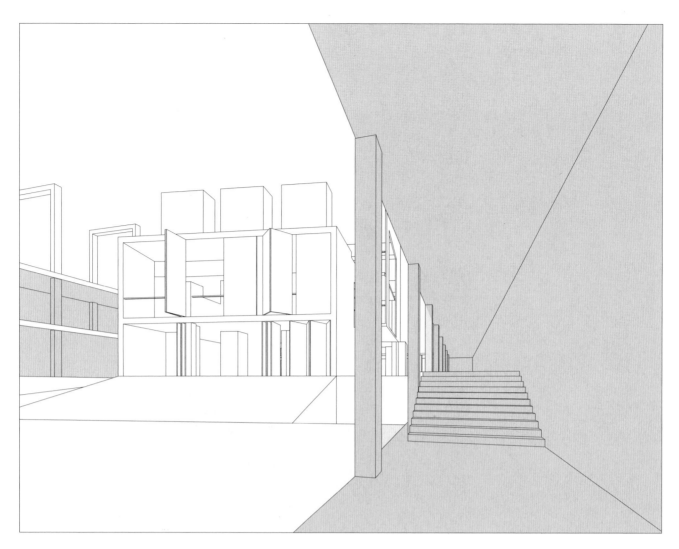

336
Climate House

The Iranian Fuel Conservation Organisation commissioned this project as a show house to demonstrate the principles of environmentally sound design. It formed part of a larger exhibition and conference centre. Designed for a site in Tehran, Climate House incorporated traditional features of climatic design such as courtyards, wind towers, re-interpreted as solar chimneys, dual orientation, and fountains to provide natural cooling to the internal spaces in hot weather. It also included a lower ground level of thermally protected inhabitable space, a traditional building practice in this region which has been largely lost. The main living space is located on the north side, while the southern aspect is protected by deeply overhung terrace areas, and the solar chimneys draw air, cooled by a pool and fountains, in and up through the house. The design promotes the idea that occupants will naturally migrate from the inner to the outer areas according to the time of year, without having to move all the furnishings and fittings. The whole development is protected from the busy street by a 'green wall', which also provides entry to the site. The project is aimed to influence the upgrading of building regulations for houses in Iran.

This project has been carried out in association with Golzari (NG) Architects.

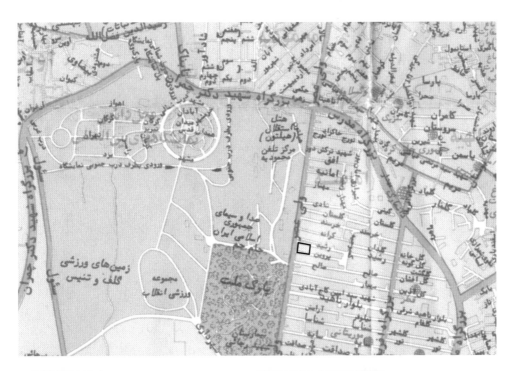

Site plan and view of site from across
Vali Asr.

1:200

0   10m

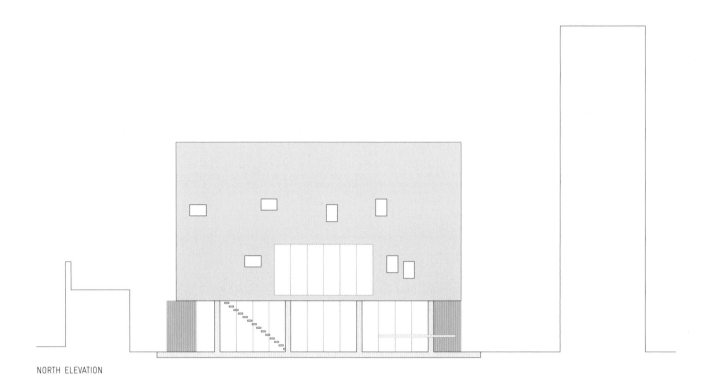

NORTH ELEVATION

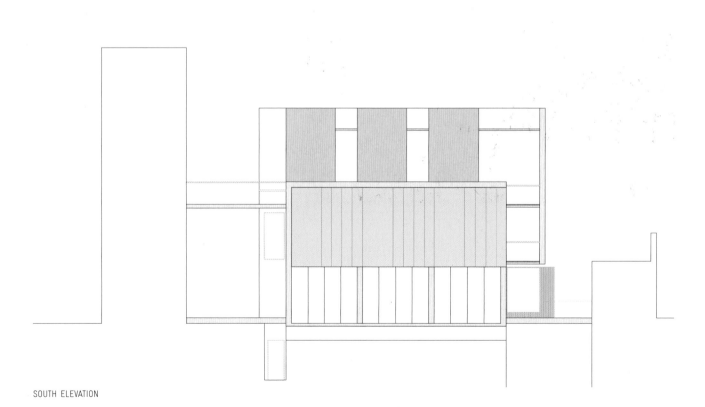

SOUTH ELEVATION

The house was designed as a show house within a larger exhibition and conference centre dedicated to sustainable construction in Tehran, Iran. Both sides have an open verandah providing cross ventilation to the interior. On the south, three large solar chimneys are visible, drawing cool air through the house. There is also a habitable basement, to which the family may retreat in the summer heat.

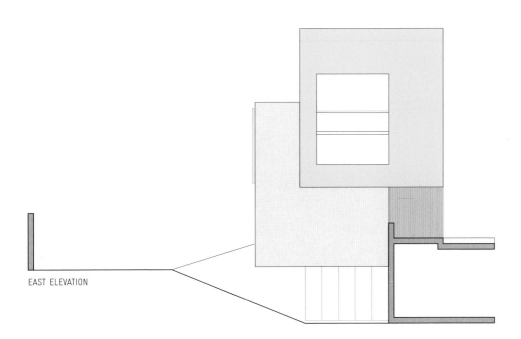

EAST ELEVATION

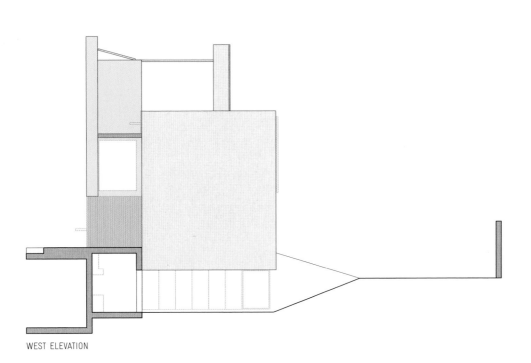

WEST ELEVATION

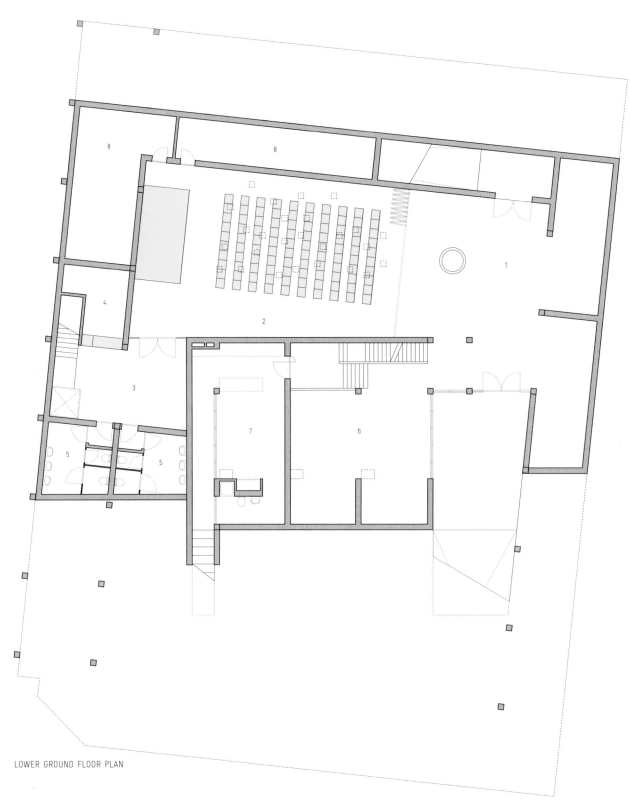

LOWER GROUND FLOOR PLAN

The extensive lower ground floor plan
has been designed as part of the
exhibition facilities. The library is within
the footprint of the house and would
be a living room to which the family
might retreat during the hot weather.

1   Exhibition
2   Lecture Theatre
3   Foyer
4   Cloakroom
5   Public Lavatory
6   Library/Family Retreat

7   Flat
8   Storage/Plant

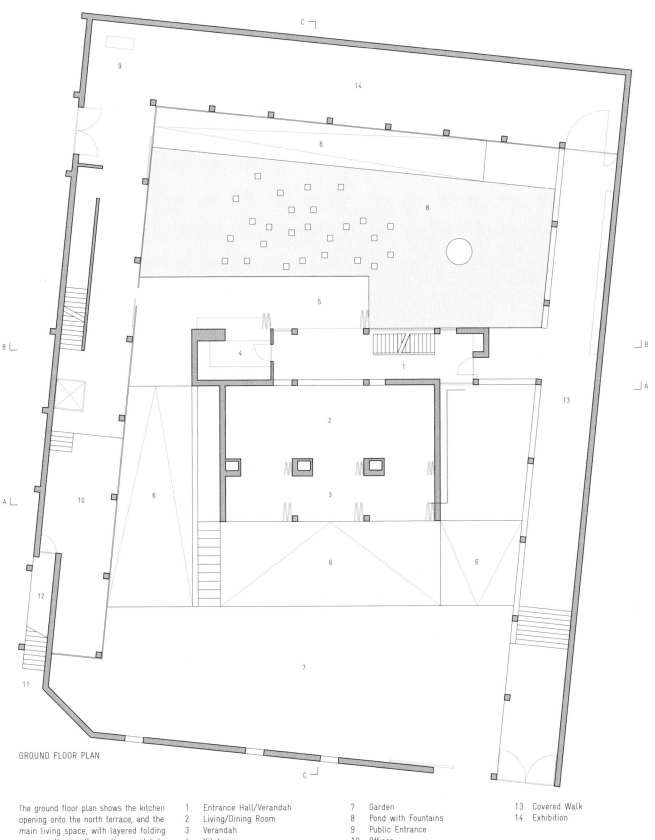

GROUND FLOOR PLAN

The ground floor plan shows the kitchen opening onto the north terrace, and the main living space, with layered folding screens allowing the south verandah to be open or closed according to need.

1   Entrance Hall/Verandah
2   Living/Dining Room
3   Verandah
4   Kitchen
5   Terrace
6   Ramp
7   Garden
8   Pond with Fountains
9   Public Entrance
10 Offices
11 Staircase to Tea House
12 Staff Entrance
13 Covered Walk
14 Exhibition

1:200

0   10m

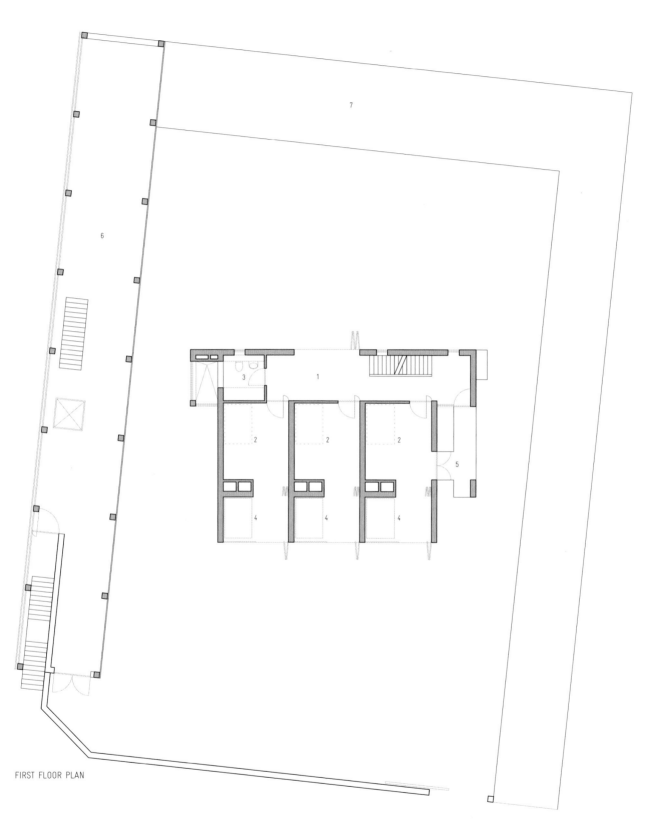

FIRST FLOOR PLAN

The first floor plan shows three
bedrooms, each with its own individual
sleeping porch, equipped with folding
screens.

1	Landing/Verandah	6	Tea House
2	Bedroom	7	Grass Roof
3	Bathroom		
4	Sleeping Porch		
5	Vertical Garden		

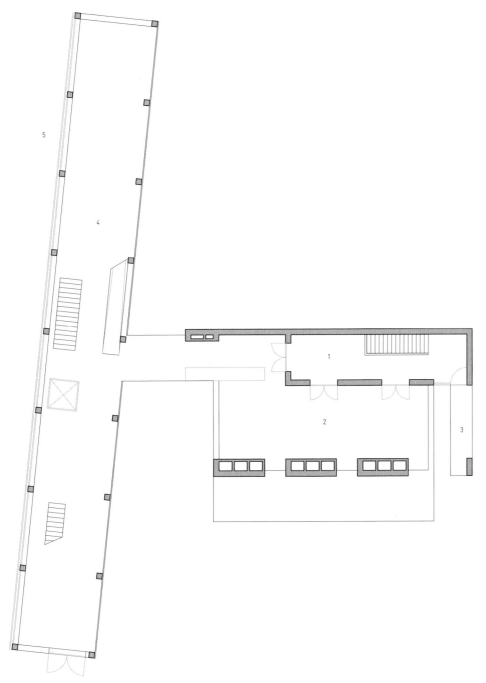

SECOND FLOOR PLAN

The second floor plan shows the roof garden and garden room, connecting to the covered second floor terrace of the perimeter building, or 'green wall', which accommodates the primary entrance to the exhibition centre on the west side on the ground floor, a public tea room on the first floor and exhibition terrace on the second and third floor.

1   Garden Room
2   Roof Garden
3   Vertical Garden
4   Exhibition Terrace
5   Green Wall

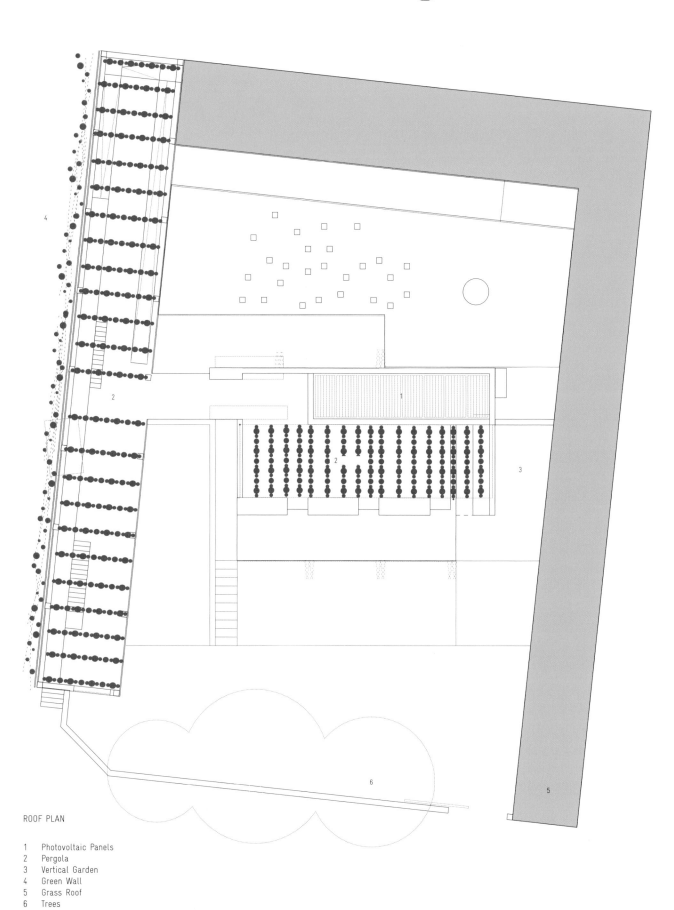

ROOF PLAN

1 Photovoltaic Panels
2 Pergola
3 Vertical Garden
4 Green Wall
5 Grass Roof
6 Trees

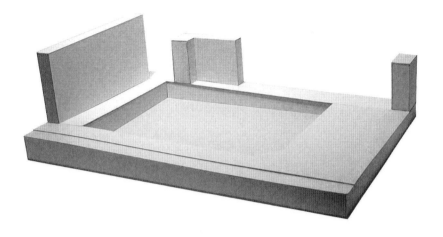

(opposite) The roof plan comprises the top of the pergola structure and an area of photovoltaic cells over the garden room, with access to the third floor level of the main entrance building. The planting scheme at roof level and trees to the south provide cool 'green' shade within the site and around its edges.

The site models show firstly the excavated site (top), the greenwall and exhibition cloister with various exhibition facilities on the lower ground floor (middle) and finally the Climate House itself located within the site (bottom).

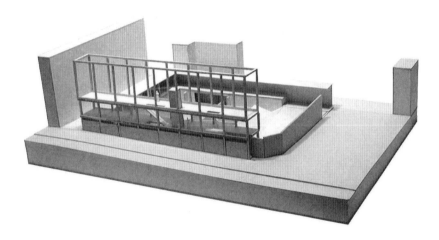

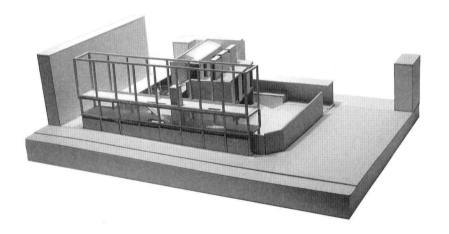

1:200

0   10m

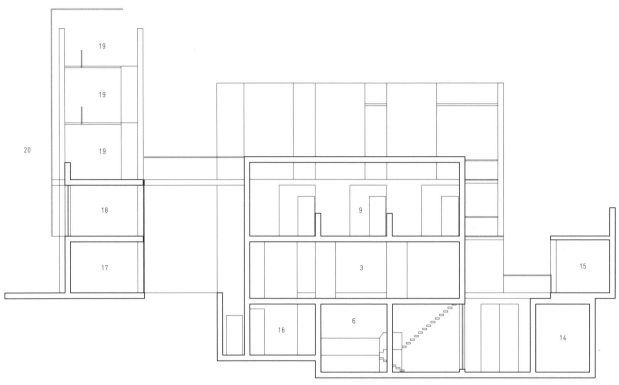

SECTION AA

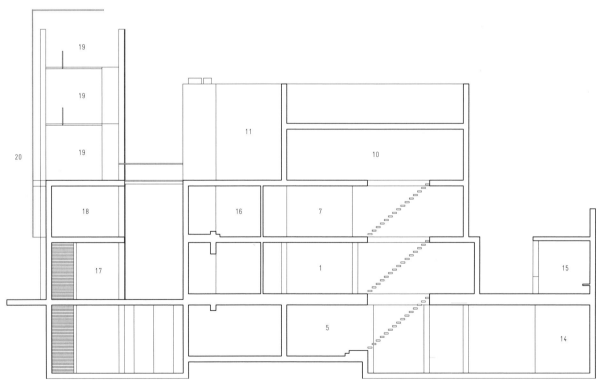

SECTION BB

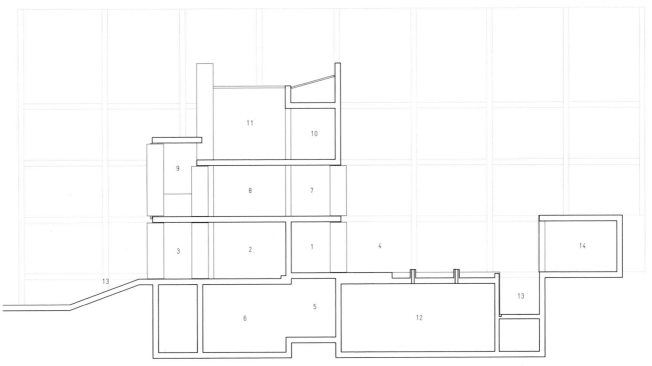

SECTION CC

Section AA (opposite top), taken from west to east, is taken in front of the solar chimneys, and through the tea house in the perimeter building, and bathroom of the family apartment in the basement. Section BB (opposite bottom), taken from west to east, through the circulation zone of the house and bridge to the exhibition terrace. Section CC, taken from north to south, through the bedroom, shows the library and lecture hall accommodation below.

1   Entrance Hall/Verandah
2   Living/Dining Room
3   Verandah
4   Terrace
5   Landing
6   Library/Family Retreat
7   Landing/Verandah
8   Bedroom
9   Sleeping Porch
10 Garden Room
11 Roof Garden
12 Lecture Theatre
13 Ramp
14 Exhibition
15 Covered Walk
16 Bathroom
17 Offices
18 Tea Room
19 Exhibition Terrace
20 Green Wall

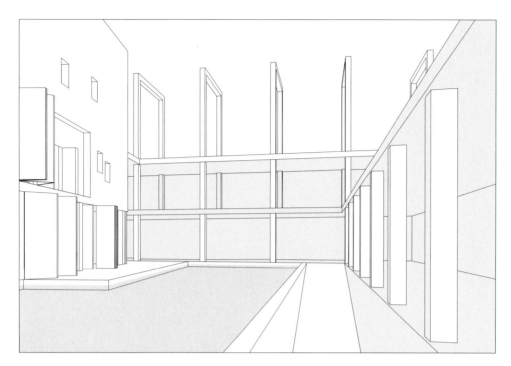

(top) North elevation oblique view across pool toward the green wall.

(bottom) Perspective view of the south facade from within the perimeter building.

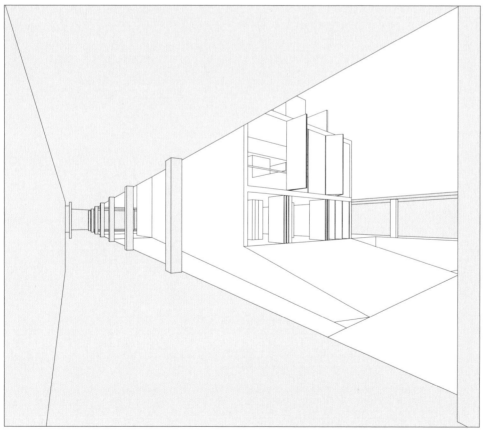

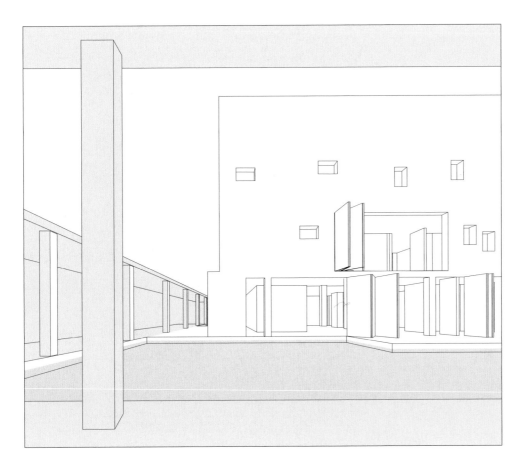

View of the north elevation from
the exhibition cloister.

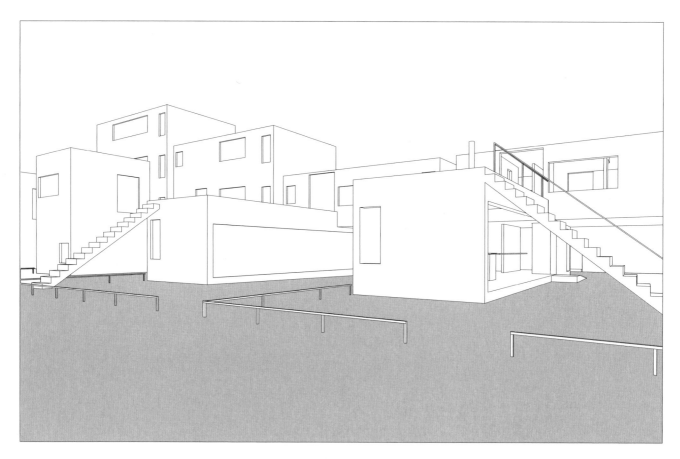

340
Swaythling Housing

Perspective of backs of houses viewed from the communal garden.

This is a scheme for prefabricated houses assembled as different combinations of stacked and joined modules made in a factory. The approach here achieves a range of different types and sizes of dwelling, which can also be adapted and extended during their lifespan to suit a household's changing circumstances. There are two basic building types: a multi-storey L-shaped structure (two to four storeys), and a single storey house. The L-shaped buildings are structurally autonomous and physically independent of the next, but address the street as a visually continuous building line, integrating private open courtyards at front and rear, and a variety of heights and rooftop profiles, including roof terraces. At the back are communal gardens. The internal space is open-plan and flexible, with additional container-style storage located under a porte cochere in the vehicular entrance courtyard at the front. The single storey house type, with the same basic features, is designed particularly for use by the elderly, disabled, or families with young children. Both building types can be extended vertically and horizontally, and customised with a range of 'extraordinary' elements including: (external) mast for tv aerial, flag pole, greenhouse, garden shed, additional storage units, photovoltaic panels, solar panels, hydroponic (vertical) garden, staircases, pergola, paving, planting, various claddings, and (internal) fireplace/chimney (gas-fired), as well as personally selected items.

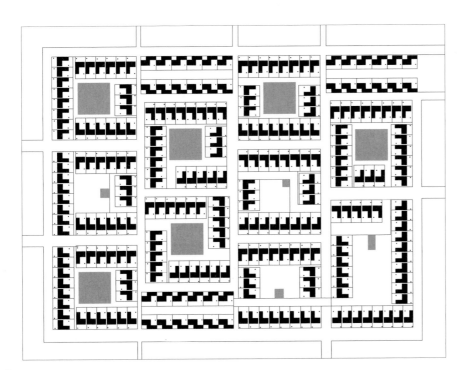

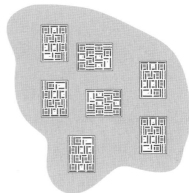

(top left) The pattern of combined building types, courtyards and gardens can be replicated and reconfigured to create a regular network of streets and squares with independent vehicular and pedestrian circulation routes.

A typical 11 hectare site can accommodate at least 40 dwellings per hectare and has the potential to provide an increase in density of up to 92 dwellings per hectare without encroaching on the public squares which measures 42 by 42 metres. It is envisaged that the public squares could contain small pavilions offering a variety of public facilities.

(top right) This diagram shows seven 11 hectare sites set in a rural location. The surrounding farmland is capable of producing sufficient biomass crop to provide each site with fuel for a district heating system, as well as parkland for recreation and leisure.

(bottom) Typical Saturday afternoon in Eastleigh town centre.

1:200

0   10m

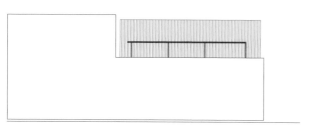

SIDE ELEVATION

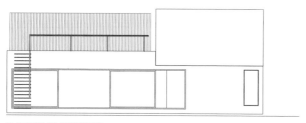

ELEVATION TO COURTYARD

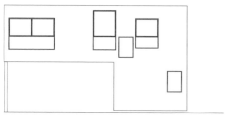

ELEVATION TO STREET

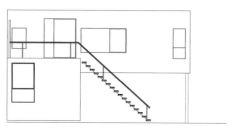

ELEVATION TO COMMUNAL GARDEN

Each house is designed with a simple facade facing the street behind a 2.1 metre high hedge or screen. Facades may be clad in a wide range of finishes depending on taste, choice and location.

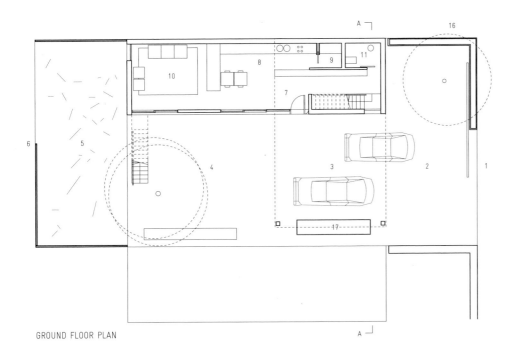

GROUND FLOOR PLAN

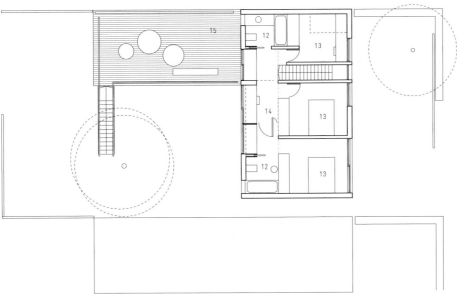

FIRST FLOOR PLAN

Two storey, three bedroom house: ground floor plan (top), showing porte cochere for car-parking underneath the front wing, and private courtyards to back and front, opening to communal garden at the rear. The first floor plan (bottom) shows the rear roof terrace, with external stair access from the courtyard, and bedrooms on the upper floor at the front, over-looking the street. Each plot measures 11 metres wide by 24 metres long.

1	Street	12	Bathroom
2	Front Courtyard	13	Bedroom
3	Porte Cochere	14	Landing/Study
4	Side Courtyard	15	Roof Terrace
5	Rear Garden	16	2.1 Metre Hedge/Screen
6	Communal Garden	17	Mobile Storage
7	Entrance		
8	Kitchen/Dining		
9	Utility		
10	Living Room		
11	WC		

1:50

0   2m

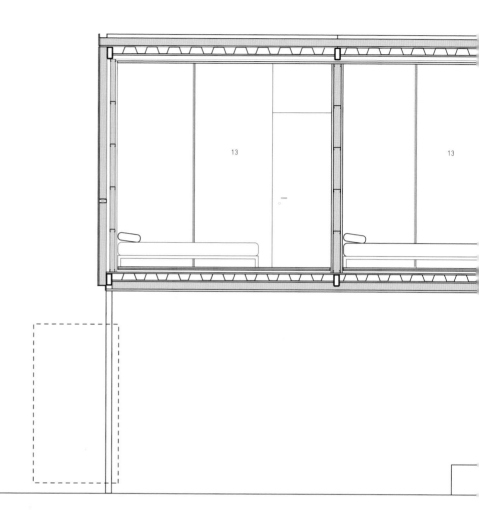

SECTION AA

A Prefabricated Modular Construction Approach

The advantages of prefabricated modular construction are:
a. Quality control of the product in the factory.
b. Spatial flexibility: units can be assembled in a number
    of different ways.
c. A range of optional/customised internal and external
    fittings and finishes.
d. Ease and speed of assembly on site, with limited wet
    trades and minimal foundations.
e. Integrated services.
f. Potential for adaptation in the future.
g. Potential for recycling.

One drawback of the prefabricated modular construction approach
is the need to provide transport from factory to site. This may
be overcome, where there is a sufficient number of dwellings
to be constructed, by constructing a factory to manufacture
the dwellings on site. The factory may be converted once the
required dwellings have been produced to provide a sports hall,
studio workshops or even a townhall.

Bedroom section of two storey three
bedroom house. The building is
constructed out of prefabricated modules
which are joined together to create
structurally self-contained dwellings,
and can be clad in a range of different
materials, depending on context.

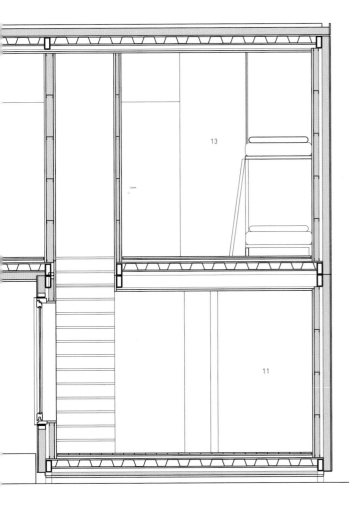

13

11

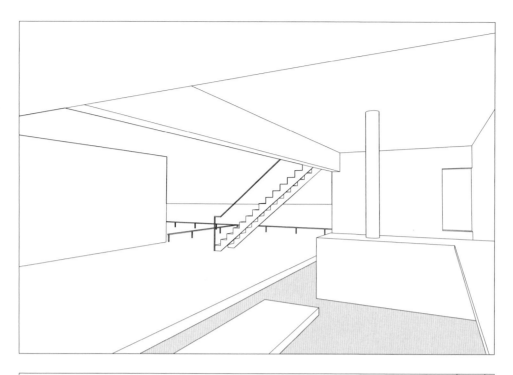

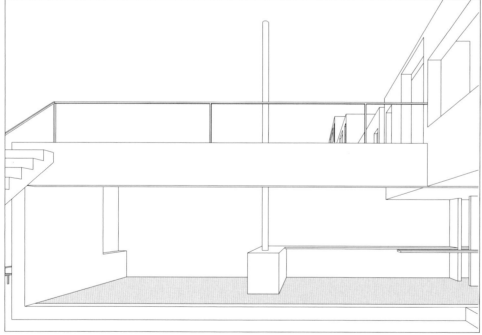

(top) View from kitchen into the private
courtyard and to public square beyond.

(bottom) View from the courtyard to the
living room with the roof terrace above.

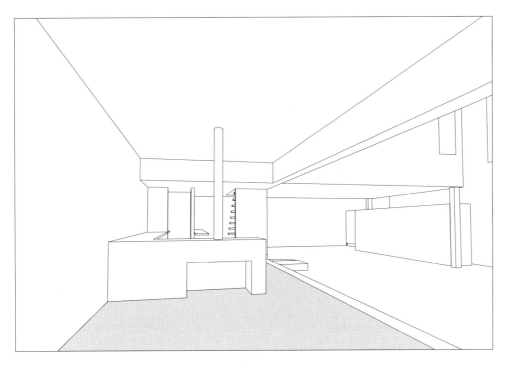

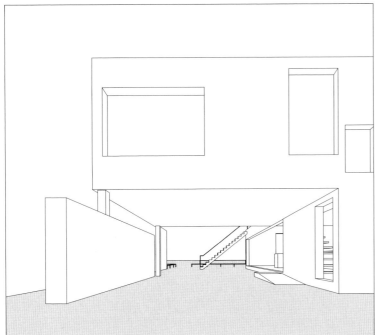

(top) View from the living room towards the fireplace.

(bottom) View of the entrance elevation, with the rear courtyard framed by porte cochere.

344
New Battery House

The new house was designed to be less visible on the site (below opposite) than the existing building: lower in height, and largely concealed from the lane behind a high hedge (above).

The site for this scheme is a five acre plot on the edge of a suburban landscape, on the one hand, and an ancient bogland on the other. An existing house was to be demolished and replaced with a modern development, suitable for contemporary living and working. The design takes into account the severe restrictions which govern new residential development in the countryside. The new house is designed to be lower in height, with a flat roof, minimising its impact on its surroundings. The rectangular plan incorporates bedrooms upstairs, and open-plan, 'loose-fit' living-space and kitchen downstairs, entered under a large over-hanging porte cochere from the west, and opening via sliding windows onto a garden terrace to the south-west. It was to be built with a stone clad steel frame, full height triple glazing and large perforated sliding screens externally. A linear single storey building at the rear of the site contains accommodation for guests and carport.

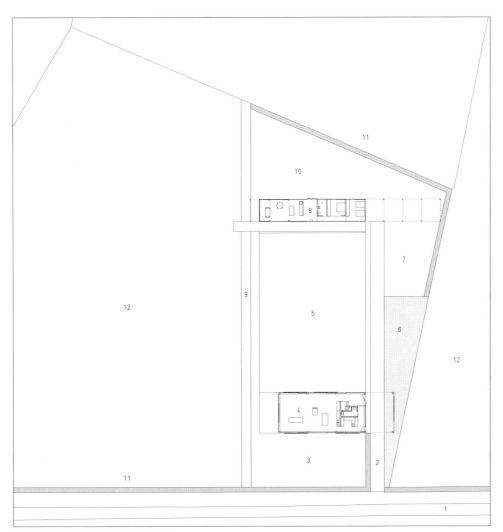

1	Lane
2	Drive
3	Kitchen Garden
4	House
5	Lawn
6	Shrubbery
7	Parking Court
8	Guest Wing
9	Canal
10	Yard
11	Hedge
12	Field

The site plan (top) is carefully layered to provide a rich, unfolding experience of open and closed vistas, solid and void, and indoor and outdoor spaces which provide an appropriate backdrop for domestic life.

The open field to the east of New Battery House is set in dense woodland with the lane to the south (bottom).

1:200

0   10m

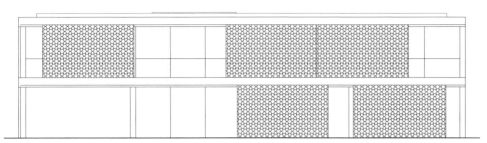

NORTH ELEVATION

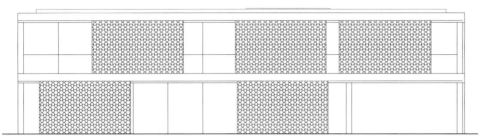

SOUTH ELEVATION

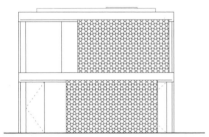

EAST ELEVATION

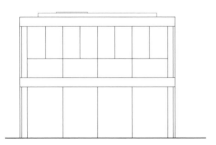

WEST ELEVATION

The house is designed as a stone-clad
steel frame, with facades of glass and
polycarbonate, and equipped with
stainless steel grill sliding screens
externally.

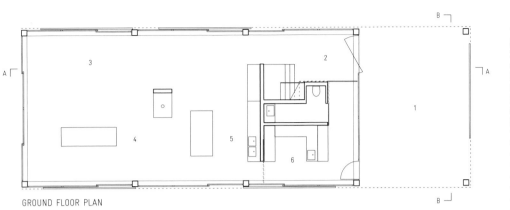

GROUND FLOOR PLAN

1   Porte Cochere
2   Entrance Hall
3   Living
4   Dining
5   Kitchen
6   Utility
7   Library/Long Gallery
8   Master Bedroom
9   Master Bathroom
10   Bedroom
11   Playroom
12   Bathroom
13   Shower Room
14   Secret Staircase
15   Sliding Skylight
16   Skylight
17   Photovoltaic Panels

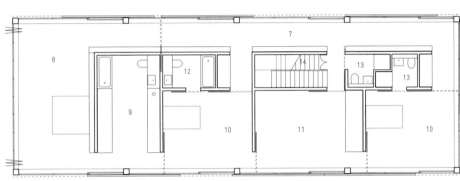

FIRST FLOOR PLAN

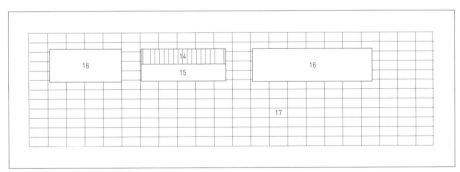

ROOF PLAN

The ground floor is planned with a central core containing staircase, kitchen, WC and utility room, and a loose-fit sequence of entrance, living, dining and service space around it contained within the external walls of the house.

The bedrooms and play room are provided with interlinking sliding doors. When open they create an enfilade of spaces along the south elevation.

A secret staircase leads to the roof and offers a vantage point over the landscape. The roof is fitted with a carpet of photovoltaic panels which provides electricity for the new house and on occasion will supply electricity to the national grid.

1:200

0   10m

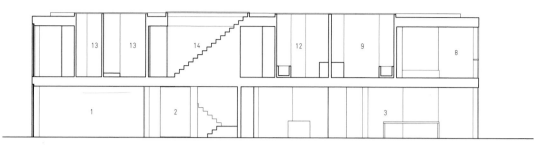

| 13 | 13 | 14 | | 12 | 9 | 8 |

| 1 | 2 | | 3 |

SECTION AA

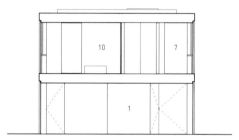

| 10 | 7 |

| 1 |

SECTION BB

The master bedroom on the west
elevation is fitted with sliding folding
windows which may be thrown back
to transform the room into an outdoor
space on warm days.

1	Porte Cochere	7	Library/Long Gallery	13	Shower Room
2	Entrance Hall	8	Master Bedroom	14	Secret Staircase
3	Living	9	Master Bathroom	15	Sliding Skylight
4	Dining	10	Bedroom	16	Skylight
5	Kitchen	11	Playroom	17	Photovoltaic Panels
6	Utility	12	Bathroom		

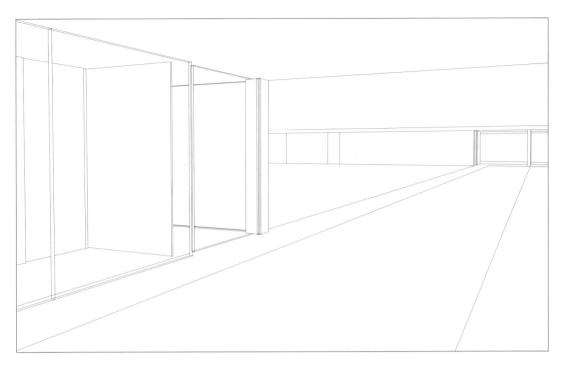

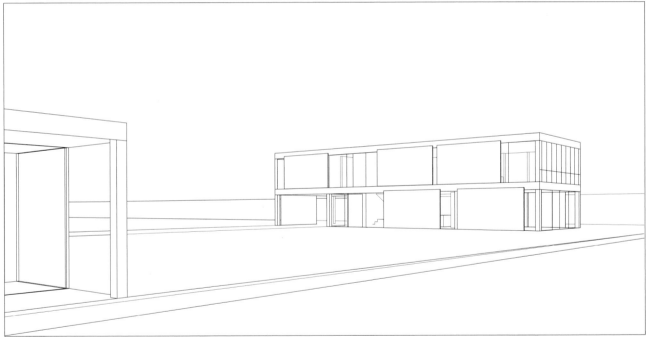

(top) View of the guest wing and lawn from the porte cochere. The main entrance door is to the left.

(bottom) View of the house across the lawn and canal from guest wing.

350
Sam House

Designed for a site on the island of St. Vincent, in the Caribbean, this project was commissioned for a couple who had been inspired by a visit to the Ideal Home Show in London, and wished to build a 'dream house' for their retirement. It is a response to the conditions of life in a hot climate, at a slower pace, with rooms opening onto a long verandah and terrace looking out to sea.

The site plan (top) and photograph
(bottom) shows the commanding
position of the site, looking out to sea.

350
Sam House

1:200

0   10m

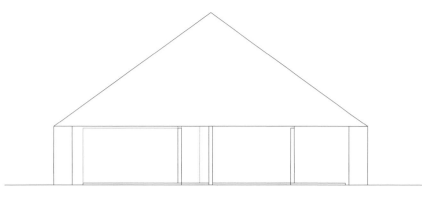

NORTH ELEVATION

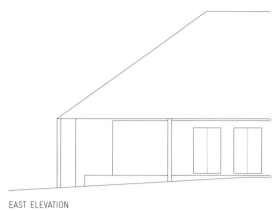

EAST ELEVATION

SOUTH ELEVATION

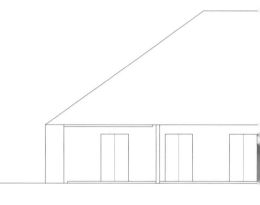

WEST ELEVATION

The elevations show the house
surrounded by a verandah on the
south, west, and north-east, with
a deep overhang on the east. It is
one storey in height with a big
pitched roof providing a large open
internal roof space.

1:200

0   10m

The ground floor plan shows the
entrance in the north-east corner,
opening into a large rectangular living-
space facing west. On the east side are
the bedrooms and bathrooms. The upper
floor plan shows a habitable area in
the truss-free roof space, which could
be used for a variety of purposes. A
gauze mesh is stretched around it to
create a flyscreen between the open
roof space and the ground floor rooms.

1   Entrance Porch
2   Garage
3   Kitchen
4   Dining
5   Living
6   Bedroom
7   Bathroom
8   Master Bedroom
9   Master Bathroom
10   Terrace
11   Verandah
12   Gymnasium/TV Room

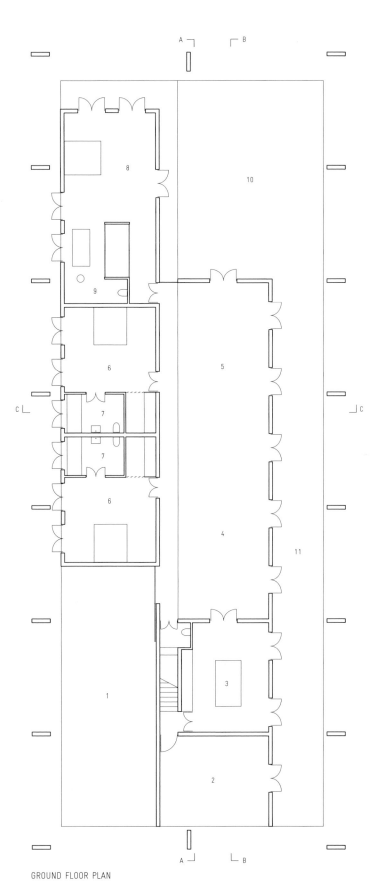

GROUND FLOOR PLAN

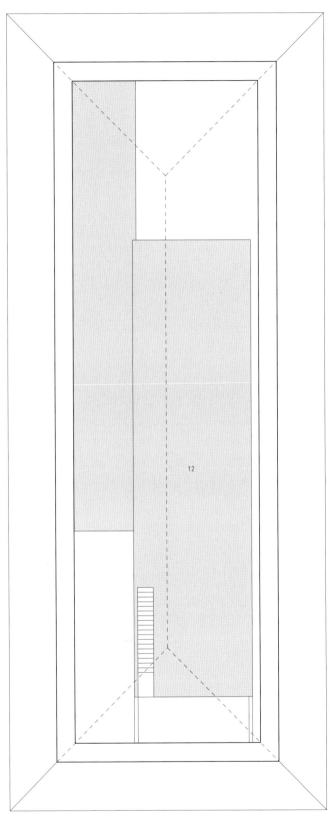

FIRST FLOOR PLAN

The house is designed with three independent but interdependent elements. It is envisaged the ground plinth and portal framed hipped roof are built first to provide a shaded working environment for building the enclosed domestic spaces.

Local materials are used throughout. The roof is constructed using concrete portal frames to provide a clear span. The roof void is ventilated at eaves and ridge to facilitate cooling of the space beneath. The roof is smooth finished internally and clad with steel corrugated sheeting externally. There are no gutters and rainwater is expected to soak away into the garden soil.

The plinth and the two joined pavilions containing the enclosed domestic spaces are constructed using painted rendered blockwork walls. All external windows are standardised timber French windows. The floors and raised plinth are finished in stone.

The pavilion containing the public rooms of the house has a flat roof finished in polished concrete. The pavilion containing the sleeping quarters is lower and open to the hipped roof. A flyscreen mesh is stretched from a ring beam along the inner edge of the portal frame columns tight over the lower pavilion and attached to the wall of the taller pavilion.

A staircase from the kitchen and garage provides access to the roof of the large pavilion which is used as a gymnasium and cinema room underneath the hipped roof.

1:200

0   10m

ROOF PLAN

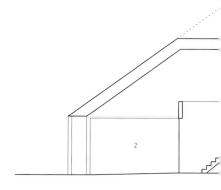

SECTION AA

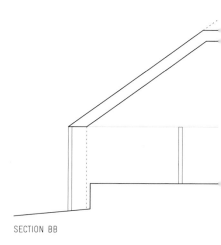

SECTION BB

1   Entrance Porch
2   Garage
3   Kitchen
4   Dining
5   Living
6   Bedroom
7   Bathroom
8   Master Bedroom
9   Master Bathroom
10   Terrace
11   Verandah
12   Gymnasium/TV Room

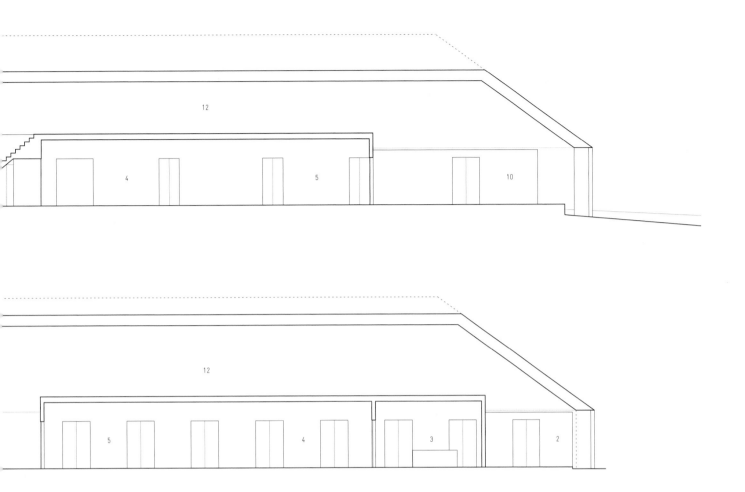

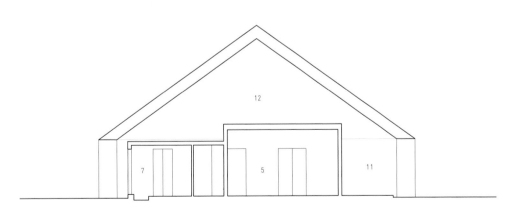

SECTION CC

(top) Aerial view of model from south west with hipped roof and supporting columns separated from the plinth on which the enclosing walls of the house are built.

(bottom) The same view with roof removed showing the volume of the principal living space raised above the horizontal fly screen.

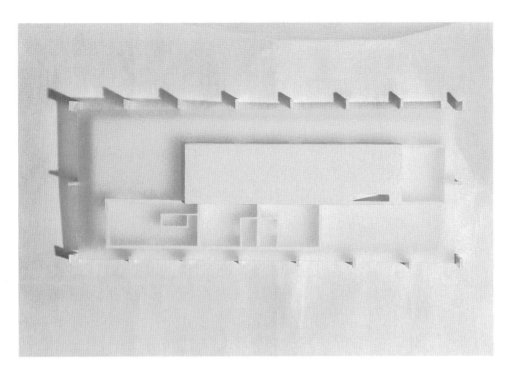

(top) Plan view of the model without
roof.

(bottom) The lipped roof forms a shaded
verandah to the west and south.

The photograph of the model demonstrates the luminous, floating quality of the house, enclosed by a thin, translucent external skin of perforated polycarbonate. The inner facade of the house, and the external stair, can be glimpsed through the large openings in the external skin, which also provide good views out from the inside. When the lights are on inside, the whole structure appears to glow like a lantern.

358
Drum House

The Drum House is a prototype for a model of vertical living which continues the genre of octagon houses established in the mid-nineteenth century, when they became rather fashionable. It was argued then that the advantage of the octagon form was that it could provide more sunlight, ventilation, and good views from every room, and made more efficient use of internal space. We think this is still true today. In this prototype, the house is elevated above ground level, and has an inner and outer envelope, with a circulation stair attached to the outer envelope. The freestanding, self-contained structure can be fenestrated and rotated to suit any orientation, making it highly adaptable to different sorts of sites.

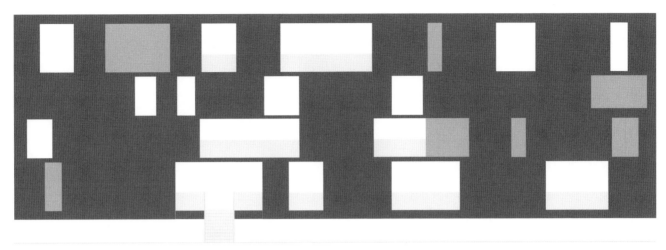

EXTERNAL ELEVATION

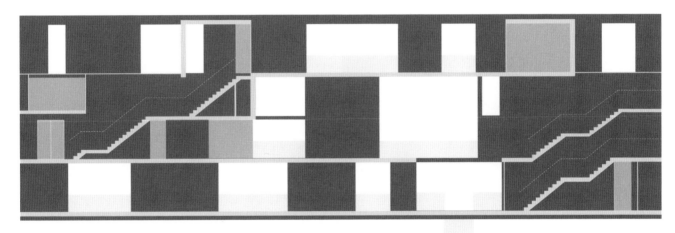

INTERNAL ELEVATION

These two drawings show the external
skin of the house unwrapped and laid
flat like a dress pattern. The internal
elevation (bottom) indicates the position
of the staircases.

358
Drum House

1:200
0   10m

EXTERNAL

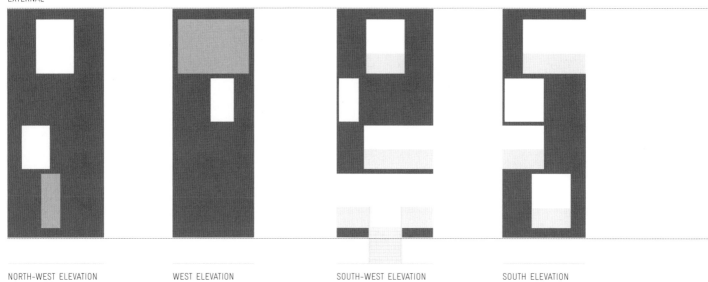

NORTH-WEST ELEVATION   WEST ELEVATION   SOUTH-WEST ELEVATION   SOUTH ELEVATION

INTERNAL

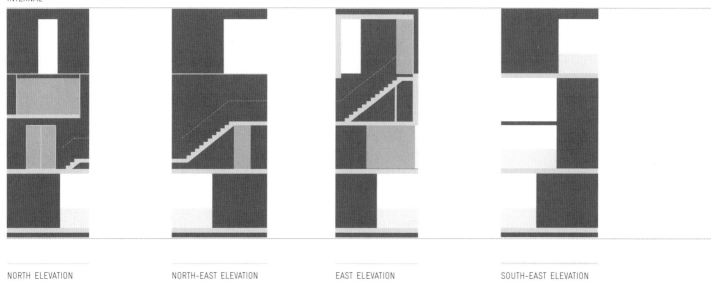

NORTH ELEVATION   NORTH-EAST ELEVATION   EAST ELEVATION   SOUTH-EAST ELEVATION

(top) External elevation separated into
eight panels which represent each side
of the octagonal plan.

(bottom) Internal elevation with location
of the floors and staircase indicated.

EXTERNAL

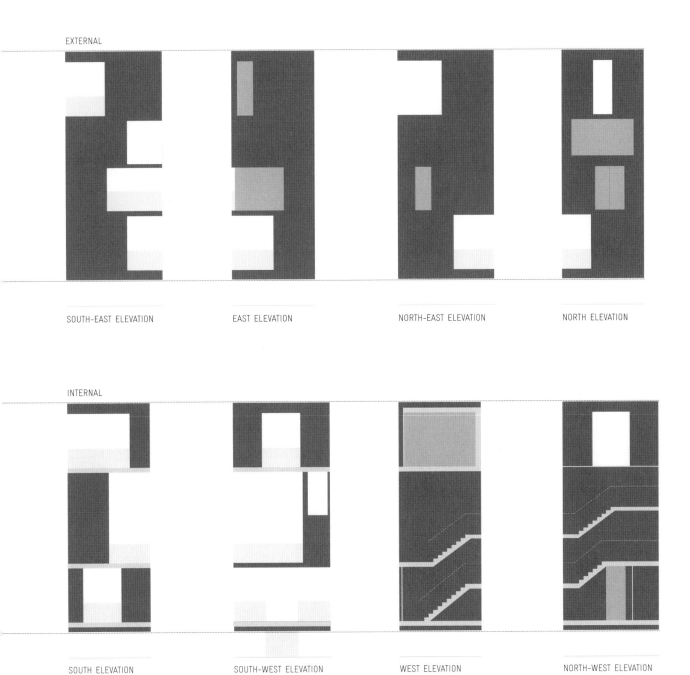

SOUTH-EAST ELEVATION

EAST ELEVATION

NORTH-EAST ELEVATION

NORTH ELEVATION

INTERNAL

SOUTH ELEVATION

SOUTH-WEST ELEVATION

WEST ELEVATION

NORTH-WEST ELEVATION

1:200

0   10m

The plans show the basement, elevated ground floor, containing children's bedrooms or a separate flat, first floor, containing a double-height living space, second floor, with study and winter garden, third floor, containing the master bedroom suite opening onto a deck, and roof levels.

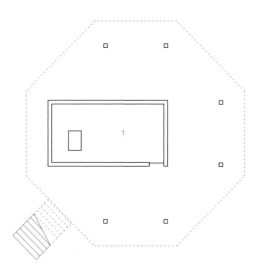

BASEMENT PLAN

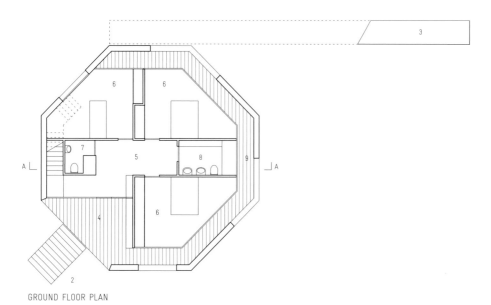

GROUND FLOOR PLAN

FIRST FLOOR PLAN

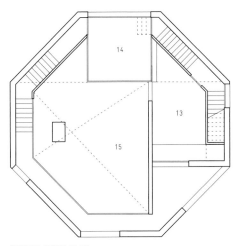

SECOND FLOOR PLAN

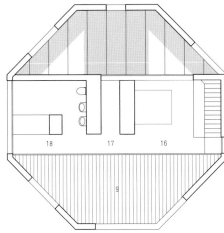

THIRD FLOOR PLAN

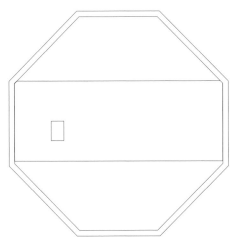

ROOF PLAN

1	Plant/Store Room
2	Entrance Staircase
3	Ramp
4	Porch
5	Entrance Hall
6	Bedroom
7	WC
8	Bathroom
9	Deck
10	Vestibule
11	Living/Dining Room
12	Kitchen
13	Study
14	Winter Garden
15	Void
16	Master Bedroom
17	Dressing Room
18	Master Bathroom

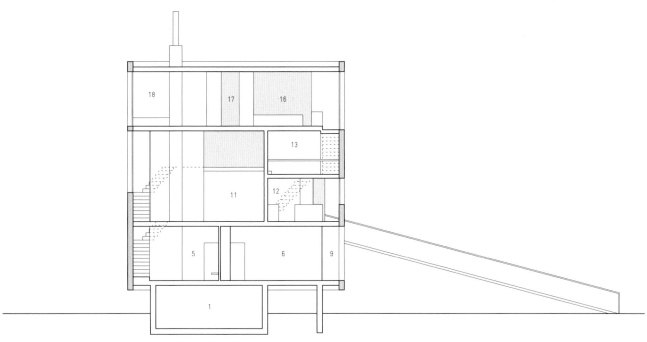

SECTION AA

The section shows ramp access to the
main entrance at first floor level, with
separate access to the accommodation
on the elevated ground floor.

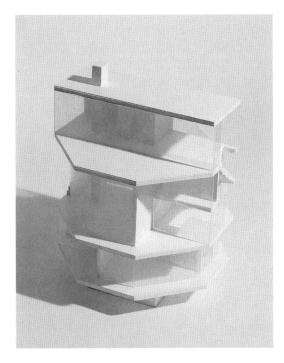

(top left) Interior and exterior spaces of the Drum House revealed as a composition of vertical and horizontal planes.

(top right) Octagonal polycarbonate envelope with openings which are either glazed or left open according to the interior functions.

(bottom) Drum House model showing how the interior and exterior spaces are contained within the perforated external wall.

(top) Model viewed from the west.

(bottom) Model viewed from the south.

(top) Model viewed from the north.

(bottom) Model view from the east with ramp to the main entrance at first floor.

ESSAYS

Reality and Project
Pierre d'Avoine

This text describes the limitations and restrictions commonly experienced by architects practising in urban Britain, and the ways in which sheer pressure on land, combined with a general preoccupation with conservation as the overriding agenda for the built environment, have shaped the direction of architecture. It sets out the case for prioritising environmental concerns, and investing in education to nurture public confidence and enjoyment in new approaches to building.

In the Vishnu Dharmottar Purana, one of India's ancient scriptures, an architect asks the sage how he should build the temple (home). He is told that besides technical studies he should know phonetics, vocal and instrumental music, dance, painting and image making. In short, he should know all the ways in which the body expresses itself and all the lifestyles, if he desires to give an appropriate dwelling to the user.

In both East and West, the architect has historically been expected to fill the role of universal scholar, with a breadth of learning and an understanding of many diverse subjects, in order to express man's harmony with the cosmos in built form, on the one hand, and, on the other, to provide the practical means for realising dwelling, workplace and community.

In the latter half of the twentieth century, however, the role and scope of the architect was significantly challenged and undermined. In that increasingly fragmented world, it became very hard to make the kind of architecture that could offer a sense of order amidst the apparent chaos: an architecture that could make connections among the disparate forces that govern people's lives.

The process of making architecture is shaped, in our practice, by a multi-cultural and global outlook that will also have meaning for the individual in his or her local context. This may have something to do with the fact that I was born and brought up in India, that I am of both Indian and European background, and that I now live and work primarily in England. It represents a rejection of narrow categories that lead to dogmatism and chauvinism. During my time at architecture school, I was encouraged to believe in a heroic monolithic modernism, cut off from the past. It was only later and quite gradually that I came to understand how much richer and varied the strands of modernism were and how much they were rooted in tradition.

It seems to me that the scope for architecture in Britain, whilst I have been practising, has been extremely restrictive. Built experimentation tends only to be permitted in interiors, and with most architecture there is little risk-taking in the area of formal language and ideas.

Our practice aims towards a rigorous approach to its work, based upon a desire to build. However, the opportunities to build at any great scale, or from scratch, have been limited. Initially, the bulk of our workload consisted of conversions, alterations and extensions of existing buildings for private and commercial clients. The relatively small scale, simple programmes and tight budgets of these projects, forced us to be inventive with and concentrate on the expressiveness of the materials themselves; particularly in terms of carefully detailed design — because everything is seen in close-up. We were also concerned with re-ordering the interiors to provide a 'centred' space as the unifying mechanism, usually by opening up the building on section within the existing envelope. The revelation of the internal re-ordering on the exterior became a critical moment in each project, and could either be delicate or forceful, ironic or blatant. The crude restrictions imposed by town planning authorities are problems we have had to face, even when working on mundane existing buildings. On the project for Sheendale Studios, which ironically is a new building, this has led to unnecessary dislocations between the interior and the exterior, which are diminishing to both the building and its locale.

This causes one to reflect on the current obsession with conservation; designing 'in keeping'; and the literal-minded, narrowly formal contextualism that the media insist is what the public wants, and that town planners increasingly demand. This has much to do with the long-standing obsession of the English with the forms of the past whenever they are in an identity crisis and the future looks uncertain.

I feel that architecture, particularly in terms of environmental issues and broader cultural issues, should be a fundamental part of the school curriculum. The layman/patron who cares about and is better informed in these matters can enjoy and contribute positively to the architectural debate instead of voting for the sentimental option of historical styling in lieu of an authentic identity.

The practice has chosen to work on a broad front and has undertaken residential projects, shops and office projects, exhibition design, cultural projects and community and landscaping projects — ranging in scale from furniture design through to masterplanning exercises. The range of work reflects our concerns, and in retrospect we have been quite selective.

The last ten years have seen the virtual demise of public sector architecture. We have had to practise in an increasingly commercial marketplace dominated by developer clients. A major part of the problem with speculative offices, apart from designing for an anonymous end user, tends to be the meanness of the brief. In the competition project for Grand Buildings in

Trafalgar Square, designed in collaboration with Nick Coombe and Pip Horne, we tried to emphasise the civic/social role of the development, whilst invigorating the brief, by balancing the speculative office requirements with a mix of leisure usage. We felt it was unnecessary to design an overtly classical facade. However, the building is carefully related to the neighbouring buildings.

Its central space is not a private office atrium, but a vertical shaft open to the sky. At the base of the shaft, a public space gathers up and focuses several pedestrian routes both above and below ground from Trafalgar Square, Charing Cross, the Strand and Northumberland Avenue. People are invited to shop and take a lift to the subterranean club and cinema, or to the rooftop restaurant, where the relationship to Trafalgar Square is established by the alignment of the glass restaurant wedge with Nelson's Column.

It is a depressing and unfortunate result of our society's present loss of nerve that the jury chose as winner a design that proposed to demolish the existing building and then develop new offices behind a replica facade.

This project, together with our scheme for newspaper offices in Richmond, the feasibility study for the redesign for Mortlake Green, and earlier community arts projects in Surrey and Birmingham, has given us the opportunity to explore the notion of a public architecture in which the social ideals of modernism still offer a broad base from which to approach the problem of making architecture. As El Lissitzky wrote, in 1930: "the basic elements of architecture in Russia in the twentieth century are tied to social revolution".

The false dialectic between traditional and modern architecture is being transcended by pressing environmental concerns. A genuine contemporary architecture must respond optimistically to the vital issues of the times. It requires a wide-ranging approach that balances technological development with ecological welfare, the needs of the individual with those of the collective, whilst seeking new ways of expressing the primary and timeless architectural impulse of place-making and shelter.

Colour and Architecture: The White House
Pierre d'Avoine

Colour and Architecture was an exhibition curated by Clare
Melhuish at the Heinz Gallery in 1993, which set out to reveal
the nuances of colour usage in contemporary buildings designed
by a range of architects from different countries, and different
climates, around the world. The exhibition was designed by
Pierre d'Avoine, and included his scheme for the White House.
In this text, he explained how the prevalence of white surfaces
provided the means of orchestrating a rich but subtle array of
coloured hues.

In England colour is used to accentuate elements very intensely
and randomly, but in India, where I was born, whole surfaces
are coloured, and gradually, in the monsoon and the hot sun,
the colour fades and peels off. I'm used to both sides and so
I'm not frightened of colour. I can use it in a garish way or
quite carefully. Because my work is planar, colour can be used
almost symbolically to give a piece a certain place and
importance, or to make distinctions between materials, so that
you get a tactile and aural distinction as well as visual.
Sometimes materials are used for their intrinsic colour — copper
that becomes patinated, steel left to go rusty, mill-finished
aluminium or fibreglass. You make discoveries, take chances
and the project becomes something else as a result.

With the White House, white was given in the name. Everything
was painted white except the hallway containing the stair, which
was yellow. Lit only from above, it was like a tower at the
centre of the house. Then there was the green garden. In the
new project the garden became an outside chamber. The only
new applied colour was the grey-green of the window frame
and lintel, which was to do with symbolising, not dissolving,
the connection between the two spaces: the most potent
connection in the house.

In the end, the whole point was the quality of the light on the
white of the walls and ceilings. The various openings were
designed to open the house up in different directions — north,
to the garden, west to the courtyard. Tinted light from the garden
reflected green on the walls. Warm orange light came from the
south and west. So from the kitchen at the heart you perceive
all the different spaces. The actual colour was never white
because it was always reflecting and vibrating with other colours,
activated by the light.

"Colour: the sensation produced by waves of decomposed
light upon the optic nerve."
Concise English Dictionary

Flowering of the New Suburbia
Clare Melhuish

In the early 1990s, economic recession bit hard in the UK. The absence of grand architectural projects encouraged architects to look closely at the conditions of everyday domestic life, taking stock of the further changes in living patterns which had emerged since the 1960s. The White House project represented a subtle re-examination of conventional models of suburban living, which led on from the Sheendale Studios development, completed in 1989, and was continued in the more radical Invisible House scheme.

The extension to the White House, in south London, completed in 1993, was not simply a beautifully conceived and crafted domestic addition, but also made a significant contribution to innovative thought about the suburban environment, and indeed, the human habitat in general. It presented the idea that the suburban environment should be of equal, if not more, interest to the architect as the metropolis. In the very ordinariness of its elements lies the promise of the special and extraordinary. Through architecture, this promise can be brought to fruition, opening the way to new perceptions about the environment and aspirations for the future: a new optimism.

The White House was an ordinary 1920s semi-detached house in a particularly leafy London suburb beside the river Thames. The clients were enthusiasts for modern architecture, and were keen to take an active and supportive interest in the architect's proposals and the realisation of the work. They had already made some significant changes to the upper floor of the house, and had put considerable effort into developing a verdant and luxuriant garden to the rear. These initiatives paved the way for the subsequent redevelopment of the back of the house.

The rethinking of the existing ground-floor living spaces, an ad hoc arrangement of pokey ill-lit kitchen and service rooms, was focussed on the garden — in particular, a magnificent wisteria, that had grown up close to the building. The new plan was based on the idea of opening a vista to the garden right through the house from the front door, framing the wisteria, and allowing warm garden light and colour to flow through the interior.

A new kitchen, dining room and sitting room were designed as part of a fluid continuum of space in which the different domains are given loose articulation, rather than being presented as completely open plan. The two more functional areas were slightly elevated, forming a transitional space between the busy core of the house (containing the staircase) and the more tranquil sitting area, set at the lower level of the garden. The connection between the sitting area and the garden, the latter transformed into a field of absorbing and revivifying contemplation, was re-forged as a fusion of internal and external spaces separated only by a glass screen of sliding doors. Under a

single deep steel beam running the whole width of the house, the screen was divided into four bays, three single, and one double filled by the wisteria, which itself provides the missing rhythmic vertical accent.

From the core of the house the wisteria can be seen along a direct visual route through the dining area, via two not-quite-aligned openings in the old structure, now pared away to the minimum. The visual and physical routes through the new plan, connecting the different spaces, both internal and external, are very important, but they do not disturb the spatial integrity of each. By glazing over the first opening from the hall into the dining room, physical, as opposed to visual, movement towards the sitting area and garden is diverted to one side, along the edge of the kitchen space. Hence both spaces are preserved intact. The dining area communes with a small west-facing courtyard, through full-height sliding doors. The kitchen acts as the fulcrum of the whole spatial sequence — the 'mother of the house'. It is designed as a single service wall along the party wall of the house, with one main element, a large work surface over storage, pulled out as a free-standing structure. Overhead, the ceiling is treated as a floating plane, marking out the kitchen domain.

The mingling of northern and western light in the interior, tinting the white walls with different reflected colours at different times of day, is part of the blurring of boundaries between inside and outside, the artificial habitat determined by a certain way of life, and the natural environment that is never quite predictable or controllable. The first phase of the project had been inspired by the idea of the wisteria becoming an organic part of the architecture. The second phase was concerned with forging a direct route at first floor level from the sleeping quarters into the garden, via a light, white-painted steel walkway that, once colonised by climbing plants, would also become a leafy pergola.

This route forms an extension to the direct passage from bed to bath which the client had already created along the front range of the first floor. It descends to the garden by a movable steel stair, operated by a winch, across the gable end of the sitting room. The winch allows the stair to be lifted into a horizontal position over the passage from the courtyard to the garden, giving access and a measure of security.

This metal structure, wrapped around the end wall of the new building whose white chimney juts up through green leaves, is the only part of the scheme which is clearly visible from the street, thus forming the sole point of direct intervention in the suburban landscape. The walkway, as an almost theatrical external extension of the house into the life of the street, gives a quite new dimension to a domestic way of life which in this country is usually highly introverted. In the sense that it provides a platform from which to view and be viewed, it represents a variation on the domestic veranda typical in hot countries, from which the life of the street might be observed and entered into without actually leaving the domestic territory — an English variation, perhaps, in that it is so closely involved with the garden.

The unusual kinetic element to the design of the walkway and stair is not simply a curiosity, but directly influences the way the house itself operates and is perceived. It represents a conception of domestic architecture which is not static and finished (by the architect), but open to physical manipulation and alteration through the participation of the user.

In common with Rudolf Schindler's Californian houses of the early twentieth century, which were an inspiration, the White House does not depend on rich and sensuous materials for its success, but follows in the same path of questioning and invention in the creation of spatial sequences and relationships, executed with spareness. In the interaction of interior and exterior, the inhabitation of the different structural elements and the contrast between movement along connecting routes and moments of stillness, where the architecture seems to pause and wait, the White House invites us to imagine new ways of domestic living, and a new future for the suburban environment.

Gone But Only In My Head
Pierre d'Avoine

This article, written in the mid 1990s, presents a critical appraisal of the architect's often awkward role in society, mediating, as observer, critic and creator, between the powerful influences of commercialism, consumerism, and authentic experience. It sums up the nature of the dilemma that faces architects, and points in the direction of the pattern book concept as a tool of re-engagement and de-mystified communication between the architect and the public.

During the 1980s our architectural practice worked both in the UK and abroad, particularly in Japan, but also in Italy and India. During this period the location of the office did not change; London remained our base. However, to an extent, we felt alienated, or exiled by the cultural climate of Britain at that time. Many architects in the UK did not seem to be connected with the cultural mainstream. Paradoxically, it seemed that some architects were living in a kind of exile within their own country. The value of their contribution to the cultural life of Britain appeared diminished, and architecture itself marginalised.

Architects have always had to go where the work is. "Have drawing board will travel", announced a headline in The Times on 2 July 1992. The article suggested that although "British architects are suffering, out of work, plans on ice, fees cut, designs bypassed, where can they turn?", recession had slowed down the rampant commercial development which changed the face of the country for much the worse in the 1980s. Even architects were heard to comment that no architecture was better than so much bad architecture. In reality, the commercial operators had already set up camp in Eastern Europe and were busy inflicting development, in the service of a capitalist vision, on countries scarcely out of the grip of communist repression. Here too lay a paradox: the moribund economies behind the Iron Curtain also left, intact but decaying, a treasure trove of architectural gems ripe for preservation and conservation.

Britain is part of a Western-centric culture that has imposed itself on the rest of the world through control of the global economy. It has been a culture of casually assumed superiority which seeks to dominate peoples who, as a result of a slower pace of material 'progress' have been perceived as 'backward'. However, this vision of the world is changing. The global hegemony of the West is breaking down as other cultures rise up the ladder of prosperity, especially China, India and the Pacific Rim countries. Simultaneously, the flowering of post-colonial theory and subaltern studies, through the work of thinkers such as Edward Said and Dipesh Chakrabarty, has established the rewriting of history from a non-Western perspective, with powerful implications for the future balance of global power and influence.

Nevertheless, in architectural terms these countries continue to look to Western models for guidance and direction, a tradition that has been sustained at least since the Renaissance. Already in 1915, the Indian writer Coomaraswamy had stated:

Let it be clearly realised that the modern world is not the ancient world of slow communications; what is done in India or Japan today has immediate spiritual results in Europe and America. To say that East is East and West is West is simply to hide one's head in the sand. [But] It will be quite impossible to establish any higher social order in the West as long as the East remains infatuated with the, to her, entirely novel and fascinating theory of laissez faire...[1]

Coomaraswamy regarded the Western model of social idealism, the cornerstone of modernism, as the only way forward for humanity. By the end of the twentieth century, however, market-led capitalism had triumphed over such social idealism. Postmodernism as a cultural theory represented a celebration of the life-style and the electronic toys of middle class affluence, while shutting its eyes both to the persistence of poverty, mass unemployment, miserable housing and low pay in the West, and to the role played by the advanced industrial nations in perpetuating the gross inequalities of the Third World. Alternatively, it simply retreated into an increasingly desperate nihilism.

The Japanese writer Tanizaki recognised the corrosive nature of cultural imperialism in his book In Praise of Shadows. He writes:

One need only compare American, French and German films to see how greatly nuances of shading and colouration can vary in motion pictures. In the photographic image itself, to say nothing of the acting and the script, there somehow emerge differences in national character. If this is true even when identical equipment, chemicals, and films are used, how much better our own photographic technology might have suited our complexion, our facial features, our climate, our land. And had we invented the phonograph and the radio how much more faithfully they would reproduce the special character of our voices and our music. Japanese music is above all a music of reticence, of atmosphere. When recorded, or amplified by a loud speaker, the greater part of its charm is lost. In conversation too: we prefer the soft voice, the understatement. Most important of all are the pauses. Yet the phonograph and the radio render these moments of silence utterly lifeless. And so we distort the arts themselves to curry favour for them with the machines. These machines are inventions of Westerners, and are, as we might expect, well-suited to the Western arts. But precisely on this account they put our own arts at a great disadvantage.[2]

Tanizaki's nostalgic musings did not anticipate the bewildering changes of the late twentieth century, by which time his country, having commodified the Westerner's machines, had become a leader among the advanced industrial nations.

Before the sudden collapse of her economy in the early 1990s, Japan gloried in her recently acquired economic pomp, rampantly acquisitive of all that was new. Everything was rapidly consumed and ejected. For a time, she drew in a vast and glittering array of performers to her court, including an influx of British architects desperately seeking work far from home, and prepared to rise to the challenge of responding to a totally different cultural context, of which few had any knowledge. For the British the invitation to the dance was a challenge to break out of the confines of a country suffering a long period of readjustment and lack of confidence following the loss of Empire and gradual economic decline. In architecture this was manifested by an increasing dislocation between theory and education, on the one hand, and, on the other, the public perception of architecture and its influence on what was actually being built.

As a new century gets under way mainstream culture seems to have re-engaged with the idea of architecture in the private domestic domain, at some levels. The media reveals an insatiable fascination with the subject of 'design' as a key to self-realisation and contentment in the home. At the same time, it continues to promote an idea of instant gratification through largely quick-fix, superficial 'solutions' which are a far remove from the principles of a holistic engagement between architecture and the choreography of living, which architects are trained in and continue to explore and evolve throughout their careers. In this context, architects, in common with artists and poets, need to be aware of the positive value of 'exile' as a mental condition, allowing them to maintain a critical relationship with society through a certain distance and subversive intent — sharing an imaginative responsibility for the continued well-being and husbandry of the planet.

Notes:

[1] Coomaraswamy, Ananda.
[2] Tanizaki, Jun-Ichiro, In Praise of Shadows, London: Jonathan Cape, 1991, pp. 19-20.

Suburbia On My Mind
Pierre d'Avoine

This essay consolidates the thinking about the future of suburbia and suburban housing models that evolved through projects such as the White House and Invisible House during the early to mid 1990s.

Environmental considerations, locally as well as globally, have forced us to re-evaluate the ways in which we plan our cities and the countryside surrounding them. Too often the suburbs and peripheral areas have been forgotten about and have evolved as indeterminate, in-between spaces – neither one thing nor the other. In the twentieth century cities vastly increased in size as the result of a global population explosion, and our traditional understanding of them was challenged. The suburbs are now where most of us live, and increasingly where most of us work too. The infrastructure and buildings represent a huge investment by the state and local communities. As architects we have to make architectural and environmental sense of the new building types that have emerged in the periphery almost without our noticing, and often without the involvement of architects at all. As a result, the quality of the suburban environment has declined; however, suburbs have immense potential. They are worthy of consideration and have value in their own right. One of our tasks as architects is to consider how these emergent models can be manipulated and tuned to fulfil this potential and, in doing so, invigorate the lives of the people who live there.

I was born in Bombay, right in the heart of the city. It has now grown into an immense conurbation that stretches for 30 or 40 miles from the tip of its southern peninsula, where the original city was founded by the Portuguese, to the point where it joins to the mainland of western India. At the time of its development, in the nineteenth century, Byculla, the neighbourhood in which my family lived and I was brought up, was a suburb of Italianate villas. It grew up around the Byculla Club, an exclusive sporting and social club – a typical product of the Raj. Byculla, only two miles from the very centre of Bombay, is considered urban rather than suburban. Today the villas and the spacious gardens have mostly gone. The Byculla Club has vanished – to be replaced by multi-storey blocks of flats whose pavements are home to squatters and whose roads are full of traffic. Bombay is not unique in this change. Charles Correa writes in The New Landscape, 1985:

> Across the globe, the towns and cities of the Third World are growing very rapidly. In most of these countries, the annual population growth rate is somewhere between two to three per cent. But the towns and cities themselves are increasing at more than double this speed. This growth is compounded by the great waves of distress migration from the rural areas. The farmlands cannot sustain the population. And so squatters come to the cities living illegally on pavements, or in whatever crevices they can find.[1]

Whereas the squatters have to live with the utmost economy in the leftover spaces of the city, it is the emergent middle classes, in their desire for more space, who are responsible for pushing the boundaries of the city ever further from the centre – so much so that the very idea of a centre becomes increasingly meaningless. Over the last 20 years, developers have started to buy up tracts of land in remote rural areas within two to three hours drive of Bombay for redevelopment as housing estates. Although these are intended primarily to provide retirement and holiday homes, it seems likely that because these estates are within commuting distance they too will eventually become part of the conurbation of greater Bombay.

We have designed a small holiday house, the Mehr House, in the foothills of the Western Ghats, about 80 miles north of Bombay. The plot is part of a small estate, one of many in the Bombay hinterland catering for its burgeoning middle class. The layout forms a suburban road pattern placed arbitrarily on the landscape. The site is remote and the developer has provided a small workforce to build houses to the designs of architects commissioned by owners of individual plots. There are no rules and the potential for visual cacophony is great. This project has been an opportunity to make a clear and direct response to climate and landscape. Working within the new tradition of reinforced concrete a simple perforated cubic form is proposed, a filter to the prevailing breezes, organised as a sequence of interlocking volumes culminating in a roof terrace and outdoor sleeping space orientated towards the view of hills to the north. A secondary arrangement of screens, blinds, canopies and shutters extends the invitation to occupation and adaptation.

In his book Bourgeois Utopias, 1987, Robert Fishman claims London is the birthplace of suburbia. He suggests the roots of the modern suburb are to be found in the ideal community established by William Wilberforce and his colleagues in the Evangelical Movement in Clapham in the late eighteenth century. Whereas the merchant class had traditionally lived and worked from the same building in the city, possibly retreating to a country house at the weekend, the Clapham Sect permanently separated the home from the workplace in order to raise their families in a more wholesome and healthy environment, away from the growing pressures of city life.

The Clapham Sect created a grouping of villas in a park-like setting. This was inspired by notions of the picturesque developed in the writings of Alexander Pope and Horace Walpole, both of whom built themselves Thameside houses in Twickenham and Strawberry Hill as embodiments of a Picturesque ideal. This ideal rapidly filtered down through the merchant class to tradesmen at the opposite end of the social scale, to the extent that even in 1750 Walpole would complain: "There is not a citizen who does not take more pains to torture his acre and a half into irregularities than he formerly would have employed to make it as regular as his cravat."[2]

Raymond Williams identified the Picturesque landscape as "being organised for consumption – the view, the ordered proprietary repose, the prospect", in contrast to "The mathematical grids of the enclosure awards, with their straight hedges and straight roads", which were "contemporary with the natural curves and scatterings of the park scenery".[3] Thus functional separation of land organised for production and for consumption was given a visual coding so powerful that we now cannot contemplate the suburb in terms other than the Picturesque.

Separation was inherent to the concept of suburbia. The growth of the suburbs was dependent on the development of easy transport connections between the home and the workplace in the centre – the railway system in the nineteenth century and the motor car in the twentieth. However, Fishman argues that it was precisely the increase in use of the motor car which ultimately caused the decline of the suburb in its traditional role as dormitory adjunct to the city centre by diffusing residential development over a wider area. He also suggests a situation has evolved where the traditional city centre has lost its pre-eminence and given way to a multiplicity of peripheral centres which are themselves interconnected.

In the East and the developing world the pressures of urbanisation have been felt to a far greater extent than the West as cities have had to cope with vast population increase, widespread poverty and the effect of rural migration. These trends were critical in Europe in the nineteenth century in the wake of the Industrial Revolution. The result of this in Europe is that over 70 per cent of the population is now urban or suburban. In Britain the population has been fairly stable at around 55 million for several decades. In London, however, the population has decreased by a million to about seven million as a result of the initiative to decentralise by building a ring of garden cities and new towns in the London hinterland. This is a very different scenario from the developing world.

The suburb is defined in The Oxford English Dictionary as a district adjoining a town, the outskirts of a town, and most surprisingly as the outskirts of a town especially formerly as the prostitutes' quarters. This latter definition of the suburb as a potentially racy and disreputable place is contradicted by the sense of the word 'suburban' – that is, lacking the good qualities of either town or country, smug, comfortable, half-cultured, and narrow in outlook. The damningly pejorative view of suburbia was summed up in a line by John Betjeman: "Come friendly bombs and fall on Slough" – and the bombing of suburbia is precisely what the filmmaker John Boorman depicted in his film Hope and Glory, 1987.

Boorman's film may be viewed as an allegory of British antipathy to and suspicion of Continental influence, whether war-like or cultural. It is a nostalgic, but at the same time critical, exploration of Boorman's childhood during the Second World War. He was (in his own words) "Born at No 50 Rosehill Avenue, Carshalton, a monotonous street of those semi-detached suburban houses of which four million were built between the wars".[4] He traces his shame at being born in Rosehill Avenue partly to the political attitudes of his father, and partly to the contumacy and disdain heaped on Metroland in the culture of the time. However, he suggests that semi-detached suburbia gave rise to a stealthy social revolution – the development of the private inward-looking world of the nuclear family, of dormitories ten minutes walk from the tube, with no roots and no past, which were home to a new phenomenon, as yet unnamed, the commuter.

Boorman argues that architects were contemptuous of the semi-d, not least because they were totally uninvolved in its design and construction. Those tasks fell to the speculative builders who surely expressed the deep unconscious fantasies of a people oppressed by the patronising values of its betters. It was the speculative builders who lured the people into an unformed fantasy using a handful of cunning design metaphors – Tudor gables, leaded window panes and bow windows, which evoked a mythic English past yet paradoxically broke free from it and pointed to a shining future. The fantasy is perpetuated today by the volume house builders, in their attempt to capture the imagination of the house-buying public after the great post war experiment to provide decent public housing for everyone was all but abandoned in the 1980s.

Both approaches to the creation of housing on a large scale, whether market-led or part of the welfare state, are different sides of the same coin. They both tend towards a form of social engineering. They both give rise to disillusion caused by failure to recognise the needs of community, place-making and quality of environment, and a failure to recognise the need to provide and maintain an infrastructure and evolve an approach which takes into account slow-moving as well as fast-moving changes.

In London the policy of a green belt has encouraged more intensive development within the city and the suburbs. However, there is a profound mismatch between the old suburban patterns of development that have evolved since the First World War and the post-industrial culture in which we now find ourselves. Too often, new development in the suburbs is inappropriate and unaffordable. An emphasis on the single family house has led to a monoculture of environmental stress and loss of public open space: lifestyles that burden working families and isolate the elderly and single.

The Invisible House is one of a series of interstitial suburban houses we are designing that has its roots in a British architectural tradition thriving until the end of the nineteenth century, when most houses were dug into the earth. This is true in particular of central London mews and the inner London suburbs where most houses have cellars or garden flats. The Invisible House has been designed for a site in Acton in west London adjacent to the A40 road. The site is part of the Goldsmiths' Estate, a typical suburban development of the inter-war period. It does not have the quality of Bedford Park, a late Victorian suburb in neighbouring Chiswick, which was 'architecturally' designed by Norman Shaw, amongst others. The Goldsmiths' Estate lacks the architectural and infrastructural merits of the earlier development, which included shops, schools, a church and public houses all within a short walk from the new metropolitan train station. This is not to say that the Goldsmiths' Estate is completely lacking in merit. It may be bland, but in its heyday it must have had a civility and modesty. It still has an openness, and the trees planted in avenues have matured and provide a softening greenness to the environment. However, 60 years on, whatever good qualities it may have had are gradually being eroded. The inevitable wear and tear on the built fabric of the suburb has resulted in a variety of changes and alterations – some good, some bad – but the general effect is detrimental.

The Invisible House may be viewed as an antidote to the over-assertiveness of much of the suburban fabric. It is not intended as a universal strategy but possibly another letter in the alphabet of building types. It is designed specifically for a suburban back garden site where it can be eased into the small scale landscapes of fences, hedges, greenhouses, garden sheds, pergolas, shrubbery, compost heaps, lawns and herbaceous borders without much disruption – low-key aspects of suburban life which can be not only enjoyable but also inspiring. By burying the building in the ground the new house becomes invisible behind a two-metre-high fence, suggesting an Eastern image of the walled courtyard, a Western image of the secret garden. It is intended to retain an element of mystery. The burying of the house allows the flat roof to continue the ground plane and provides garden and car space. It affords integration and involvement with the earth, recognition that man mediates between earth and sky.

The potential of The Invisible House as both dwelling and workplace is released by organising the internal plan as a series of loose-fit, interconnected spaces around the central courtyard. The organisation of the house also means that it neither overlooks nor is overlooked by its neighbours. Generous light is provided to the interior and the glass walls focus the view from the surrounding rooms into the intensely private courtyard. The ceiling to the living room is raised so that the garden above it provides a vantage-point over the wall, humanising the austere introversion of the basic concept. The roofs are turfed and climbing plants encouraged to grow over the open frame, so that the Invisible House, when viewed from the surrounding houses, and as the vegetation matures over time, gradually disappears.

A slightly modified version of the project received planning permission in 1994 after a two-year battle with the local planning authority. Permission was conditional on lowering the raised garden to prevent overlooking of neighbours' property, thus ensuring their privacy. However, a cursory examination of the situation would reveal that the gardens of the existing semi-detached houses are anything but private and may be readily viewed from the first floor windows of several of the neighbouring houses. It suggests a certain arbitrariness in the application of rules and regulations which seem to address a frozen moment. In the resulting project for the Invisible House the carefully evolved spatial balance of the original design is upset and the frustration is that, afterwards, the garden may still be raised without reference to the authorities by simply building up the level of earth. Even in 'derided' suburbia the difficulty of trying to invest a project with subtlety and depth in conception and execution is evident in the face of a rigidly imposed bureaucratic vision for a public realm. When new development is planned, difference is mistrusted in favour of outdated precedent and a false image of continuity. It has become easy to understand the coarse materialisations, couched in deep ironies, that increasingly constitute the built fabric of our environment as sign and image become almost everything.

In Japan where we have worked on projects for over a decade it can sometimes seem that this is all that is on offer. The difference there is a cultural confidence and powerful economy which has indulged formal experimentation. The architect Tom Heneghan has written that "Despite the appearance of Japan's cities – which are certainly not for the 'aesthetically squeamish' – modern architecture is central to the culture of the Japanese."[5] The suburban edge of Otsu, a small town on the southern shore of Lake Biwa near Kyoto, is a typical Japanese suburb in many ways but also untypical in that the site of our project, a huge shopping and entertainment building for a commercial client, is on land reclaimed from the lake. The context is one of violent juxtapositions of scale – the scrappy mat of two and three storey buildings dwarfed by the more recent lakeshore development. An outline plan was already in place for a warehouse-like structure extending to the limits of the triangular site that is bisected by a canal. The client wanted ideas for the appearance, image and atmosphere of the building and provided us with two reference photographs to work from – the QE2 and Frank Lloyd Wright's Guggenheim Museum. Our scheme concentrated on the skin of the building—treated like the metal-clad hull of a container ship overhanging a continuous shop window around the base, the entrance sequence, internal T-shaped atrium and roof. The entrance is located over the canal, between the main shopping building and the smaller entertainment building, which is lifted up over a sheet of water viewed from inside through its glass underbelly. The roof is used for car parking but is mainly additional space for entertainment, including outdoor cinema and garden parties.

The Otsu building pays homage to the delirious merged projects of Toyokazu Watanabe. The combination of given images is developed with other themes to express the client's cultural and civic aspirations for the project in a fictional narrative based on the story of Romeo and Juliet. Through this device we try to reveal the building by focusing on detail and event in the Japanese tradition of expanding experiential space "by 'killing' (slowing down) time."[1] The skin of the building becomes a kinetic backdrop onto which the communal fantasies of suburban Otsu are projected.

In Britain the retreat by the state from the social aspirations of modernism into the embrace of the market economy is one of the reasons why social cohesion is breaking down. This fragmentation has also been viewed positively as "... the sign of a society in which difference and discontinuity rightly challenge ideas of totality and continuity."[2] One suspects it is not only discontinuity and difference themselves that lead to withdrawal and atomism in our society. Our collective fear of the future is no doubt fuelled by rapid unpredictable change. It may also be caused by the rapacious suburbanisation of the globe that leads, paradoxically, to sensations of homogeneity and sameness. The most potent narrative in the history of suburbia is the triumph of 'middle culture' and 'middle place'. The suburban house is still the prototypical Englishman's castle and in middle England even the blandest suburb achieves antique value by virtue of its age. Nevertheless, the very somnolence of suburbia can sometimes be a reactor for the imagination and trigger inventions and events that could never have been initiated anywhere else. We used to view it as a containing edge to the urban and perhaps never really anticipated a time when the suburb and its network of roads would completely swallow up the country and the city. Ultimately, a mutant sub-urban future is not necessarily a psychological problem but one of environmental concern — the profligate misuse of land and resources.

The notion of the environment expressed by the word 'ecological' envisages a balance between all things; man and nature, nature and technology and so on, including the balance between the social physical active man and the inner psychological spiritual man. There are no divisions in reality. These dichotomies are useful devices for analysis, but the message of ecology is clearly that the world is one and everyone is responsible. Life in the suburban soup doesn't have to be a thin diet of gruel when the ingredients — so multifarious and potentially delicious — offer us the promise of a feast that could sustain us all.

Notes:

[1] Correa, Charles, The New Landscape, Bombay: The Book Society of India, 1985, p. 9.
[2] Fishman, Robert, Bourgeois Utopias.
[3] Williams, Raymond.
[4] Boorman, John.
[5] Heneghan, Tom.

245

The Invisible House: The Architect as Anthropologist of Suburban Life
Clare Melhuish

The Invisible House scheme was designed as a model for a new approach to development in the suburbs, based on the principle of densification. It pre-dated the government-led initiative at the end of the 1990s to encourage high-density development in cities, as a way of resolving the housing shortage. The project tapped into the potential represented by the extensive landscape of back gardens, some lovingly cultivated and enjoyed but many abandoned and left to go to seed, which is concealed behind the inner city and suburban street frontages of British cities.

The suburb should be a rich field for anthropological research. On the surface often monotonous, repetitive, and apparently blank, offering very little to the stranger, yet underneath, behind closed doors, a fertile seed-bed for all sorts of unexpected cultural activities and manifestations. One only has to think back over the history of popular music and fashion in London since the 1960s, and the people who made it, to realise what an enormous contribution the suburbs have made to the dynamic alternative cultural scene which has given Britain a high international profile.

The work of Pierre d'Avoine Architects has consistently engaged with the issue of suburbia, exploring both in the UK and abroad — in India, Japan, Ghana, and the West Indies — how to develop a new approach to suburban development. It has been motivated by a refusal to accept the straitjacket of prescribed models of development imposed by British planning authorities, or the market-orientated certainty of the volume house builders that the key to sales is an endless recreation of the suburban semi, replete with Tudor gables and bow windows, evoking a mythical, idyllic, but essentially false English past. Both are founded in a superficial appraisal of the existing architectural forms, and in a deeply conservative view of the social structure and norms of suburban living, based on a nineteenth century idea that has been superseded by social and technological change. By contrast, the Invisible House represents an investigation of new forms that reflect the great changes that have taken place in suburbia. The concept is based on an understanding of the anthropology of architecture, or the meaning that lies behind the spatial organisation and architectural forms that evolve during certain periods of social history in specific places.

The Invisible House was designed for a small site at the end of a back garden in what is now an inner suburb of west London, and represented a test case for a new approach to suburban redevelopment. It provoked an intense reaction both on the part of neighbours and the planning authority, which was almost entirely negative in character. The scheme was initially refused planning permission on spurious grounds — over-development, substandard accommodation, and being 'out of character' — despite the fact that the house could not be seen at all from the street, being substantially dug into

the ground around an open central courtyard. The roof was treated as a garden and car parking bay, thus merging with the immediate, low key landscape of back gardens, potting sheds, and garages, and the entire structure was completely concealed from the road behind the existing garden fence.

This curious state of affairs was eventually rectified when the planning refusal was overturned at appeal. However, it raised some interesting issues. The building was regarded as an intrusion, although it was invisible. In some way, which no one could quite articulate, it was a subversion of what was perceived to be the existing order — even though the surrounding area, close to the A40, was a far from homogeneous mixture of housing and unattractive out-of-scale industrial development which people seemed happy to accept, despite a level of general environmental decay.

The site lay within the Goldsmiths' Estate, a typical suburban development of the interwar period, which lacked the architectural and infrastructural merits of earlier developments inspired by an ideal of country living within commuting distance of the city on the new public transport links.

The architects of these earlier developments took as their model a version of the English, verging towards the German, vernacular which could be easily reproduced on a large scale to provide housing first for the middle classes and later for the masses. One such example of the latter is the Old Oak estate, close to the site of the Invisible House, developed by the London County Council between 1913 and 1920. With its pointed gables, prominent chimney pots, and steeply pitched roofs, it was intended to create a village-like, pastoral environment, apart from the city, but — planned around a railway station rather than a church — within easy access of it by means of the Central London Railway.

Such development promoted what John Boorman depicted in his film Hope and Glory, 1987, as a private, inward-looking world of the nuclear family, smug, half-cultured and narrow in outlook— a view commonly shared by the intelligentsia. Yet the suburbs constructed earlier this century have been progressively absorbed into the city as its boundaries have expanded outwards, bringing the original ideals of apartness, and quasi-pastoral low density into question. The structure of the nuclear family has broken down to a great extent: household units in the suburbs are far more varied than they were when these communities were originally built. Cultural homogeneity has gone, and with it, the common dream of a mythical English past, as ethnic communities have expanded and taken root; and traditional commuting patterns have dramatically altered, with the rise of decentralisation and working from home. These factors imply significant change in the culture of the traditional suburb.

The Invisible House was the result of first-hand observation and personal experience of these developments, combined with a deep-seated concern for the degradation of the suburban environment that has resulted from a failure to evolve new directions and models for the future. It was intended as the first in a series of proposals for different types of interstitial suburban buildings.

As such, the Invisible House project has its roots in traditional English architecture up to the end of the nineteenth century – not superficially, in terms of its architectural language, but in the fact that it was dug into the ground, as most houses used to be. However, the dark, dank cellar is replaced by a light, open central courtyard, around which the living accommodation for one or two people is arranged behind glass walls. The layout is informal and flexible compared to traditional house-plans (still reproduced on an ever meaner scale in speculative housing developments). It recognises the relaxation of lifestyles which has occurred, and the increased scope for sensuousness offered by domestic life today: a hedonism which would have been frowned upon in the society of the late nineteenth and early twentieth century, and was completely denied in the original suburban house.

Although the traditional attic has gone, its place is taken by a wall of storage, forming, as it were, the anchor of the building against which is fixed the main entrance descending from the garden level, via a lean-to conservatory, into the living accommodation. The stairwell runs parallel with a linear plinth linking the living room fireplace, a long work surface forming the kitchen, and the bathroom at the other end, next to the bedroom. Kitchen, bathroom and fireplace are all accommodated within this major structural and symbolic element.

The car has, more than ever, a role to play in the suburban lifestyle, despite the campaigning efforts of environmentalists, and this fact is recognised in the proposal. The car is parked on the roof of the house, surrounded by all the conventional elements of the suburban garden. From the surrounding houses, little more than the garden, sometimes with people in it, and car can be seen, as normal. As the planting grows, the structure of the house will gradually disappear into the landscape of fences, hedges, pergolas, shrubbery, flower beds, and compost heaps. It is at one and the same time a paragon of modesty and introversion, and, in its abstract architectural language and unconventional relationship between earth and sky, a formidable piece of self-expression. Paradoxically, these are equally recognisable as powerful elements of the suburban tradition, where introversion is read in the deserted streets, representing a denial of public space, and self-expression in the strange colonies of garden gnomes, the stick-on porches and fancy front doors: the treatment of the front of the house

and apron of garden as an intermediary zone of presentation and display.

The Invisible House is seemingly introverted but is intended to provide the potential for social interaction. It could function as a 'granny flat' or workspace ancillary to an existing house (or houses) and in that way could act as the catalyst for a more communal lifestyle accommodated within the back garden sites. An increase of density handled in this way could invigorate and enrich the suburban environment, by recognising and giving form to the cultural changes which have taken place and will continue to do so in the future.

Affecting Architecture: Challenging the Politics of Indifference
Pierre d'Avoine

This essay was written as preparations gathered apace for the celebration of the Millennium in Britain with a plethora of expensive new public buildings, some of uncertain function. It argued for the continuing importance of street planning, and street life at a quite intimate, domestic scale. Modern cities, having suffered the ravages of 'rationalising' redevelopment in the name of modernism after the Second World War, with great clearances of the tight-knit, historic environment, were starting to witness a steady privatisation of their public spaces by commercial interests and occupation, backed by a political agenda.

This essay attempts to address our present-day notion of public space, which, for me, still seems to contain a mythic sense of a time when the world we inhabited was completely open. "The origin of Common Land is a most obscure problem in English history... Common Rights were not something specifically granted by a generous landlord, but were the residue of rights that in all probability antedate the idea of private property in land, and are therefore of vast antiquity."[1] Settlement of the land gave rise to complex issues of ownership, possession of property and the pragmatic modification of what we imagine to be our common rights. In the West we at last sense, perhaps collectively for the first time, the limitations of mechanistic order and the Cartesian grid of the Enlightenment that the architects of the Modern Movement promised would relocate us all in the unlimited free space of utopia. We live in an altogether less predictable and dirtier place today.

Architecture has its mythic dimension, too. The fantasy of the architect as individual creator is still part of the popular imagination and continues to be peddled by a media bloated on the cult of celebrity. Yet we know that man-made environments, even the smallest villages, require something other than individual will and action to create and sustain them. The population in Britain is now predominantly urban. Today the vast majority of us live in sprawling towns and cities. The countryside is something we have chopped up with thousands of metalled roads so that our resultant sense of it as the land is lost. The economies of speed have resulted in waste. Once we could envisage the land as an ample fabric studded with the products of man, but today it is no longer secure as the soft endless matrix of earth and vegetation of our childhood imagination.

Even the biggest cities in the middle ages were contained by walls. After the Norman Conquest in the eleventh century, countryside that was not wilderness, was cultivated by a feudal society organised in rigid hierarchies. Ownership of the land was in the domain of a few powerful families; life for all but the few was unimaginably hard. The population was tied to the land by its serfdom under the lord of the manor but, though the previous communality in land had been destroyed, people

still had Rights of Common to graze cattle, gather wood, cut turf and fish. The population was also connected to the land by a cyclical way of life governed by the seasons. In this essentially non-urban scenario man and woman could see themselves as part of nature. We still think, perhaps, of a remote golden age when the land was open and people were free to wander where they chose. This may be the basis of our understanding of common land, but even in early nomadic tribal societies there must have been negotiation, some form of control over the allocation of pastures for grazing and cultivation, and limitation to the idea of freely accessible physical space.

In the period after the Norman invasion land was increasingly privatised on a piecemeal basis. By the time of the English Civil War, in 1642, nearly half of the agricultural land had been enclosed. In the eighteenth and nineteenth centuries the accelerated enclosure of the land was accomplished by acts of Parliament and in the process huge numbers of the peasantry were dispossessed of their property rights and cleared off the land. The waves of distress migration from country to city which began as a trickle in the middle ages turned to a flood in the period after the Industrial Revolution. Village life may have offered continuity, community and stability to its inhabitants, but it must also have been stifling and narrow. To men and women in the repressive agrarian society of the middle ages the city must have meant a certain kind of freedom: freedom from serfdom, freedom to change and to reinvent themselves. However, the Industrial Revolution, which was a major factor in shaping the current environment of our towns and cities and the countryside surrounding them, created a revulsion toward the city. Its effect has been degrading to the land generally and degrading to the great mass of displaced men and women who provided the cheap labour force necessary to work in the mills and factories. For the majority in the nineteenth century the city had become the ultimate enclosure.

The extreme changes brought about by the Industrial Revolution were catalytic to Socialist movement. The creation of the Labour Party was seen as a way for the vast numbers of working class people to exercise power in the running of the state. However, there was a divergence of opinion as to how the English variety of socialism was to develop. An early Fabian tract of 1886 stated:

English Socialism is not yet Anarchist or Collectivist, not yet defined enough in point of policy to be classified. There is a mass of Socialist feeling not yet conscious of itself as Socialism. But when the unconscious Socialists of England discover their position, they will also probably fall into two parties: a Collectivist party supporting a strong central administration and a counterbalancing Anarchist party defending individual initiative against that administration.

This position was voiced earlier by Michael Bakunin at the Congress of the International at The Hague in 1872. Bakunin suggested that though Marx and the anarchists wanted the same thing — which was the complete triumph of economic and social equality — Marx wanted it through the establishment of an authoritarian and centralised state which would own and control all the land, whereas the Anarchists wanted "the reconstruction of society and the unification of mankind to be achieved, not from above downwards by any sort of authority, nor by socialist officials, engineers, and other accredited men of learning — but from below upwards, by the free federation of all kinds of workers' associations liberated from the yoke of the state."[2]

When I came to live in England in 1962 the welfare state was well established. The welfare state proposed a notion of a common good — a common or public realm — and was viewed as one of the great achievements of Britain's Labour Party in the aftermath of destruction and social upheaval caused by the Second World War. Although it had been organised from the top downwards the welfare state was a safety net intended to provide even the poorest with decent education, healthcare, housing and other 'social services'. As children we took it for granted. As children we assumed it had always been there and, looking back, it seemed a humane and worthwhile enterprise.

The operation of the welfare state has not been completely successful but at least a state bureaucracy with a strong concern for social welfare provided a degree of stability that the market-led philosophy of the 1980s all but destroyed. This philosophy provided the Conservative Government with the policy weapons to control the trade unions and introduce privatisation. The same philosophy gave us a deregulated banking system and credit boom that was passed off as an economic miracle. Although this boom dissolved into a painful recession Britain still continues in the grip of market-based enthusiasm. Markets are conditioned by short-term and limited vision. Moreover they have extremely weak self-regulating properties and very little tendency to stability. In the nineteenth century socialism took root because the lived experience of the market was cruel. It ultimately threatened both production and the livelihoods of working men and women.

Our generation was apathetic when the Conservative government, under Margaret Thatcher, set about dismantling the welfare state in favour of a 'privatisation' of the common good. Thatcher was quoted as saying, "There is no such thing as Society. There are individual men and women, and there are families. And no government can do anything except through people, and people must look after themselves. It's our duty to look after ourselves and then to look after our neighbour."[3] Thoreau put it another way in his essay "On the Duty of Civil Disobedience". He states, "I heartily accept the motto — "That government is best which governs least"; and I should like to see it acted up to more rapidly and systematically. Carried out, it finally amounts to this, which also I believe — "That government is best which governs not at all"; and when men are prepared for it, that will be the kind of government they will have."[4]

For Britain the tyranny of an unfettered market has led to short-term success for some and potential long-term disaster for everyone. The most for the least in the shortest possible time may be desirable in certain circumstances, but this view, if it dominates, impoverishes culture and increases the fragmentation and alienation of the body politic. Turning architecture purely into a manufacturing process — fast-track design, fast-track construction — may be appropriate for the motorcar, but despite Le Corbusier's famous maxim, houses are not machines and may only be mass-produced convincingly with the support of an environmental infrastructure. Our towns and cities have been carefully redeveloped to give primacy to the motorcar: in the space where metaphor collides with reality our sense of 'the public' is confused because the streets themselves are filled with thousands of mobile capsules of essentially private space which must not touch except by mistake and which create conditions of anxiety and environmental pollution.

In architecture the great postwar experiment to provide decent housing for everyone, which reached its apogee in the 1960s, was all but abandoned in the 1980s. I grew up in west London suburbia and had friends whose families had been 're-housed' on the new housing estates. These consisted of more or less Corbusian slabs raised on columns mixed with low rise blocks in open landscaped parks and had replaced streets of Victorian terraced housing. A tabula rasa was never a realistic possibility. The job was never completed, could never be completed, and we have always had to contend with the uneasy juxtaposition of new with old.

The modern movement architects demanded the freedom of Cartesian space for the new architecture in the same way that large open sites were used in Paris during the French Revolution for festivals celebrating citizenship. However, these huge events, intended by the organisers, including the artists David and Quatremere de Quincy, to generate a sense of "patriotic happiness, perfect equality, and civic fraternity", were apparently scenes of confusion and apathy. Richard Sennett in his book Flesh and Stone, 1994, suggests that these festivals "... mark a point in Western civilisation where the visceral experience of freedom was dispelled in the name of a mechanics of movement — the ability to move anywhere, to move without obstruction, to circulate freely, a freedom greatest in the empty volume." I understand the utopian impulse behind Le Corbusier's Radiant City to lie in just such Enlightenment ideas where the specificity of place is disregarded in favour of an overriding abstract ideal of unlimited space. It becomes apparent that wide open space accessible to all does not necessarily work as 'public space' whereas the street traditionally did.

The patronising paternalism inherent in the welfare state provided an opportunity for well-meaning experiments in social engineering. However, the apparently simple-minded way in which the architectural ideas of Le Corbusier and others were adopted for re-housing the working class and rebuilding the city centres of post war Britain have proved to be disastrously divisive socially and were used to discredit at least two generations of architects. A reaction to Le Corbusier and The Athens Charter had been formulated by Team X in the 1950s but the protagonists had not discovered the means to advance beyond the architectural language and spaces of new brutalism. Nevertheless, the integrity of these architects, their search for authenticity, their awkward invention and their resistance to the superficial has been inspirational today when we are almost overwhelmed by the mediated images of mass culture.

I left architecture school in 1975 in the midst of a recession caused by the first oil crisis. The economy had commenced the uncertain cycle of boom and bust that we now accept as the norm. I found myself working part time in an office and rebuilding the small terraced house in Twickenham in which I lived. I was interested in the subversive individualism of architects like Rudolph Schindler and Konstantin Melnikov. At the same time I was reading Robert Venturi's Complexity and Contradiction in Architecture and felt liberated by its eloquent range across a wide sweep of architectural history, and justified in my search for an architectural expression related to the mess of ordinary life.

The house became something of a test bed for ideas about identity — within personal space and with relation to the perceived community. This whole drama was played out on the front doorstep, opening straight onto the pavement. The house was at the top end of a cul de sac and for me it became vital to restore the public front facade carefully. The sash windows were repaired, the brickwork repointed and the front slope of the roof reslated. This was not to deny the drastic changes made to the interior but to relate to the established conventions of the Victorian street. The dislocations of the interior were presented on the side elevation, which opened onto a small garden. The treatment to this gable wall was intended to offer the community of the street a symbol that was both personal and communal.

In the meantime the street was undergoing great changes as the older working class residents, who mostly rented their houses, either died or moved away and the houses passed on to their children or were sold to young middle class people.

The appearance of the street changed drastically and older conventions were replaced in a frantic period of do-it-yourself. The long terrace lost its consistency, as individual houses were altered without paying any attention to their neighbours. This rampant self-expression was the tip of an interior iceberg and was extended to the street itself, which became filled with cars parked outside their owners' houses. This all happened over a period of several years. It was very stimulating to live in such a mixed community. But it made me feel mixed-up and luddite to have strong sentiments about the indifference to and abandonment of a communal urban order, expressed in the modest architecture of a narrow Victorian cul de sac, in favour of an introverted individualism.

This microcosmic example is part of a greater trend towards atomism in society. We witness the spectacle of the city turning in on itself at the same time that the clear distinction between city and countryside is no more. The public domain of the city is being steadily deregulated and privatised and, in the process, society fragments and order breaks down. The new 'public' spaces of the city are privately developed and are experienced as mono-cultural zones. For example, in the ubiquitous themed shopping malls controlled by private security guards and where, culture is experienced in relation to shopping. One must conform to certain codes and conventions of dress and behaviour to gain entry. There may be pleasures to be had in introversion but the link between the realm of the individual and the civic has to be recreated for a humane society to exist. Homogeneity is not an answer, the street as a spatial matrix still offers the opportunity to resist segregation and for meaningful, non-violent cultural mixing. New mechanisms have to be found to make public space at the point of transition between and within different worlds. These mechanisms could be elisions that combine beauty, grace and authenticity with a necessary grit and friction to stimulate a challenge to the politics of indifference.

As Charles Taylor has put it:

> What our situation seems to call for is a complex, many-levelled struggle, intellectual, spiritual, and political, in which the debates in the public arena interlink with those in a host of institutional settings, like hospitals and schools, where the issues of enframing technology are being lived through in concrete form; and where these disputes in turn both feed and are fed by the various attempts to define in theoretical terms the place of technology and the demands of authenticity, and beyond that, the shape of human life and its relation to the cosmos.[5]

The more repressive the bureaucratic state the greater the challenge to make public space without people resorting to ever more unconventional and subversive strategies. Self-regulation and balance are difficult to maintain all the time and become a cause of antagonism between marginal groups and the mainstream of society. The latter often dramatically overreacts and in the process infringes the rights of all of us – witness the Government legislation to prohibit 'travellers' from moving around the country. The dilemma is how to allow for spontaneity, flux and dynamism in the public arena without tipping over into chaos and disorder.

The Queen's Silver Jubilee in 1977 was a public holiday. Across London, street parties were held in celebration. These appeared to be spontaneous events but actually entailed preplanning, most probably with the approval of the forces of law and order. Streets were closed off in makeshift fashion and access by cars was limited; house fronts and garden fences were made festive with bunting and trestle tables were laid down the middle of roads; children painted their faces, people ate cake, talked to strangers and even danced. For a few fleeting hours the space of the street was transformed. The buildings were the same as before but by adjusting the rules and by bringing on some props it became a very different public place and one we perceived as quite unexpectedly normal. The temporal nature of the transformation was the most remarkable thing. The next day things returned to a more usual normality. The reasons for celebration may have been banal but our view of the monarchy was probably more innocent then. Any irony and cynicism co-existed with a genuine feeling of communality and wonder at the modest pleasures of social life to be had in the city.

The government's plans to celebrate the millennium could not have been more of a contrast. Huge sums of money were spent on a vast gestural architecture of consumption – the public spaces static and pictorial – that was not even accessible to everyone because of the high cost of entry to the sites. As a nation we witnessed the strange and fluid moment in the Christian calendar in the current English fashion: strapped to the wheel of fortune, looking backwards, eyes firmly fixed on a tired tableaux displaying all our yesterdays.

Notes:

[1] Ivan Illich quoted by Francis Reed, On Common Ground, Working Press, 1991.
[2] Michael Bakunin, "Letter to the Internationalists of the Romagna", 28 January 1872, quoted by Colin Ward, Anarchy in Action, George Allen and Unwin, 1973.
[3] Woman's Own, 31 October 1987.
[4] "Essay on Civil Disobedience", in Walden, Airmont Books, 1965.
[5] "Against Fragmentation", in The Ethics of Authenticity, Harvard University Press, 1992.

Slim House: Model Terrace for Concept House 99
Pierre d'Avoine

The proposal for Slim House, winner of the Concept House competition in 1999, sets out the programme for a new terraced house of the future, with the potential for large scale prefabricated production, and construction for under £50,000.

A. The proposal
Slim House provides a contemporary design solution for a speculative reinterpretation of the British urban terrace house. It is an innovative design prototype that could be easily mass-produced using readily available materials and prefabricated components. The proposal explores and subverts the normative model of the urban terrace house which, to date, has imposed certain constraints on the development and provision of new housing for the future.

Slim House
The design of Slim House is based on 5 fundamental principles:

1. Loose-fit/flexible accommodation
The Slim House plot is five metres wide by 25 metres long. Slim House is a mainly single storey building (90 square metres) that forms a linear volume extending from front to back across the footprint of a traditional terrace house and its back garden. At the front is a double-height room addressing the street, with the other rooms behind it entered off a wide corridor/long gallery 16 metres in length. All the rooms have full-height glazed sliding doors opening onto paved, tree planted courtyards that bring generous light into the linear volume. There are four habitable rooms and two bathrooms. The layout provides flexible accommodation for varying patterns of occupancy by up to five inhabitants. The accommodation is primarily residential, but can easily be adapted for home working and even incorporate a small shop. Rear access is preferable, but not essential.

2. Raised threshold
The raised area between the front door of Slim House and the pavement forms a covered threshold that provides a secure individual 'porch' large enough for parking bicycles. The raised area is enclosed by painted metal railings with an entrance gate and ramp up from the pavement. The 300 mm high ramp facilitates movement for prams and wheelchairs. Public utilities may be housed in an easily accessible compartmentalised duct below the raised threshold.

3. Roof garden
The roof garden is situated on top of Slim House and is laid with a 'soiless lawn' and paved pathways. Each Slim House has individual access to the roof garden by a staircase from the double-height front room. Privacy and safety are ensured by the provision of low, wide hedges, railings and proprietary heather screens around the edges of the open courtyards. The roof garden almost doubles the amenity space for each Slim House. The roof garden on top of each Slim House may be private, but the potential for shared use is much more exciting. Communal gardens may be extended across the top of whole terraces, possibly linked to neighbouring terraces, to create an extensive car-free landscape above street level for cultivation and leisure.

4. Active facade with urban(e) front and DIY back
The orderly, urban(e) front and ad hoc DIY back of the traditional terrace is compressed into a single vertical element with front and back elevations forming the street facade of Slim House above the porch. It is set forward of the house, providing a screen to a private yard above the porch. The active facade is designed to be regular so that it may be duplicated in terraces to form a greater whole, while allowing scope for individual variation within the overall framework. The urban(e) front could be designed in a traditional way in streets where the conventions of good neighbourliness may have to be respected, for example in conservation areas. Its design is intended to be fundamentally flexible and adaptable, capable of responding to different types of location and also to technological developments and cultural changes in a particular neighbourhood. The urban(e) front might then be developed as a sign/hoarding, a street light, a solar panel, a satellite dish, topiary wall, etc., subject to planning permission and consultation within local residents' associations. It may be solid, perforated, translucent, transparent or a combination of these qualities, and it could be built in a sound-absorbing construction to act as a buffer against the traffic noise of city streets. The DIY back of the facade offers Slim House inhabitants the opportunity to customise their individual environment to suit their particular lifestyle. It could be used as a vertical vegetable garden, fitted out with built-in garden shed, cold frame, dovecote, grey water storage container, etc..

5. Vertical extension
Slim House has been designed so that the double height front room at ground floor may be subdivided horizontally to provide a separate first floor room. The double-height front room, which forms a pavilion structure at first floor located between the active facade at the front and roof garden behind, may be extended upwards to provide a third storey. The staircase access to the upper storeys could be screened off at ground floor level, with a separate secondary entrance into the house, so that the vertical extension may be used independently as a workplace/office, etc..

Model Terrace
The Model Terrace has been designed for new contexts and existing urban settings. The proposal attempts to define and respond to the needs of contemporary inhabitants and anticipate

future developments in cultural, ecological and economic terms. The 25 x 25 metre site for the Model Terrace accommodates a row of five Slim Houses. The linear unit accessed from street front and mews back is extremely efficient in terms of land use and built form. When developed into Model Terraces the Slim House offers a new urban pattern for high-density development, suitable for all age groups, that combines the best aspects of the more modest traditional urban terraces with a new elevated garden cityscape protected from noise and traffic fumes by the active facades, yet open to sunlight and offering residents the opportunity for extensive perambulations, long green vistas and open skies.

B. Cost and finance
The scheme can be built within the specified budget of £50,000 and it is commercially viable. The internal gross floor area is 87 square metres. The build price is £42,721 at £493/square metre gross floor area (excluding foundations, services below ground, external works, landscape, contractor's profit/overheads, unfitted furniture, professional fees).

Superstructure	£30,806.00	(£356/sq m)
Internal finishes	£3,449.00	(£40/sq m)
Fittings and furnishings	£2,250.00	(£26/sq m)
Services	£5,366.00	(£62/sq m)
Site preparation	£850.00	(£10/sq m)
TOTAL	£42,721.00	(£493/sq m)

C. Choice of materials
The structure, being predominantly timber, has a low embodied energy value. The prefabricated components enable efficient mass production off site and the potential for recycling in the future. Most of the materials specified are available from local builders' merchants or DIY stores.

D. Structural engineering and building construction
Each Slim House is designed to be structurally self-contained. The basic stability is provided by steel frames which span across the five metre width of each house plot and carry horizontal loads in that direction without the need for internal columns or cross-walls. The front frame is triple height to support the facade. In the longitudinal direction timber stud panels, clad on both sides with 12 mm plywood, provide stability and comprise the main outer walls of each unit, as well as carrying vertical loads.

The floor and roofs are made of pre-assembled panels of timber joists, with timber boards on top. The roof of the first floor study structure is made of steel sections which are bolted together and also clad with timber panels, so that it can be dismantled and re-assembled if required for a second floor extension.

E. Environmental engineering
The proposed scheme incorporates features in its fabric and layout that will lead to a highly energy efficient development that should achieve a National Home Energy Rating (NHER) of 10. The layout of the buildings on the site minimises the area of exposed external wall. Where the walls are exposed they can be very well insulated using double insulated stud wall construction. The high thermal capacity in the roof reduces the heat loss below that to be expected from a well insulated roof. Water falling on it is only drained off during exceptionally wet weather. It is generally retained on the roof for maintaining the planting without the need for irrigation. Water can also be conserved by the use of grey water, with a storage tank incorporated into the facade structure. With high levels of insulation and airtightness a simple combination gas fired boiler provides heating to radiators and hot water with a very good Standard Assessment Procedure for NHER's. Pipework is distributed through the floor structure. A raised threshold enables an efficient distribution of mains services. The facade structure allows every house to add a solar panel to provide heat for free hot water in the summer. The compact plan also improves the economic viability of a combined heat and power scheme to provide electricity for the development and to meet the heating requirements by using the waste heat from electricity generation. The annual energy bill for heating, ventilation and hot water should be less than 50 kilowatt hours/square metre per year. The courtyard arrangement provides day-lighting and a secure environment so that windows can be left open to provide night ventilation during hot summer weather. There is potential for stack effect ventilation in the bathrooms and kitchen, depending on the height of the surrounding buildings, avoiding the need for electric fans. The potential of fluorescent and low voltage fittings can be exploited to create appropriate lighting levels in the house and, externally, in the landscape.

F. Production
The scheme has the potential to act as a 'show house', as well as being suitable for mass production.

G. Programme
Each house is designed to be delivered to site in components that can be carried on lorries and quickly assembled. For the exhibition, where no foundations are required, this can be done in a matter of days.

Slim House will be capable of construction on the exhibition site at Earl's Court within ten days.

Interstitial Space: The Ideal Home Show
and DIY culture
Pierre d'Avoine and Clare Melhuish

The concept of 'interstitial space' has been integral to the practice's engagement with the suburban landscape, and the development of a 'pattern book approach'. This essay throws light on the meaning of the concept of interstitiality, and discusses the design of Slim House, as a response to those conditions, and to the need for an engagement with a mass market for more original design ideas with 'DIY' potential.

The word 'interstice' is defined in Chambers Dictionary as "a small space of interstitiality between things closely set"; 'interstitial' is the adjective that defines "that which occurs in interstices, chinks, crevices and gaps." As an architectural practice, we have always had an interest in the kind of architectural space which is not necessarily about smallness per se, but certainly about an attitude of anticipation, opportunism, invention and pragmatism in response to awkward and irregular bits of the city and the physical environment in general.

In countries like Britain, which are so urbanised and densely populated, the landscape has essentially become an urban continuum: not a megalopolis exactly, but more a 'super-conurbation' of fairly evenly distributed population density with the occasional plot of wilderness ring-fenced and protected from encroachment – or packaged for our enjoyment and pleasure. We have to accept that the landscape has already been designed, at least once, and that the task for most of us is to rethink and rework various parts of the landscape to suit evolving conditions, particularly where certain bits have run down or worn out. The landscape we have inherited is not a blank canvas awaiting a grand gesture to fill its empty spaces. The architectural process is more about working with the detail, which offers the potential for individual expression.

Our approach starts with a self-conscious resistance to the concept of the masterplan in favour of a kind of "action planning", as defined by architect and planner Otto Koenigsberger. Koenigsberger, who played an important role in developing responsive planning strategies for rapidly developing cities in the tropics, emphasised the need for local knowledge as a foundation for the evolution of mosaic-like action programmes in such places. His approach points towards an engagement with the notion of interstitial space, existing at every scale and encompassing the minutiae of the domestic environment as well as the grander territory of the city region and beyond, understood as the theatres of the everyday and more ceremonial performances of human life. By closely observing, participating in, questioning and documenting those performances and their dramatis personae, the architect, following in the footsteps of the ethnographer, may evolve a better understanding of the anthropology of modern life as the basis for a responsive architecture.

In 1998, the practice won the Concept House 99 competition, with its Slim House: Model Terrace proposal. This was a response to a brief for a contemporary reinterpretation of the British urban terrace house. It was conceived as an innovative design prototype that could be easily mass-produced, using readily available materials and prefabricated components, and inserted into existing urban settings or new contexts at different scales. The proposal explores and subverts the normative model of the urban terrace house, which to date has imposed certain constraints on the development and provision of new housing for the future. For instance, the 'loose-fit' accommodation allows variations in patterns of occupancy by up to five inhabitants over time. At the front is a double-height room addressing the street, with the other rooms laid out behind it in a linear plan, entered off a wide corridor/long gallery 16 metres in length. All the rooms have full-height glazed sliding doors opening onto paved courtyards that bring generous light into the linear volume. The front room can be subdivided, if required, to create an upper level space which could be used as an office or, alternatively, as a living room over a ground floor shop unit.

The traditional back garden, which in big cities is commonly small, overshadowed, and overlooked, was relocated to the roof of the Slim House and laid with a lawn and paved pathways. The roof garden almost doubles the amenity space for each Slim House, and offers the potential for shared use as an extensive car-free landscape above street level, which can be used for cultivation and leisure.

The traditional facade was reconceived for the Slim House as a detached vertical, 'active' element rising above the porch to create a protective screen from the street. Immediately behind it, located on top of the porch at first floor level is a so-called "back yard", while the facade structure itself could be turned into a vertical vegetable garden, or fitted out with built-in garden shed, cold frame, dove cote, grey water storage container, etc.. The urban(e) front could be designed in a traditional way in streets where the conventions of good neighbourliness may have to be respected—for example, in conservation areas – or alternatively, be developed as a sign/hoarding, a streetlight, a solar panel, a satellite dish, topiary wall, etc., subject to planning permission and consultation within local residents' associations. It might be solid, perforated, translucent, transparent, or a combination of these qualities, and it could be built in sound-absorbing construction to act as a buffer against the traffic noise of city streets. Its design is intended to be fundamentally flexible and adaptable, capable of responding to different types of location and also to technological developments and cultural changes in a particular neighbourhood.

As part of a Model Terrace, Slim House attempts to define and respond to the needs of contemporary inhabitants and anticipate future developments in cultural, ecological and economic terms. The 25 x 25 metre site for the Model Terrace accommodates a row of five Slim Houses. The linear unit, accessed from street front and mews back, is extremely efficient in terms of land use and built form. When developed into Model Terraces it offers a new urban pattern for high density development, suitable for all age groups, that combines the best aspects of the more modest traditional urban terraces with a new elevated garden cityscape protected from noise and traffic fumes by the active facades, yet open to sunlight and offering residents the opportunity for extensive perambulations, long green vistas and open skies.

The design of the Slim House partly developed from the earlier Invisible House project, which started as a workshop, held at the Dublin Architecture Winterschool in 1991, on the theme of architecture and literature. The Invisible House site epitomised the kind of interstitial space with which the work of the practice has been concerned. The workshop investigated notions of ordinariness and domesticity, the suburban environment and the way that people become so familiar with their surroundings that they start to disappear from their perception. It also addressed the idea of an avant-garde in architecture, questioning the shock tactics of Dada and Surrealism and the way architecture as an academic discipline always seems to appropriate ideas from other disciplines, including semiotics, anthropology, philosophy, art and literature in order to justify itself, or present itself as forward-looking. According to Umberto Eco there is an inevitability about this situation because, although within architecture there are possibilities of the poetic function and self-reflection, the architect is, nevertheless, "obliged in his work to think in terms of the totality".

The workshop drew on material from Flann O'Brien's book The Third Policeman, which evokes quite strongly the idea of interstitiality:

As I came round the bend of the road an extraordinary spectacle was presented to me. About a hundred yards away on the left hand side was a house which astonished me. It looked as if it were painted like an advertisement on a board on the roadside... It looked completely false and unconvincing. It did not seem to have any depth or breadth... As I approached, the house seemed to change its appearance. At first, it did nothing to reconcile itself with the shape of an ordinary house but it became uncertain in outline like a thing glimpsed under ruffled water. Then it became clear again and I saw that it began to have some back to it, some small space for rooms behind the frontage. I gathered this from the fact that I seemed to see the front and the back of the building simultaneously from my position approaching what should have been the side. As there was no side that I could see I thought the

house must be triangular with its apex pointing towards me but when I was only 15 yards away I saw a small window apparently facing me and I knew from that that there must be some side to it...

Once inside what turns out to be a police station, the narrator discovers that he is not actually in the building but in the walls of it.

The first project for the Invisible House may be viewed as a response to this idea of the elusive in the built environment, and an antidote to the over-assertiveness of much of the suburban fabric. It was not intended as a universal strategy but possibly another letter in the alphabet of building types, which celebrated the everyday, low key aspects of suburban life.

Slim House was constructed as a show house at the Ideal Home Show in London in 1999. In this context, it became part of a phantasmagoria of images and artefacts which represented the idealised, but at the same time attainable, embodiment of a culture's desires and aspirations. Re-presented in this way, it became embedded within the realm of a 'do-it-yourself' popular culture, which might be said to have its spiritual home in the suburbs, and it became dislocated from the normal channels of architectural discourse — even though its approach was seen by some as radical.

The Ideal Home Exhibition had its inception in 1908 as part of an extraordinary range of exhibitions in London that year. There was the Franco-British Exhibition at White City and the Hungarian Exhibition at Earl's Court. Other exhibitions included the Heavy Motor Exhibition, the Sociological Society's Toy Exhibition, the Orient in London, Home Art and Industries and the Brewer's Exhibition. These were intended as venues for the promotion of commerce and trade but were also intended to cater to the public demand for large scale entertainment and a popular culture of the spectacular which continues to this day. The Ideal Home Exhibition catered to the emergent mass market, in particular the newly affluent lower middle classes, with a dual intent — to educate and to entertain. Home-making was presented as both scientific and glamourous. The exhibition was sponsored by The Daily Mail, founded by Lord Northcliffe in 1896 specifically to appeal to the new mass market created by the spread of literacy. But it appears that the middle culture associated with The Daily Mail and the Ideal Home Exhibition today was vilified by the intelligentsia from the beginning. According to John Carey, "Northcliffe aimed the Daily Mail specifically at clerks. The whole paper, said one intellectual critic when it was first published, "reeks of the concerns of villadom" with its cycling column, its fashion section and its home hints. The periodicals Titbits and Answers, and the department store Selfridge's, were likewise seen as components of clerk culture."

The advertising department of The Daily Mail devised various publicity stunts in the battle with other newspapers, in particular the Daily Express, to attract more readers. Exhibitions were a useful form of publicity in addition to the more usual bill-posting and roadside hoarding. The building industry presented The Daily Mail with its goal—an industry with an almost inexhaustible capacity to supply any demand that could be created by advertising. The fact was that firms in the house building industry depended for business on the recommendation of the architect. In return for a 15 per cent commission on orders, architects recommended fittings and decorations to house purchasers. This was presented by Wareham Smith, the advertising manager of The Daily Mail, as restricting freedom of choice. He was quoted as saying,

> Their hold (the architects' that is) was so complete, in fact, that the home builder was left with no say whatever in the construction of his house, choice of fitting and decoration... Our task was clear. It was important to undermine the influence of the architect without delay, remove his stranglehold from the whole industry – 'clean up the racket', as my American friends would say. I was determined that the public should know the various and multitudinous things in existence which could make a house a home.

Smith was in effect instrumental in the advent of DIY. By persuading manufacturers and retailers of items connected with interior decoration to advertise in The Daily Mail newspaper as well as in the trade press he had a considerable influence on patterns of shopping and consumption and was also instrumental in reducing the architects' role as middleman. But, by way of giving something back to architects in return for this challenge to their business, Smith devised a competition.

> A big prize would be offered for a design for an Ideal Home, surrounding the home with all the materials and gadgets that would contribute to its amenities and comfort. The title of the Ideal Home Exhibition was therefore designed to please architects, who also must have realised that their business would be stimulated by the publicity-grabbing exhibition medium.

The Ideal Home Exhibition has always aimed for mass consumption and mass appeal. Although it has at various times built "houses of the future", the context in which these projects, often by notable architects, are presented make it difficult to view them as other than novelties.

It has always been a problem because the houses are shown as a collection of competing individual buildings, usually in a prosaic suburban setting, although sometimes against incongruously beautiful landscape backdrops.

The extraordinary numbers of visitors to the ideal Home Exhibition reached an all-time high of 1,329,644 in 1957. A year previously Alison and Peter Smithson designed a House of the Future, reintroduced to the exhibition for the first time since the 1930s. It is always presented in terms of its sci-fi interior, without any clue as to how the project would appear either in a setting composed entirely of similar houses or in the context of the existing environment. The emphasis on gadgets was apposite. But the Ideal Home Exhibition has been used overwhelmingly by house builders to promote their latest models – invariably based on a traditional English style. More recently, the adventure and fun associated with the show has had to be shared with the rise of other forms of competing entertainment such as television and theme parks. As a result of this dilution of its impact, there has been a loss of confidence in its role as educator of the public in all aspects of the home environment, or as a disseminator of new ideas. As a venue for architects to promote their ideas about housing it has never seemed quite serious enough.

In Britain the postwar adoption of a modernist approach to mass social housing by successive Labour and Conservative governments probably created an atmosphere of complacency among architects in the pursuit of commissions and in the communication of their ideas about housing to the public. As a result there has been a mistrust of them by the public, who continue to perceive architects as the prime instigators of built experiments in social engineering. The public that can afford to put its trust in the volume house builders, who base their marketing strategies on the car industry and offer them aspirational images of the good life – usually diluted versions of Georgian architecture or mock Tudor. Historically, architects have produced pattern books to promote themselves and their ideas. The last time that an architect in Britain succeeded in promoting a new vision for the domestic environment was when Lawrence Weaver consistently featured Lutyens in the pages of Country Life at the turn of the century. Lutyens, however, only built houses for a particular social class. In America, the architect Frank Lloyd Wright achieved a crossover success. On the one hand, he influenced a whole generation of architects in the USA and Europe with the Wasmuth portfolios he published at the turn of the twentieth century, while, on the other, he published ideas for affordable housing in American women's magazines, acquiring considerable popular appeal.

In Europe and America, architects have, from time to time, succeeded in penetrating the public consciousness through show houses constructed for major exhibitions – for example, Mies van der Rohe's country house for a bachelor at the Berlin Building Exhibition of 1931, or Marcel Breuer's show house at MOMA in New York in 1949. Le Corbusier's Pavilion de l'Esprit Nouveau exhibited in the International Exposition of Decorative

Arts held in Paris in 1925 was somewhat different in that the show house was a full-scale mock-up of a dwelling unit from a proposed apartment building. In the 1940s and 50s in America, John Entenza published a series of freestanding suburban houses, known as the Case Study houses, in his magazine Art and Architecture. These were aimed at prospective middle class clients and were aspirational in intent.

In Britain, unlike Europe and America, the use of show houses as a medium to expound new ideas on housing has been limited, partly because architects have been blocked by the system from contributing to the debate on this subject, but also perhaps because they have been unwilling to engage with the populist and mainstream. Today, however, it is impossible to operate outside the conflation of culture and consumption. As Charlotte Raven has noted:

> Whatever its ostensible subject, the subtext of a modern work of art [in this case architecture] is the sycophantic/ dominant relationship of market to consumer. There is no other subject matter nor any possibility of stepping outside this economy. In other words culture is commodified. No longer offering a refuge from the market or a critique of its operations, it simply exists to reflect the status quo. Even when it seeks to challenge it, it finds itself deployed as propaganda for the tolerance and inclusiveness of the system it was trying to undermine.

It is important for architects to establish a presence within this system that allows the possibility of supplying an emetic, which might create a terrible stink at the time, but ultimately help to fertilise the ground for new possibilities to flower in future. In other words, architects need to find ways of being simultaneously engaged with the mainstream and capable of providing a subversive input that can stimulate change and progress in the long run. The Concept House competition provided the ideal opportunity to explore these possibilities, challenging the orthodoxy of the volume house builders, which is essentially anti-urban, but also falling in line with current government initiatives to promote ideas for brownfield sites while preserving the green belts around cities.

Since establishing our practice 20 years ago nearly all our work has been for brownfield sites. Architectural practice in London provides very little scope for any other kind of work, and so, inevitably, becomes embedded in what we have called an interstitial approach, fusing our interests in building, urban typology and cultural anthropology with an enthusiasm for detailed scrutiny of the built environment.

Monad House: Thoughts on a Design Approach for a Welsh House for the Future

Pierre d'Avoine and Clare Melhuish

The design of Monad House, runner-up in the Welsh House for the Future Competition in 2000, represented a slight shift of focus away from the specifically suburban and towards more extra-urban and rural contexts for new housing. Furthermore, it focused attention on the question of cultural context defined by regionality. This essay explored the implications of those notions for the design of domestic buildings in an era defined by globalisation.

"But now, what generic building shall we choose at last, to stand example for the whole Welsh art of building? The farm, only the farm!"
The Matter of Wales: Epic Views of a Small Country, Jan Morris

In designing a Welsh 'House for the Future', we wanted to avoid reproducing an explicit version of the historic vernacular — an approach which risks devaluing and destroying the original in the long run; but we also rejected any need for irony or kitsch in reinterpreting Welsh cultural traditions to make them meaningful for our times and for the future. Our intention, then, was to generate a reinterpretation of a vernacular which was not necessarily about imitating historic forms or using authentic materials, but about continuing and reinvigorating the spirit of a tradition in such a way that it can continue to evolve, adapt and mature over the years indefinitely. We were interested in deflecting the overwhelming emphasis placed on material progress and consumer empowerment in much of the debate about future social change. While these issues have a place in ensuring the possibility of equality for all, in terms of material and physical comfort, we would suggest that they should be integrated within a more holistic vision of life in the future, based on environmental sustainability, and a sense of cultural identity.

Although we have drawn on a perception of Welsh cultural traditions and aspirations in our design, it is clear that the issues facing Welsh society as it moves into the next century are fundamentally those of Western society as a whole. Wales as a regional identity is also part of a wider European and global entity increasingly unified through the operation of the media and telecommunications, and by common economic interests. This is the time to build up regional identity as a strong foundation for a confident presence on the European and global stages. We would suggest that while the use of recognisable symbolic architectural elements in our proposal may provide the basis for a cultural-national discourse, they are ultimately intended as part of a process in which Wales and Welsh identity is positioned on a much broader platform.

In The Matter of Wales, her 'definitive' account of Welsh culture, Jan Morris points out that the Welsh have never historically evinced a great interest in constructing grandiose works of architecture, or indeed in building cities. The most dramatic and striking edifices are the castles built to subdue the Welsh,

while the real strength and identity of Welsh culture is to be found in the simple, plain chapels and vernacular buildings embedded in the countryside, gradually added to and elaborated by their occupants through the years. The typical Welsh farm, writes Morris, "stands sheltered in the lee of a hill, and it has a small scrubby garden in front of it, with a low stone wall and a central pathway to the front door.... It is not a very tidy place. Its outbuildings, barns and garages are cluttered any old how around a concreted yard..." The St Fagan's Museum of Welsh Life is a living document of these building traditions. It has an important role to play not only in heightening awareness of Welsh history and identity, but also of the ways in which Welsh culture and society may develop in the future, especially since the establishment of the new Welsh Assembly.

The competition for a House for the Future focuses attention on changing patterns of family and working life. There has been much public discussion throughout the Western world about the demise of the traditional nuclear family and the development of different family configurations — changes which are closely associated with the emergence of new working patterns, for example the increase of women working outside the home. These factors suggest a decline in home life but in fact it would seem that the development of increased working from home by both sexes, due to advances in communications technology, may have precisely the opposite effect, restoring the home to its historic status as a centre of production inhabited at all times of day and night by varying configurations of adults and children in ever-changing versions of the pre-nuclear extended family. These positive and exciting developments make the domestic house a stimulating subject for architectural speculation.

In this context, we would suggest that the typical Welsh farm model is highly appropriate as a basis for an architectural proposal for a House for the Future — in both rural and urban/suburban contexts. It provides a flexible, loose-fit system of associated buildings gathered around a sheltered open space, which can be added to or compressed as required. It is made of tough, plain materials capable of withstanding the inclement weather conditions, characteristic of Wales. It is above all not a finite, self-conscious stylistic statement, but a highly serviceable working model based on the principles of organisational, spatial, and technological adaptability. We have used these as the basis for the design of the Monad House — a 'simple organism' generated by a concept of 'domestic measure', being the desirable width for a linear form which can be extended, contracted and wrapped around space to adapt to requirements as they change through the years.

A House for the Future

Our proposal for a House for the Future in Wales is very much intended as a serious contribution to the debate about our society and housing in the next century, grounded in the reality of continuous, gentle, incremental change, based on existing traditions and expectations. It is not intended as a dramatic, futuristic statement based on architectural stylistic novelty, but as a subtle reinterpretation of familiar forms and ideas, which gradually release fragments of radical insight as the project is explored. The building form and construction is elemental, but allows for shifts of scale, contrasts of room heights, long views through the house, and a manipulation of the building skin using techniques of layering to achieve openness, transparency, thermal and acoustic insulation, shading and privacy as required and which together offer a richer experience of domestic living than the conventional norms. It also provides a framework which can easily accommodate advances in the development of building materials, energy conversion technology and electronic communications systems in a form which is neither overbearing nor intrusive, yet establishes the domestic unit on a firm footing within the global communications network, and a realistic and acceptable model for a way of life built on low energy consumption, renewable power and a closed cycle of waste. It offers the potential for self-sufficiency and strengthened local relationships, reducing the need for unsustainable dependence on national and international structures.

We would suggest that this approach is very much in tune with the tradition of earthy radicalism, which has found its natural home in Wales over the last few decades. As a crucible for the alternative technology movement, founded at sites such as Machynlleth, Wales has been at the forefront of the development of environmental action and awareness, which, as we move into the next century, has been generally recognised as the foundation on which any vision of the future must be built; for without it, there will be no future. Low-tech environmental advances spearheaded in Wales are now widely accepted as the basis for radical changes, which must take place in global living patterns in the future.

The Monad House also builds on and re-presents qualities of Welsh culture and identity going back further into history — as far as they can be synthesised into some form of national identity across a region of marked contrasts and distinct traditions. We would suggest that there is a certain traditional reticence in terms of formal and visual expression in Welsh culture, which is embodied in the vernacular architectural palette of plain pebbledash or grey rendered cottages and functional Spartan chapels, the lack of indigenous grand houses, and the muted hues of the native woollen industry. Yet the cultural legacy of non-conformism constitutes a somewhat deceptive overlay for the irrepressible fervour, enthusiasm, imagination and romanticism that is manifested in Wales' enduring literary and musical traditions; from the marvellous canon of the Mabinogion to the work of Dylan Thomas, or from the poignant folk tradition to the outpouring of stirring hymns in the nineteenth century.

Then there is the landscape: a rich, varied, mysterious rural landscape of incredible beauty which has inspired artists, architects and writers of all sorts throughout the centuries. The Welsh landscape was instrumental in the development of the aesthetic theory of the picturesque in the eighteenth century through the writings of the Welshman Uvedale Price. The harsh man-made landscape of the Industrial Revolution, for which Wales is also famous, was being formed at the same time, and must also be taken into account.

We would like to propose that these aspects of formal reticence are fused with imagination and romanticism in the Monad House to achieve a form of architectural expression which grows out of contrasting landscapes and aspires, above all, to a simple and inspiring beauty. A vernacular building may be usefully defined as one in which the space plans are generic and general-purpose, and the grammar of construction economical and prudent, while the specifics of material, style and finish are left to the builder and dweller. As a rule, this is completely misunderstood by the volume house-building companies of today, which manufacture various vernacular 'styles', with great emphasis being placed on an elaborate subdivision of rooms internally according to specific functions. The Monad House represents a protest against this misunderstanding. It aspires to establish principles of design and construction for the domestic environment which may provide the most appropriate and flexible response to changing living conditions, and which may engender a freedom of spirit in the dweller.

The subdivision and increasing specialisation of rooms in a house has developed alongside the notion of domesticity and domestic life itself, based on a distinction of living space from the space of work. In fact this is a modern invention, emerging only in the early 1800s. It became increasingly significant as the concept of leisure time developed in the post war years, and boom in consumer spending-power boomed. Now it seems that technological and economic developments, and associated social change, are causing clear distinctions to break down once again; most surprisingly, the wealth of leisure time promised by mechanisation and computerisation does not seem to have materialised for the working population. Many people complain that they are working longer hours than ever before. The boundaries between domestic life and work are for many people becoming increasingly blurred. This is a fact the design of the Monad House recognises and aims to accommodate in a positive and inspiring way, through a fundamentally generic and general-purpose approach to design of domestic space.

From Climate House, Tehran, to New Housing at Eastleigh, Hampshire (Swaythling)
Clare Melhuish

This essay was written for an Iranian architecture magazine, Sakht, and set out to draw parallels between the contingencies of practising in very contrasting cultural contexts in an era of globalised production. Both projects focussed on the need to establish more sustainable planning and construction practices, while responding to the particular needs of different types of communities.

The projects for Climate House in Tehran and new housing at Eastleigh in south-east England are situated many thousands of miles apart, and represent architectural propositions which are highly specific in each case to a markedly different cultural and physical context. Yet they also share a great deal in common, namely a design approach driven by the need for radical overhaul of the construction industry and current thinking about new building, in response to a global environmental and social crisis which is now generally acknowledged.

In the UK developers, planners and architects have come under intense pressure to develop an ecological approach to new development, as the government faces the need to provide 4 million new homes by 2010. This requirement has been stimulated by demographic changes, in particular the steadily shrinking size of the typical household as more and more people opt to live alone, without children, or in small family units. The greatest demand for housing is in the south-east of the country, where employment opportunities are concentrated, but where land is in relatively short supply and prices are high. This has generated intense debate about the rights and wrongs of building on hitherto untouched greenfield sites or, alternatively, recycling so-called brownfield sites and increasing density in existing settlements. Although the latter option has been recommended by the government's advisors, such sites usually come with many problems, such as contamination by industry, awkward access and small size, making them relatively unattractive to developers.

Climate House, Tehran
The approach to the Climate House project in Tehran was stimulated by experience of working in this context of heightened environmental awareness in the UK, particularly as it relates to housing design, along with observation of the extent of environmental damage in other countries, like Iran, where the relatively cheap price of fuel has encouraged the construction industry to cast off constraint with regard to energy consumption. The design draws directly on research and expertise developed over a number of years through a progression of residential and housing projects for the UK and elsewhere, in particular Pierre d'Avoine Architects' competition-winning Concept House scheme of 1999, but translates this very specifically into the cultural context of Tehran. The idea for the Climate House emerged as a result of a series of study visits made to Iran

by Nasser Golzari with students from Oxford Brookes University, during which the issues raised by observation of traditional construction methods, their inherent environmental integrity, and the cultural structures which they support, provided the basis for subsequent work. At the same time, the Concept House scheme was presented and well-received in Iran, prompting the notion of forging a common project, specifically addressing environmental issues, for a site in Tehran.

The primary aim with the Climate House was to produce a building with a certain degree of thermal mass. In essence, the building is designed as a manifesto for an environmental agenda in the construction industry, and to that end will function as a show house and exhibition centre open to the public and professionals.

The use of a thick enclosure to the house, which will most probably be constructed out of reinforced concrete, with insulation wrapped around the outside, and timber-framed windows, emulates traditional building methods insofar as it immediately provides a level of thermal mass to reduce heat loss and gain. This fundamental principle is combined with a number of other design strategies drawn from regional traditions that ensured a degree of climatic comfort over centuries. Such traditions have been discarded in favour of thin cavity walls air-conditioning systems, of which high embodied levels of fuel and energy consumption, in addition to the inherent unhealthiness, are their major drawbacks. One of the key aspects of the design is the incorporation of a lower-ground level of thermally-protected inhabitable space in an attempt to reclaim and revive a very long-standing custom, now almost disappeared, for which Tehran and the south of the country were famous. A second aspect is the use of two courtyards, one on the north and one on the south side, for winter and summer occupation. These generate a system of circulated air enhanced by a series of solar chimneys, based on the traditional wind tower, and water features, including a pool, and fountains as well as a more contemporary 'shower tower'. Finally, the design looks to the traditional custom of relocating from one part of the house to another during the cycle of the seasons, as a very simple method, adapted to modern use, of exploiting the climatic contrasts represented by different orientations within any particular site. In addition to these tactics, the scheme incorporates an extensive system of planting, in order to create a network of naturally shaded areas.

The site provided for the Climate House by the Iranian Fuel Conservation Organisation in association with District 2, is a typical urban plot to the north of Tehran. It is located on a corner, addressing the busy thoroughfare of Vali Asr Street on the west side. The scheme wraps the boundaries with built-up edges containing circulation and ancillary spaces, while the house itself, as the main exhibition piece, is situated in the centre of the site, with open courtyards on the north and south sides. Orientated north-south, it sits slightly skewed in relation to the orthogonal site plan, so that the relationship between the buildings and intervening spaces is infused with a particular dynamic quality.

The western edge of the site is marked by a commanding four storey structure addressing the main road. This structure is designed as a 'green wall', which offers protection from the strong west sun and polluted atmosphere of the city beyond, and declares the existence of an environmental oasis, with its own micro-climate, behind. The building contains the primary entrance and reception area at street level, a tea-house on the first floor, and exhibition space on the second, enclosed within a densely planted pergola construction rising two storeys. The north and east sides of the site are wrapped around by a one storey covered walkway leading into exhibition space, and thence into the house itself. The south of the site is enclosed by a high wall in which the vehicular access point is located.

The key to the environmental success of the project lies in the carefully balanced relationship between the buildings and the open spaces. The two courtyards work together to maintain a system of air-flow throughout the site, the northern courtyard being designed for air-cooling, with the pool, fountains and shower tower operating a continuous circulation of water, while the southern courtyard is designed to harness the warmth of the sun, channelled into solar chimneys built into the structure of the house on its southern aspect. These are faced in glass at the upper level, painted black on the inside to absorb maximum levels of heat. As the heat rises through them into the atmosphere, assisted by mechanical fans within, water-cooled air from the northern courtyard is sucked through the main living spaces of the house and up the chimneys in its wake. In this way, the scheme aims to manufacture a carefully balanced micro-climate even in the absence of naturally occurring winds, which has historically made the use of the traditional 'wind catcher' difficult in Tehran.

While the main body of the living space is located on the north side of the solar chimneys, the southern aspect is occupied by deeply overhung terrace areas equipped with folding windows and louvered shutters at the outer and inner edges. These are designed to allow a natural migration of the occupants from the inner to outer areas according to the time of year, without necessitating the full relocation implicated by traditional house design. Today, due to the number of fixed appliances associated with contemporary living-patterns, this has become almost unthinkable.

The flat roof of the building has been designed specifically to address the thermal inadequacy of thin traditional roofs, being semi-covered by a pergola, for additional shading, and by a roof of photovoltaic and solar panels over an enclosed garden room. The planting on the rooftop is supplemented by a vertical garden on the east side of the house, rising from the first floor upwards.

The main public functions of the building are accommodated predominantly at the lower-ground level. A lecture hall is sited underneath the north courtyard, illuminated from above by 'sun pipes' — apertures that penetrate through the pool and roof construction of the hall, and allow both light and air to filter through the space. The library occupies much of the lower-ground level of the house itself, and lies adjacent to a small self-contained flat. These spaces are reached by a ramp leading down from the street entrance, along the edge of the covered walkway, although the living accommodation also has its own separate entrance via a staircase from the south side.

The Climate House is intended to provide an exemplar of environmentally sustainable design. Underscoring the viability of traditional principles of construction translated into contemporary usage, and the continuing relevance of regionally-specific cultural norms as the driving force behind contemporary design from place to place, it challenges the misperceived hegemony of a so-called 'globalised' industrial culture. For a team of architects based in Europe, but enjoying strong personal and professional links with Iran, it provides an exciting opportunity to share knowledge and develop the cross-cultural channels of communication which are vital to the advance of an environmentally sustainable architecture in the future.

Eastleigh, Hampshire (Swaythling), UK

In the summer of 2002, architects were invited to participate in a competition to design 500 new houses for an unspecified greenfield suburban site in the environs of Eastleigh, near Southampton in south-east England. The competition was organised by the local borough council in conjunction with a local housing association, which will build and manage the development as part of a 10 year regional housing strategy specifying a requirement for 5,570 new dwellings in the county, with particular provision to be made for single-person households and accommodation for the disabled and elderly. A proportion of the houses were to be designated for sale on the private housing market, but a significant number were to be retained by the housing association for rental.

This competition demonstrates very clearly the typical characteristics of the current housing situation in the UK, particularly in the south-east. It presented an exciting proposition;

an opportunity to design from scratch a substantial development housing a whole new community of people. Yet at the same time participants had little information about the intended future occupants of the development. They could only judge the possible tastes and requirements of the inhabitants by the general social characteristics of the area, which is relatively affluent, with good employment opportunities, and culturally quite homogeneous with few ethnic minority groups compared to other parts of the country.

The brief made it clear that the winning scheme must be 'aesthetically' appealing to the end-user, and the panel of judges included several representatives of local residents' groups. In the UK generally, in both urban and rural areas, planning authorities favour 'traditional' styles of new building and obstruct the aesthetics of the modern, regarded as threatening the viability of a historic cultural heritage already dramatically eroded by the forces of industrialisation. There is a powerful assumption that such censorship is an accurate reflection of the desires and aspirations of the general public. However, the recently specified necessity for new buildings to meet standards of environmental 'best practice' has the potential to end a tired debate about 'styles' and open up new avenues of design which draw on the principles, rather than the superficial appearance, of traditional building, and translate them into the context of contemporary technologies and living patterns with refreshing, culturally meaningful results.

These were the ideas that lay behind the development of the practice's submission for the Eastleigh competition. Recent research published in the UK has underlined the problems associated with a predominantly outdated housing stock, a lack of innovation in housing design and a reluctance to increase housing density above conventional suburban standards. These problems are being not only fundamental to a crisis in housing provision, but major causes of social and environmental erosion. The submitted outline scheme aimed to address these issues directly, proposing a volumetric modular approach to fabrication and construction, in conjunction with a simple gridded solution to the planning of the site, which would allow various permutations of interlocked streets and squares developed in differing densities as required. As architecture designed for present-day living, it was founded in five basic principles:

#1 open dialogue
#2 a creative approach to the brief
#3 the landscape/urban conditions of the area
#4 ecological requirements
#5 cost-use calculations for efficient, economic
    construction and maintenance

The proposal comprises two basic building types: a multi-storey L-shaped structure, and a single-storey house. The first type consists of a flexible system of stacked and joined units which can be configured to provide a variety of flats and houses, and is designed to fit a standard 11 x 24 metre plot. Although each building is structurally autonomous and physically independent of the next, they are arranged in a linear sequence and address the street as a visually continuous building line, within which private open courtyards at front and rear, and a variety of heights and roof-top profiles is integrated. Each house enjoys vehicular access from the street and pedestrian access from the communal gardens, intended for leisure or cultivation, on the other side. The internal layout is essentially open-plan and flexible, allowing for reorganisation to suit changing household configurations over a period of time, while the flat rooftops, a potential source of contention from an aesthetic point of view favouring the traditional, allow for use as additional outdoor terrace space, and also for vertical extension if required.

The two- or three-bedroom single-storey house is designed particularly for use by the elderly, households including a member who may be wheelchair-bound, or families with young children. Like the L-shaped model, each house is structurally autonomous and separated from the next, but en masse they form a visually continuous building line. The design principles are the same, with increased potential for vertical extension to provide linked or self-contained accommodation. This might be domestic in nature, to accommodate members of the extended family, or carers, but it could also offer office accommodation for residents working from home, as service industries explore the possibilities offered by 'tele-working' technology to increase flexibility in working practices for their employees.

The advantage of the volumetric modular system is that it offers standardisation and quality control alongside the potential for customisation and personalisation. A range of 'extraordinary' elements offered by the developer (e.g. greenhouse, storage units, photovoltaic panels, pergolas, fireplaces, etc.) are combined with items chosen by residents themselves. This represents a response to the emphasis placed on providing scope for individual choice within the context of mass housing provision—which in itself represents a backlash against the standardisation and 'anonymity' of mass housing in previous decades. The desire to exercise rights of individual expression may be perceived as a very Western preoccupation, while at the same time it may be better understood against the background of intense industrialisation and its impact on UK culture.

The proposed modular system itself is a sophisticated development of earlier systems of prefabrication. 'Engineered construction', as it is called, is now making an impact in the construction industry for many reasons, in particular cost certainty, quality control, and enhanced response to environmental issues. Clients can inspect their buildings during the construction process, in a clean dry factory environment that is more akin to the electronics and automotive industries than to a traditional building site, and expect the product to comply with projected building regulations for at least the next 50 years. As only premium quality products, achieving wherever possible an 'A' rating in the Green Guide for housing, are used in the construction process, it is estimated that the building infrastructure itself will last for a minimum of 100 years.

In addition this method of construction offers inherent spatial flexibility, since units can be assembled in a number of different ways, as well as ease and speed of assembly on site, due to limited wet trades and minimal foundations. Its steel frame assures greater strength and durability of construction than could be provided by an alternative material such as timber, This construction withstands permanent conditions, when it must resist vertical and wind loads, and the process of lifting for transportation to site and assembly. A steel frame can also be recycled – an important environmental consideration.

The maximum size of each volume is limited by the practicalities of transportation. The modules are bolted together at floor and ceiling levels, then anchored to the ground by micropiles attached to the bottom frame, eliminating the need for extensive excavation work. The windows are timber-framed, and the external walls can be clad in various finishes, to be agreed upon with residents at the discretion of the developer, and reflecting regional building traditions: they might include timber boarding, clay tile hanging, brick slips, render, slate, stone or metal sheet.

The proposed site layout provides for an inherent porosity and interconnectedness to the development. It eliminates cul de sacs and provides a system of car-free public spaces, while also ensuring the viability of defensible space in the immediate environs of the dwellings. At the same time, the street network provides for easy accessibility by vehicular traffic.

The disposition of houses around larger communal gardens allows for densities of at least 40 houses per hectare, and as much as 92 dwellings per hectare if required, while maintaining an open garden area of 42 x 42 metres (1,764 square metres). This is in line with current recommendations for increased densities in new developments, and provides for some 500 to 600 houses on a notional 11 hectare site. The garden zone could also be made available, however, for the erection of additional free-standing buildings accommodating cultural, educational and leisure activities, or commercial and retail uses, representing considerable potential for future development of the social and physical infrastructure.

The communal gardens, or public squares form part of a greening strategy that also includes private courtyards and gardens enclosed by tall hedges, screening walls and railings to provide for privacy and security. The squares are connected by pedestrian pathways, which are car-free extensively planted spaces open to sunlight and fresh air.

The environmental strategy is driven by a concern to minimise the impact of the development on the environment and the local infrastructure, particularly as it will be located on a greenfield site. It is based on the following principles:

a   Minimised heat loss, through insulation, airtightness and re-use of waste heat from exhaust air in conjunction with mechanical ventilation
b   Minimised services installation, by locating ventilation and plumbing within central prefabricated units
c   Use of CHP and Biomass, fuelled by crops and woodland planted around the perimeter of the site as parkland
d   Water conservation, using spray taps, low volume cisterns, recycled rainwater, and septic tanks and reed-beds for waste water treatment
e   Reduction of electricity requirements, by designing for high levels of internal daylight, and use of low energy artificial lighting, plus photovoltaics on south-facing roofs, financed by government grants

One disadvantage of the volumetric modular construction approach is the environmental impact of transporting the units to site. It is proposed that this problem could be eliminated by fabricating the components in a factory set up on the site itself, and converting the building afterwards into a social facility.

One of the jury's most significant comments on the Eastleigh submission was that it was not immediately recognisable as a prefabricated scheme. This demonstrates its success in overcoming the anonymity associated with mass produced construction, and establishing a distinctive materiality and identity expressive of its specific cultural and physical context. Likewise, Climate House demonstrates that there is no need for an explicitly 'ecological' project to subject or sacrifice architectural aesthetic integrity to the demands of the technical solutions. Thus although the Eastleigh scheme is designed for very different conditions, and on a markedly different scale from that of the Climate House in Tehran, both projects represent a manifesto for the production of culturally appropriate, aesthetically refined forms of new architecture based on the principles of environmental sustainability. These forms are combined with, and enhanced by, the best of present day manufacturing processes applied to the construction industry.

Housing and Cultural Identity in Non-Metropolitan and Rural Areas: The Future of Prototypes for Innovation in Housing
Pierre d'Avoine and Clare Melhuish

This proposal, submitted to the Royal Commission for the Exhibition of 1851 in competition for its Research Fellowship in the Built Environment 2003, was short-listed along with four others. The theme for the Fellowship that year was Housing in the twenty-first century, and the proposal set out a brief for ethnographic research into the culture of modern-day non-metropolitan and rural communities, providing the basis for a series of design propositions for new housing models in those types of settings. The aim was to shift the focus away from cities and issues of urban development, which had been at the heart of the government-led debate around housing for a decade.

Research Objectives:
We wish to investigate how to deliver appropriate new models of housing for non-metropolitan areas in the twenty-first century, using the research methods of anthropology — namely ethnographic fieldwork, comparative study, and analysis — in conjunction with those of architecture (surveying, mapping, imaging) as the basis for the development of a set of theoretical design proposals capable of implementation. Following the upheavals in the UK rural economy of the last few years, and the pressure which has come to bear on farmers, in particular, to diversify, the question of development in general, and housing provision in particular, in non-metropolitan areas has taken on a renewed urgency.

Brief:
To research and critique the culture of housing development currently offered by the typical volume house builder in conjunction with planning authorities, examining the chain of connection between land ownership structures, government and local authority policy, local economy, physical infrastructure, community aspiration, and daily patterns of life in a particular setting.

To investigate and analyse collective and individual experience of architectural materiality and space in non-urban housing development, and its effect on cultural identity and social cohesion, stressing the importance of an interdisciplinary approach crossing the boundaries of architecture and anthropology as the key to a proper understanding of this relationship, and to the development of an approach to the design of new housing prototypes for society today and in the future.

We will consider how far housing in today's society reflects the shift from an industrial/agricultural to a consumer economy, and whether an understanding of physical materiality and space has been displaced by a preoccupation with form and visual image — buildings as icons of symbolic meaning. We will consider what images and ideals of non-urban living may be promulgated through buildings by volume house builders, and how these match, and influence, social structure and

perceptions of cultural identity. We propose to explore the potential of new housing design prototypes to alter received ideas about life in non-urban areas.

Our aim is to identify a particular case study, or pair of case studies, for research and analysis during the first year of the study, followed by a second year of work on developing alternative design prototypes based on our findings. We will examine our findings against the context of historical exemplars and theoretical prototypes for non-urban development (for example, Frank Lloyd Wright's Broadacre City, or Le Corbusier's Pessac), with a view to re-evaluating a range of options, and assessing what they may have to offer in the evolved, and evolving, cultural context of today.

We will offer the design prototypes we develop as theoretical models for dissemination, but also as practicable propositions appropriate for implementation through collaboration with industry partners.

The Key Issues Expanded
During the years since New Labour came to power, the economy and culture of the countryside has been very visibly in a state of crisis. The scale and impact of the BSE and foot and mouth disasters has brought rural communities into the foreground of the national consciousness, and the long-running political campaign to ban fox hunting has provided a focus for a growing urban — rural rift vividly embodied in the mass demonstrations organised by the Countryside Alliance in London. The Labour government and its policies have been openly accused of demonstrating a bias towards urban culture, and a lack of connection with, or understanding about rural life — to the extent of "driving thousands of law-abiding citizens to consider civil disobedience".

John Prescott, the Deputy Prime Minister, is currently promoting a campaign (the Sustainable Communities Plan) to build hundreds of thousands of new homes in four key areas outside the metropolitan centres, but to date there is scant information as to what models of planning and design are to be used in these initiatives. They will be 'urban' in terms of density, services, and transport links, but it is unclear whether they are to be conceived as self-contained suburban centres, or as commuter 'villages' serving London. It seems wholly inappropriate that Prescott has chosen to make a study visit to the controversial neo-traditional town of Seaside in Florida, as a source of ideas for the development of new non-urban 'sustainable' communities in Britain. But the fact is that very little work has been done in Britain on the development of housing and community prototypes for non-metropolitan areas, revealing a glaring lack of engagement with the conditions and prospects of contemporary non-urban life and culture.

Since the publication of Sir Richard Rogers' Urban Task Force research document, Towards an Urban Renaissance, and the subsequent government White Paper, all the emphasis in the housing debate has been on the shortage of available land to meet the identified housing shortfall, and the need to promote development on recycled brownfield sites within the curtilage of urban areas. However, recent research published by the Campaign for the Protection of Rural England (CPRE) claimed that many of the volume house builders are in fact sitting on large and valuable land banks which could be available for new housing in non-metropolitan areas.

Planning restrictions on new housing in the countryside have been extremely onerous, yet the rural landscape is peppered with examples of repetitious, poor-quality, mono-cultural, car-dependent residential developments delivered by the established mass house builders. The scale and ubiquity of this type of 'Brookside-style' development shows that planning authorities and their committees are prepared to enter into working partnerships with these parties — perhaps spurred on by the fear of blight, as house builders sit on sites — while actively obstructing smaller-scale construction initiatives by lesser-known parties offering unfamiliar products. John Prescott is looking to these same partners to deliver his Sustainable Communities Plan. Yet he has, himself, condemned the quality of 'Noddy box veneer housing' blotting the countryside without regard for local environment or culture, echoing CABE's criticism of developers for producing "incredibly low quality housing."[2] Furthermore, it has been suggested by Design for Homes' David Birkbeck that many such companies face possible extinction, due to the growing difficulty of raising finance in this country for a product increasingly recognised as not worth investing in.[3] If this happens, mass housing construction in this country could simply grind to a halt.

In the Housing Design Awards (Home: A Place to Live) last year, the vast majority of awards went to urban schemes, and the jury noted the dearth of innovative good design in rural areas, compared to the progress that has been made in metropolitan housing. (One exception was the Newhall development outside Harlow, which effectively embraces an urban scale, density, and typology). This fact indicates a failure of confidence in designing for contemporary rural communities, resulting from a significant lack of research into contemporary rural culture and land-use, and a reliance on profitable, national house-types.

However, the successive crises in the rural economy have forced a reconsideration of what rural communities need and want to survive and to nurture their cultural identity in the twenty-first century. Following the decimation of farming by foot-and-mouth, the government has emphasised the need to promote a 'sustainable, diverse, adaptable and competitive industry'. This means not only bigger farms, but new initiatives in sports and leisure (e.g. equestrian centres), tourism (e.g. holiday chalets), retail (e.g. farm shops), specialist agriculture (including organic farming), and woodland management, as explained in the government's Rural White Paper, Our Countryside: the Future, published November 2000.

This document actively promotes the notions of sustainable modernisation, expansion and diversification in rural communities, including the re-use of existing buildings for business purposes, and the construction of isolated new dwellings where necessary to accommodate employees for reasons of husbandry and welfare at or near their place of work. This is the key proposed policy amendment contained in the revised version of PPG7 (The Countryside—Environmental Quality and Economic and Social Development) published in 1997, which is currently out in draft form for consultation. However, most development should continue to be focussed in and around existing towns and villages. Also, the policy exception contained in the existing PPG7 allowing large, high quality houses to be built in the open countryside has, controversially, been removed [a year after submission of this research proposal, this clause was, equally controversially, reinstated].

While the White Paper suggests a reassessment of the conditions facing countryside dwellers, and a need to engage with the realities of survival and quality of life in the rural economy, it appears to offer little support for the idea of an evolving, dynamic planning framework which actively promotes opportunities for diverse, small scale, innovative building initiatives in the 'action planning' tradition, offering a quick and sensitive response to changing local economic and cultural conditions. It remains far from clear, then, what form 'good quality, sustainable development' is likely to take during the next few decades, and how it is to be delivered.

Overview of Rural Context

When recently the Land Registry recently made its services available on-line, it was pointed out that land ownership in England remains far from transparent; indeed, the ownership and use of some 40 per cent of land in this country is undocumented. The countryside is largely owned by historic landowners, but worked piecemeal by tenant farmers, with relatively little control over the land they occupy, for minimal or non-existent profits. Figures just released by the Royal Institute of Chartered Surveyors (RICS) reveal that 45 per cent of smallholdings changing hands are now being acquired by "professionals seeking sanctuary from the stresses of city life", rather than farmers, because of the difficulty of making a living from them.[4] England has never embraced large scale, industrial agriculture in the way that countries such as Holland and Denmark have done, and where it does exist it has generally been at the expense of diversity, both environmental and cultural, imposing homogeneity over a landscape which traditionally has been highly varied. Rural productivity has been subsidised for years as part of a tacit understanding of the farmer's role being not simply that of economic producer, but also a manager, or steward, of the rural landscape. But the idea of 'access for all' has also been part of this deal: the idea that, in exchange for national support, agricultural communities must also accept that the rest of the population also has a claim on the countryside, and a right to its use and enjoyment. This universal claim to the landscape has not necessarily been accepted by those who live in and make their livelihoods from it.

The complexities of the system are manifested in the distinct small scale, piecemeal quality of the English countryside, its network of public footpaths, and its national parks. But the full implications for post-industrial rural life in the twenty-first century need further investigation. We know that the majority of British city dwellers hanker for the countryside. Some have second homes there, and many will eventually leave the city to live in rural areas, while sustaining their economic ties with urban centres. Those working in local agricultural economies often find it hard to survive, and will migrate to urban centres. The new influx of non-farming urban professionals has the potential to exacerbate cultural tensions, even where they take on certain responsibilities for the land. Where farms are broken up and sold off in lots, whole new communities of people may be created almost overnight, having a very different relationship to the land, and different living patterns, from those of their predecessors. But there has been insufficient debate as to how these communities co-exist, and how shifting economic and cultural identities may most appropriately be expressed in the built habitat and the planning framework that determines its shape.

Theoretical Perspective

In order to develop fresh ideas about rural housing in the twenty-first century it is necessary to examine contemporary British cultural attitudes towards rural living, the constitution of the communities which live outside the cities, and the various means by which they realise their sense of belonging in the landscape. It is also necessary to develop a critical theoretical perspective within which to discuss and analyse these issues. This will involve considering the impact of cross-cultural influences resulting from the development of a multi-ethnic society, comparison with urban attitudes, and with the values of other European cultures close to our own. We propose to explore the nature of 'affinity to', use of, and identification with the land in contemporary consumer society — notions which might be thought of as redundant — with reference to concepts of consumption, appropriation, and sustenance, and

to examine the ideologies which have helped to shape the relationship between society and the landscape over previous centuries and into the twenty-first century. We will consider these concepts in close relation to the social and economic structures that govern rural life, the British land ownership system, and as part of a holistic overview of practices and models of land use relevant to both town and country.

Notes:

[1] David Lidington, Conservative environment spokesman, The Guardian, 1 November 2003.
[2] The Guardian, 21 October 2003.
[3] Architectural Association symposium 'Home Front: new developments in housing', 17 October 2003.
[4] The Guardian, 1 November 2003.

Further Reading

1. Books featuring houses/interiors by PdAA, amongst other contemporary designers

Modern House 2, Clare Melhuish. Phaidon London 2000, pb 2004

Prefab, Alison Arrieff and Bryan Burkhart. Gibbs Smith 2002

Heroic Change: Securing Environmental Quality in Thames Gateway London, Thames Gateway London Partnership/Arup London 2001

Ancient and Modern, Cynthia Inions. Jacqui Small 2001

Space Within: Reshaping the Home for Contemporary Living, Jane Withers. Quadrille 2000

Home and Garden Style, John Brookes and Eluned Price, Ward Lock1996

Contemporary Details, Nonie Nieswand. Mitchell Beazley 1992

The New Moderns: Interior Design and Architecture for the 1990s, Jonathan Glancey and Richard Bryant. Michell Beazley 1990

2. Architectural/Historical Background

'Home Front: New Developments in Housing', Architectural Design July/Aug 2003, guest-editor Lucy Bullivant. John Wiley 2003

Experimental Houses, Nicholas Pople. Watson Guptill 2000

The Un-Private House, Terence Riley, Museum of Modern Art New York 1999

Home: the Twentieth Century House, Deyan Sudjic. Laurence King London 1999

Women and the Making of the Modern House, Alice T. Friedman. Harry N. Abrams 1998

Key Buildings of the 20th Century, Vol 1: Houses 1900–1944, David Dunster. Architectural Press1985

The Dream of the Factory Made House, Gilbert Herbert. MIT Press 1984

Robert Smythson and the Elizabethan Country House, Mark Girouard. Yale University Press 1983

Case Study Houses, 1945–1962, Esther McCoy. Hennessy + Ingalls 1977

The Place of Houses: Three Architects Suggest Ways to Build and Inhabit Houses, Charles Moore, Gerald Allen, Donlyn Lyndon. Holt, Rinehard and Winston, 1974

The English Country House: An Art and a Way of Life, Olive Cook. Thames and Hudson, 1974

European Domestic Architecture: Its Development from Early Times, Sherban Cantucuzino. Studio Vista, 1969

The Four Books of Architecture, Andrea Palladio, (with intro by Adolf K.Placzek). Dover Books on Architecture 1965

The New Small House, F.R.S.Yorke and Penelope Whiting. Architectural Press London 1953

Georgian London, John Summerson. Penguin London 1991 (1st pb 1945 by Pleiades Books)

Modern Ideal Homes for India, R S Deshpande. Aryabhusan Press 1939

3. Design and construction manuals and websites

Floor Plan Manual: Housing. Birkhauser 2004

You Can Do It: the complete B&Q step-by-step book of home improvement. Thames & Hudson 2003

The New Home Plans Book, David Snell and Murray Armor. Ebury Press, 2003

Building Your Own Home, David Snell and Murray Armor. Ebury Press 2002 (17th ed)

The Housebuilder's Bible, An Insider's Guide to the Construction Jungle, Mark Brinkley. Burlington Press, 5th ed 2002

The New Autonomous House, Design and Planning for Sustainability, Brenda and Robert Vale. Thames and Hudson, 2002

Patterns of Home: The Ten Essentials of Enduring Design, Max Jacobson, Murray Silverstein and Barbara Winslow. Taunton Press, 2002

New House Book, Terence Conran. Conran Octopus 1999

http://www.channel4.com/life/microsites/0-9/4homes/grand_designs/build_for_yourself.html

Grand Designs: Building Your Dream Home, with Kevin McCloud. Channel 4 Books 1999

4. Social Context

Home Cultures, eds Victor Buchli, Alison Clarke and Dell Upton. Cross-disciplinary journal from Berg Publishers, 2004–, published in March, July and November.

The Value of Housing Design and Layout, CABE/ODPM/Design for Homes, 2003

Home Possessions, ed Daniel Miller. Berg 2001

Social Housing in the Future: A Rural Perspective (Social Housing Forum 5), Mark Bevan, IPPR 2000

Ideal Homes? Social Change and Domestic Life, Tony Chapman and Jenny Hockey. Routledge 1999

Apartment Stories: City and Home in 19th-century Paris and London, Sharon Marcus. University of California Press 1999

An Archaeology of Socialism: the Narkomfin, Victor Buchli. Berg 1999

The Ideal Home through the Twentieth Century, Deborah Ryan. Hagar Publishing 1997

Architecture and Anthropology (AD Profile 124), Clare Melhuish. Academy Editions 1996

English Domestic Environments 1914–2000, Alison Ravetz and David Turkington 1995

So Long As it's Pink: The Sexual Politics of Taste, Penny Sparke. Pandora 1995

Modernity: An Ethnographic Approach, Daniel Miller. Berg 1993

Consuming Technologies: Media and Information in Domestic Spaces, Roger Silverstone and Eric Hirsch. Routledge 1992

Domestic Architecture and the Use of Space, Susan Kent. CUP 1990

Blueprint for a Green Planet, John Seymour and Herbert Girardet, Dorling Kindersley, 1987

Housing: An Anarchist Approach, Colin Ward, Freedom Press London, 1983

Land for the People, compiled by Herbert Girardet. Crescent Books 1976

5. Policy Documents (UK)

Towards An Urban Renaissance, Urban Task Force, 1999

Our Countryside: the Future, government White Paper, 2000

Towards Sustainable Housing: building regulation for the 21st century, Robert Lowe and Malcolm Bell: a report prepared for the Joseph Rowntree Foundation. Leeds Metropolitan University, Leeds 1998

PPG7 The Countryside – Environmental Quality and Economic and Social Development, ODPM London 1997

Draft Planning Policy Statement (PPS) 7 – Sustainable Development in Rural Areas, ODPM London

House Credits

109 Sheendale Studios
1987–1989

Richmond, Surrey, UK

Client:
Pitfield d'Avoine

Design team:
Pierre d'Avoine
Geraldine Flashman
William White
Andrea Wilson

Structural engineer:
John Davis

Main contractor:
Dakin Construction Ltd

Landscape contractor:
HMT Building Services Ltd

Photography:
Richard Bryant
Peter Cook

151 White House
1989–1992

Barnes, London SW13, UK

Client:
Sir Giles and Lady
Montagu-Pollock

Design team:
Pierre d'Avoine
Miraj Ahmed
Carol Nayler

Structural engineer:
John Davis

Main contractor:
HMT Building Services Ltd

Photography:
Jeremy Cockayne
Alberto Piovano
Guy Montagu-Pollock

175 Invisible House
1991–1992

Acton, London W3, UK

Client:
Pierre d'Avoine

Design team:
Pierre d'Avoine
Gerard Roberts

Structural engineer:
John Davis

Model (timber):
Paul Berry

Model (card):
Pereen d'Avoine
Pierre d'Avoine

Photography:
Pierre d'Avoine
David Grandorge
Guy Montagu-Pollock

175 Invisible House 2
1997–1998

Acton, London W3, UK

Client:
Pierre d'Avoine

Design team:
Pierre d'Avoine
Tom Emerson

Structural engineer:
Dewhurst Macfarlane
and Partners

Environmental engineer:
Max Fordham and Partners

Quantity surveyor:
Dobson White Boulcott

Piling consultants:
VSPC Ltd and British Steel

Model (card, acrylic, felt):
Talar Koumoudjian
Tom Emerson

Photography:
Tom Emerson

195 Mehr House
1994–1995

Khadi, Maharashtra, India

Client:
Surinder Nath Mehr

Design team:
Pierre d'Avoine
Alessandra Maiolino
Carina Richards

Structual engineer:
John Davis

Model:
Carina Richards

Photography:
Guy Montagu-Pollock

254 Highstone Rooftop Houses
1998–1999

Camden, London NW1, UK

Client:
Clare Melhuish

Design team:
Pierre d'Avoine
Noemie Laviolle

Structural engineer:
Dewhurst Macfarlane
and Partners

Quantity surveyor:
Dobson White Boulcott

Model:
Noemie Laviolle

Photography:
Noemie Laviolle

255 Slim House
1998–1999

Ideal Home Show, Earls Court,
London SW6, UK

Client:
DMG Angex

Design team:
Miraj Ahmed
Pierre d'Avoine
Alex Ely
Tom Emerson
Kim Fichter
Talar Kouyoumdjian
Noemie Laviolle
Zak Marshall

Structural engineer:
Jane Wernick Associates

Environmental engineer:
Max Fordham and Partners

Quantity surveyor:
Dobson White Boulcott

Models:
Noemie Laviolle
Talar Kouyoumdjian

Photography:
David Grandorge

Co-ordinator:
Louise McKinney

Architect liaison:
Lucy Marston

PR:
Articulate Communications

255 Slim House 2
1999–2000

Leeds, Yorkshire, UK

Client:
Yorkshire Housing Association

Design team:
Pierre d'Avoine
Tom Emerson

Consultant:
Yorkon Ltd

Structural engineer:
Jane Wernick Associates

Environmental engineer:
Max Fordham and Partners

Quantity surveyor:
Dobson White Boulcott

Model:
Zak Marshall

Photography:
David Grandorge

261 Big House
1999–2002

Mortlake, London SW14, UK

Client:
Crispin Kelly, Baylight
Properties plc

Design team:
Miraj Ahmed
Pierre d'Avoine
Tom Emerson
Svinder Singh Sidhu
John Southall

with

Aleksa Gibson
Greg Ross
Susanne Schmelcher

Structural engineer:
Dewhurst Macfarlane and
Partners

Environmental engineer:
Max Fordham and Partners

Quantity surveyor:
Smith Turner Associates

Model:
Jason Lawrence
Zak Marshall

Photography:
David Grandorge

264 Monad House
1999

Museum of Welsh Life,
St Fagans, Cardiff, Wales, UK

Client:
National Museums and
Galleries of Wales and
BBC Cymru Wales

Design team:
Pierre d'Avoine
Tom Emerson
Clare Melhuish

Consultant:
Wayne Forster, Welsh School
of Architecture

Structural engineer:
Dewhurst Macfarlane and
Partners

Environmental engineer:
Max Fordham and Partners

Quantity surveyor:
Dobson White Boulcott

Models:
Stephanie Macdonald

Photography:
Tom Emerson

Project manager
DCA (Cardiff) Limited

265 Maisonette
1999–2002

Kentish Town, London NW1, UK

Client:
Marjorie Jones

Design team:
Pierre d'Avoine
David Edwards
Tom Emerson
Zac Marshall
John Southall

Structural engineer:
John Davis

Quantity surveyor:
Dobson White Boulcott

Contractor:
John Perkins Projects

Model:
Zac Marshall

Photography:
David Grandorge

269 Pudding Mill House
1999

Marshgate Lane, Stratford
Marsh, London E15, UK

Client:
Annabel Elston and Peter Miles

Design team:
Pierre d'Avoine
Tom Emerson

Consultant:
Parklines (Buildings) Limited

278 Piper Rooftop Houses
2000–2003

Fulham, London SW6, UK

Client:
Crispin Kelly, Baylight
Properties plc

Design team:
Pierre d'Avoine
Tom Emerson
Noemie Laviolle
Greg Ross
Ute Schmittlutz
John Southall

with

Susanne Schmelcher
Svinder Singh Sidhu

Structural engineer
(to building fabric):
Waterman Partnership
(to modules): Atelier 1

Environmental engineer:
Max Fordham and Partners

Quantity surveyor:
Smith Turner Associates

Main contractor:
Hanson TIS

Model:
Noemie Laviolle

Photography:
David Grandorge
Greg Ross
Pereen d'Avoine

307 Baffoe House
2000–2001

Accra, Ghana

Client:
Ernest Baffoe

Design team:
Pierre d'Avoine
Svinder Sidhu

Model:
Max Beckenbauer

Photography:
David Grandorge

319 Collins House
2001

Chelsea, London SW3, UK

Client:
Richard Collins

Design team:
Pierre d'Avoine
Ute Schmittlutz
John Southall

Model:
Max Beckenbauer
Ute Schmittlutz
Svinder Sidhu

Photography:
David Grandorge

**335 Rough Grounds –
Octagon House
Belvedere
Lodge**
2002–

Educational Equestrian Centre,
Westonbirt, Gloucestershire, UK

Client:
Simon and Rebecca Wilson
Equine Consultancy Group

Design team:
Pierre d'Avoine
Carlos Cottet
Greg Ross
Colette Sheddick
Svinder Singh Sidhu

Structural engineer:
Dewhurst Macfarlane
and Partners

Environmental engineer:
Max Fordham and Partners

Landscape consultant:
Allan Moss Associates

Planning consultant:
Haston Reynolds Partnership

Quantity surveyor:
Dobson White Boulcott

Model:
Dimitri
Tom Housden
Colette Sheddick
Svinder Singh Sidhu

Photography:
David Grandorge

336 Climate House
2002–

Vali Asr, Tehran, Iran

Client:
Iranian Fuel Conservation
Organisation

Architect:
Golzari (NG) Architects in
association with
Pierre d'Avoine Architects

Design team:
Pierre d'Avoine
Carlos Cottet
Aleksa Gibson
Madeleine Dignam
Nasser Golzari

Philippe Haag
Greg Ross
Susanne Schmelcher
Svinder Singh Sidhu

Structural engineer:
Ali Tavakoli

Environmental consultants:
Fergus Nichol (LEARN at LMU
and Oxford Brookes University)
Sue Roaf (Oxford Brookes
University)
Mike Wilson (LEARN at LMU)

Environmental engineer:
Anthony Judd Associates

Model:
Pereen d'Avoine
Nikolay Shahpazov

Photography:
Greg Ross

340 Swaythling Housing
2002

Eastleigh, Hampshire, UK

Client:
Swaythling Housing Society

Design team:
Pierre d'Avoine
Carlos Cottet
Aleksa Gibson
Clare Melhuish
Greg Ross
Susanne Schmelcher
Svinder Singh Sidhu

Structural engineer:
Atelier 1

Environmental engineer:
Max Fordham and Partners

Quantity surveyor:
Dobson White Boulcott

Consultant:
John Thompson, Hanson TIS

Model:
David Roy

Photography
Greg Ross

344 New Battery House
2003–2004

Wilmslow, Cheshire, UK

Client:
John and Charlotte Thompson
JTC Developments Ltd

Design team:
Pierre d'Avoine
Clare Melhuish
Greg Ross
Colette Sheddick
Svinder Singh Sidhu

Structural engineer:
Atelier 1

Planning consultant:
Emery Planning Partnership

350 Sam House
2003–2004

Ratho Mill, St Vincent,
West Indies

Client:
Mr and Mrs C.G. Sam

Design team:
Pierre d'Avoine
Clare Melhuish
Greg Ross
Colette Sheddick

Photography:
David Grandorge

Model:
Nikolay Shahpazov

Photographic Credits

351 Drawing/Modelling Workshops

Additional drawing and modelling for inclusion in the book

with thanks to:

Miraj Ahmed
Pereen d'Avoine
Polly Bansal
Max Beckenbauer
Sigrun Birgisdottir
Saff Gama
Mari Inoue
Lefkos Kyriakou
Marine Leblond
David Roy
Svinder Singh Sidhu

special thanks to Greg Ross, Nikolay Shahpazov and Colette Sheddick

358 Drum House
2003–2004

Design team:
Pierre d'Avoine
Sigrun Birgisdottir
Carlos Cottet
Greg Ross
Colette Sheddick
Svinder Singh Sidhu

Model:
Tom Housden
Greg Ross
Nikolay Shahpazov
Colette Sheddick

Photography:
David Grandorge

Pereen d'Avoine
p148(top, bottom)

Pierre d'Avoine
p19, p38(top, bottom), p40, p57, p101(top, bottom), p104(top, bottom), p105(top, bottom), p120, p185

Ernest Baffoe
p153, p159(middle, bottom)

Richard Bryant/Arcaid.co.uk
p20 (top), p24(bottom)

Jeremy Cockayne/ Arcaid.co.uk
p34(right), p36

Peter Cook
p18, p24(top), p25(top, bottom)

Tom Emerson
p54(top, bottom), p55(top, bottom), p67(all), p97(left), p106, p107, p114(top, bottom), p115(top, bottom), p116(top, bottom), p117(top, bottom)

David Grandorge
p71, p74, p76(top, bottom), p77(top, bottom), p79(top, bottom), p80(all), p82, p88(top, bottom), p89(all), p90, p97(right), p98(top, bottom), p99(top, bottom), p100(top, bottom), p102(top, bottom), p103(top, bottom), p123(top, bottom), P124(all), p125(top, bottom), p126, p127(top, bottom), p137, p144(bottom), p146(top, bottom), p147(bottom), p149(top, bottom), p150(top, bottom), p151(bottom), p152, p159(top), p160, p166(all), p167(all), p183(top, bottom), p212, p220(top, bottom), p221(top, bottom), p222, p229(all), p230(top, bottom), p231(top, bottom)

Noemie Laviolle
p64(top, bottom)

Zac Marshall
p121

Parklines (Buildings) Limited
p129

Guy Montagu-Pollock
p26, p33(top, bottom) p34(left), p39(all), p44(top, bottom), p45(top, bottom), p46(all), p56, p62(top, bottom), p63(top, bottom)

Alberto Piovano/Arcaid.co.uk
p20(bottom), p27, p35(top, bottom), p37(top, bottom), p198(bottom)

Greg Ross
p48, p136, p144(top), p147(top), p151(top), p169, p193(all), p199(bottom)

Caliston Garvey Sam
p213

Colette Sheddick
p129

Essay Publication Acknowledgements

Reality and Project was originally published in the catalogue to the exhibition Four British Architects, held at the 9H Gallery, London, 1990.

Colour and Architecture: The White House was originally published as part of the exhibition Colour and Architecture, curated by Clare Melhuish and designed by Pierre d'Avoine, for the Heinz Gallery, London, 1993.

Flowering of the New Suburbia was published in Building Design, 26 November 1993.

Gone But Only In My Head was originally published in Architectural Design. Profile 115, British Architects in Exile, 1995.

Suburbia On My Mind was first published in Scroope 9, in 1997, and was based on a lecture given by Pierre d'Avoine at the Architectural Association and Cambridge School of Architecture the previous year.

The Invisible House: The Architect as Anthropologist of Suburban Life was originally published in Architecture and Anthropology, guest editor Clare Melhuish, AD, Profile 124, Academy Editions, 1996.

Affecting Architecture: Challenging the Politics of Indifference was originally published in the catalogue to the exhibition In Search of Public Space: Four Architects from London, featuring the work of Pierre d'Avoine Architects along with three contemporaries at the De Singel Gallery, Antwerp, in 1997. It was subsequently republished in Accommodating Change: Innovation in Housing, the book published by Circle 33 Housing Group in association with the Architecture Foundation, to accompany the eponymous exhibition in 2002.

Interstitial Space: The Ideal Home Show and DIY Culture was originally presented, under the title 'Interstitial Space', as a lecture at the RIBA by Pierre d'Avoine, in November 1999.

Monad House: Thoughts on a Design Approach for a Welsh House for the Future was originally published in Touchstone, the official journal of the Royal Society of Architects in Wales, May 2000.

From Climate House, Tehran, to New Housing at Eastleigh, Hampshire (Swaythling) was originally published in Sakht magazine Vol 4 No 23 March and April 2003.

Biographies

Pierre d'Avoine runs an architects office based in London and practices internationally with work in Japan, India, Italy, Ghana, the West Indies and in Tehran where he designed the Climate House, an experimental project for The Iranian Fuel Conservation Organisation, in association with Golzari (NG) Architects. The work of the practice includes housing, offices, mixed-use developments, urban design, interior design and public art projects, and has been widely published and exhibited. In 1999 the practice won the Concept House competition with Slim House, a prototype of which was built at the Ideal Home Show that year.

Pierre was born in Bombay, moved to London when he was 11 and studied architecture at the Birmingham School of Architecture in the 1970s. He set up Pierre d'Avoine Architects in London in 1979. Pierre is a visiting professor at the Welsh School of Architecture, Cardiff, and has taught at the Architectural Association, the Bartlett (UCL), the University of Bath, the Royal College of Art, Oxford Brookes University, Buckingham Chilterns University College and Chelsea School of Art. He has also lectured and broadcast extensively in the UK and abroad.

Clare Melhuish is author of Modern House 2 (Phaidon 2000), and Reviews Editor on the new cross-disciplinary journal Home Cultures (Berg Publishers). She is currently working on an ethnography of inhabitation at the Brunswick Centre, a 1960s mixed use development by Patrick Hodgkinson in central London.

She was brought up in London, and graduated in History and History of Art from Christ's College Cambridge in 1985, leading to a career as an architectural journalist and writer. She was Round-Up Editor for Architectural Design, Reviews Editor of Building Design, and a columnist for the Architect's Journal, as well as working closely with her father, the late Nigel Melhuish, during his 10-year editorship of Church Building magazine, and contributing to a wide range of other publications. She conceived and guest-edited Architecture and Anthropology (AD Profile 124, Academy Editions 1996), and wrote the monograph Odile Decq:Benoit Cornette (Phaidon 1996). She curated the exhibition Colour and Architecture at the Heinz Gallery (1993, designed by Pierre d'Avoine), taught a course in architecture and anthropology at the Architectural Association, and collaborated on a number of design projects with Pierre d'Avoine Architects.

In 2001 she received a Master of Arts in Material Culture from the Department of Anthropology, University College London, leading to doctoral research in the area of modern architecture and cultural identity, focussed on the case of the Brunswick. She is affiliated to the Faculty of Design at Buckinghamshire Chilterns University College, and supported by the Arts and Humanities Research Board, while establishing her own research consultancy in collaboration with Pierre d'Avoine, and pursuing her writing and critical practice in the field of architecture and culture.

She lives in London with Pierre d'Avoine and their two sons Ivan and Reynard.

Acknowledgements

Thanks to Duncan McCorquodale and Black Dog Publishing.

Thanks to Ben Chatfield and Mark Hopkins of bc, mh for designing this book.

Thanks to all our clients, consultants and members of the office who collaborated on the houses presented in this book.

Thanks to our families and friends for their support and encouragement.

This book is dedicated to a most wonderful daughter Molly d'Avoine — 31 May 1984 to 20 May 2004